Approaches to Social Enquiry

Norman Blaikie

Polity Press

First published in 1993 by Polity Press in association with Blackwell Publishers Ltd.

Reprinted 1995 (twice)
Transferred to Digital print 2003

Editorial office:
Polity Press
65 Bridge Street
Cambridge CB2 1UR, UK

Marketing and production:
Blackwell Publishers Ltd
108 Cowley Road
Oxford OX4 1JF, UK

Blackwell Publishers Inc.
238 Main Street
Cambridge, MA 02142, USA

ISBN 0 7456 1172 9
ISBN 0 7456 1173 7 (pbk)

A CIP catalogue record for this book is available from the British Library.

Library of Congress Cataloging-in-Publication Data

Blaikie, Norman W. H., 1933–
    Approaches to social enquiry/Norman Blaikie.
      p.   cm.
    Includes bibliographical references and index.
    ISBN 0–7456–1172–9. – ISBN 0–7456–1173–7 (pbk.)
    1. Social sciences-Methodology.   I. Title.
    H61.B4776   1993
    300'.72–dc20   93–19942
                                        CIP

Typeset in 10 on 11 pt Times
by Graphicraft Typesetters Ltd., Hong Kong

Printed and bound in Great Britain by
Marston Lindsay Ross International Ltd,
Oxfordshire

Contents

Part III Some Methodological Issues

Figures and Tables

Preface

While this book is primarily a textbook for students of social science, it is also intended for both novice and experienced social researchers. The issues covered lie at the heart of the social science enterprise and must be addressed if progress is to be made beyond the present uncertain state.

In addition to reflecting on my own research experience, the book has emerged from nearly twenty-five years of teaching courses in philosophy of science and social science, methodology of social research, and quantitative and qualitative research methods, at both undergraduate and postgraduate levels, to students from many disciplines. I came to the conclusion very early on that an understanding of ontological and epistemological assumptions, of logical and methodological issues, was important if students were to avoid perpetuating the mindless and sometimes sophisticated empiricism that frequently passed for social research.

While the theoretical and methodological issues have changed during this period, the fundamental philosophical questions have remained. The growing recognition of paradigmatic pluralism has made the need to address these questions more urgent. However, this task is doubly difficult for both students and their lecturers; not only are the issues complex, with a variety of positions adopted and advocated, but there is also a vast literature that needs to be covered to deal with them. Few texts, if any, come anywhere near resolving these difficulties.

The issues involved in these questions are likely to challenge taken-for-granted beliefs and assumptions, to require students to examine critically both their ideas about research and the core elements of their worldview. In my experience, they have found this process to be, simultaneously, both disturbing and stimulating. With very few exceptions, students have told me that the effort and discomfort has been well worthwhile. Most have found the experience to be of vital importance to their intellectual development; it has had a significant and lasting benefit for their capacity to undertake useful research and for their understanding of social science in general. I hope this book will make the task more manageable.

While the book spans a wide range of positions in philosophy, social theory and methodology, it is necessarily selective in the writers discussed. I have chosen to review and critique a range of approaches to social enquiry rather than advocate a specific approach, but I suspect my own preferences will be in evidence. Readers are encouraged to evaluate these approaches, and their accompanying research strategies, and to choose an approach which suits their purpose, prejudices and personality.

I am indebted to the many students who have travelled this path with me over the years. They have provided me with the need to grapple with these issues, they have forced me to reflect on my own position, they have taught me a great deal, and they have confirmed that the task is necessary and worthwhile.

Norman Blaikie

1

Introduction

Empirical social science must start from a properly articulated philosophical base if it is to be successful. The philosophy of the social sciences cannot be an optional activity for those reluctant to get on with the 'real' empirical work. It is the indispensable starting-point for all social science.

Trigg, *Understanding Social Science*

Purpose of the Book

Over the past thirty years, the social sciences have been plagued by theoretical and methodological controversies. The demise of the 'orthodox consensus' and the emergence of new philosophies of science and social science have been followed by a period of dispute between a variety of theoretical perspectives and approaches to research. The issues and dilemmas which have been exposed by these contemporary controversies are not new, although their nature may now be better understood. Their ingredients can be traced back to philosophical traditions which were established last century, but which have their roots in antiquity. What is new is that scientists, and social scientists in particular, can no longer ignore them as being the pastime of philosophers. Social enquiry has lost its innocence. Social researchers must now face up to and deal with a range of divergent, if not mutually exclusive, choices which lead to fundamentally different research strategies and have the possibility of producing different outcomes.

Much has been written about the paradigmatic disputes within the philosophy of science, their relevance to the social sciences, and the nature of and differences between theoretical perspectives. Each tradition has had its champions, its followers and its critics, and there has been the inevitable rise and fall in what has been regarded as fashionable approaches. At the same time, a wide diversity of methods of social enquiry is now recognized and accepted, and these have been expounded at great length in innumerable texts. For the student of social science, and the novice researcher, the task of coming to grips with the range and diversity of even the basic literature across these fields of academic endeavour is daunting, if not impossible. A common solution to this problem is to adopt one path from the intersecting maze, one paradigm or theoretical perspective, and travel along it with blinkers firmly in place. Another is to be uncritically eclectic, gathering up and combining bits and pieces of various approaches. While it may have been possible to sustain such behaviour in the past, it is no longer defensible. More sophisticated solutions are required. However, the magnitude of the task of coming to grips with the alternatives poses considerable problems for both the novice and the experienced researcher.

This book provides a comprehensive and critical review of the alternative approaches to social enquiry now available, and it outlines four major research strategies associated with these approaches, either singly or in combination. A vast range of literature from the philosophy of the natural and social sciences, and from social theory and methodology, is reviewed. Its purpose is to provide social researchers with the basis for evaluating the relevance, and the strengths and weaknesses, of these major research strategies for particular research projects, and to facilitate the making of informed and defensible choices. A sequel to this book will elaborate a new method within one of these strategies, a method which the author believes provides the best solution to the dilemmas with which these choices have to deal.

Some Basic Questions

A number of fundamental questions set the scene for the examination of these dilemmas. These questions confront both new and inexperienced social researchers alike and are the same questions which continue to raise problems for those experienced researchers who take time to reflect on their activities. Some questions relate to fundamental philosophical issues while others have to do with practical aspects of undertaking social research. The way the major approaches to social enquiry respond to these questions will be explored.

The status of social science as a science has been a matter of considerable debate.

What Kind of Science is Social Science? Unfortunately, there is no simple or straightforward answer to this question. Rather, it presupposes two other questions which have been the source of considerable controversy among philosophers and social scientists for about a hundred years. The first, which assumes that social science is possible, raises the issue of what methods are appropriate for the social sciences if they are to be regarded as 'real' sciences.

Can the Methods of the Natural Sciences be Used in the Social Sciences? Some writers have taken the view that social life does not lend itself to any kind of scientific investigation; in contrast to natural phenomena, human beings have the capacity to make decisions about their actions and these decisions have a component of 'free will' which undermines any attempt at explanation and prediction. Other writers have argued that there is no aspect of the social world that is not amenable to the application of *the* scientific method, or at least some kind of scientific method. In view of the success of the natural sciences, many authors have argued that the social sciences should adopt the same methods, the same strategies that have been used for generating and testing theories. Between these two extremes lie a number of intermediate positions which include the view that as the social sciences and natural sciences deal with fundamentally different subject matters they are of necessity different kinds of science. However, this question requires some specification of the methods that are appropriate for the natural sciences. What has come to be regarded as *the* scientific method has itself been a matter of much controversy. Philosophers now tell us that the common-sense view, of scientists making careful observations and conducting experiments which lead to scientific 'discoveries', is not only logically unsatisfactory but also does not reflect good scientific practice.

Assuming that some kind of social science is possible, in order to begin to establish what methods might make social science a real science it is necessary to answer another question.

What are the Appropriate Methods of the Natural Sciences? It is no longer possible to provide *one* prescription for *the* scientific method. Answers fall into three categories. One proposes that scientific research begins with pure observations, and generalizations or theories are produced from them. The second argues that scientific research begins with a tentative theory which is expected to explain some observed phenomenon, and observations are made to test whether this theory can be accepted. The third proposes that, as observed regularities are produced by hidden mechanisms, it is necessary to build models of these mechanisms and then to look for evidence of their existence.

It is worth noting that many natural scientists appear to have been trained to use a particular method or set of methods uncritically, and that they are not aware that a choice has been made. However, in the social sciences, controversies have raged for decades about whether the methods of the natural sciences can be used in the social sciences and, if not, what methods are appropriate.

Unfortunately, there are no simple answers to these questions; a wide range of views persists with continuing debate between the adherents of the various positions. The differences between these positions centre on two further basic questions.

What is the Nature of the Reality to be Investigated? How can Knowledge of this Reality be Obtained? These two questions require assumptions to be made about the elements that make up the reality addressed by a discipline, how they are arranged and how they behave, and the specification of the procedures that are regarded as being appropriate for gaining knowledge of this reality. One common assumption is that reality exists independently of the researcher's activities and that it can be reliably observed by the use of the senses. Another assumption is that reality is what the concepts and theories of the social scientist say it is; it can only be known through the use of these concepts and theories. These are matters of ontology and epistemology, concepts that will be elaborated shortly. For the moment, the important point is that the assumptions and choices that are made in response to these questions, either overtly or covertly, have significant consequences for the conduct of social enquiry, and for its outcomes.

In addition to these fundamental questions, there are others of a more practical nature which deal mainly with aspects of the research process. To begin with, a critical element in the design of any social research is the specification of the questions which the research is intended to answer. At the end of the day, the researcher wants to be able to say something about the problem being investigated; research questions provide direction for this quest.

What Kind of Research Questions can be Asked?   Social research is about exploring, describing, understanding, explaining, predicting, changing or evaluating some aspect of the social world. Research questions which cover these activities can be grouped into three main categories: 'what', 'why' and 'how' questions. 'What' questions are concerned with the exploration and description of some phenomenon, 'why' questions are concerned with understanding or explaining some characteristics of the phenomenon, e.g. its regularities, and to make predictions about aspects of it possible, and 'how' questions are concerned with practical outcomes, with ways in which change might be brought about.

Having settled on suitable research questions, the next issue is how they will be answered. For the practitioner, the problem is:

Where Does Research Begin?   Are the answers to research questions to be found by gathering data and generalizing from them, by finding a suitable theory that will provide some hypotheses to test, or by constructing a model of hidden mechanisms? The answers to this question will depend on which category of research question is being addressed. 'What' questions can be dealt with by making appropriate observations or measurements. However, this process is not as simple as it sounds; descriptions of what we believe we have observed may not be, perhaps cannot be, pure descriptions; the observer is, after all, an active participant in the process. Answering 'why' questions is even more complex as it involves dealing with theory in one form or another. And this raises some further questions for the social researcher.

What Does a Theory Look Like? Where Does a Good Theory Come From? Will a New One Have to be Constructed? How are Theories Tested and Validated?   These questions deal with what is usually referred to as the logic of scientific method. Approaches to social enquiry, and their accompanying research strategies, provide their own particular answers to these questions.

Another issue which differentiates the approaches concerns the relationship between how the people to be investigated talk about their world and how the social scientists talk about it. This is usually referred to as the relationship between lay concepts and technical concepts, between the language of social actors and the language of social scientists.

What is the Relationship between Lay Language and Technical Language? Should the accounts of social life be expressed in the language of the participants or the language of the expert? Some approaches to social enquiry adopt what might be described as a 'top down' approach to research in which the concepts and theories within the discipline are applied to and/or are tested in some social situation. The concepts or 'theories' of the participants are considered to be at best, unreliable, and at worst, irrelevant. Other approaches adopt a 'bottom up' approach and argue that all accounts of social life must either be expressed in the language of the participants, or at least be based on the way they conceptualize and understand their reality. Of all the questions being examined here, this is the most central one to the choice of research strategy, and the most controversial.

There is a companion question to the issue of the relationship between languages.

What is the Relationship between the Researcher and the Researched? This question touches on a number of issues. Social researchers can do research *on* people, *for* people or *with* people. In the first case, the researcher is the expert and the researched are merely subjects or respondents; the research is being undertaken primarily for the benefit of the researcher, although the results may be intended to benefit 'society' in some way. In the second case, the researcher is still the expert, but acts as a consultant; the researcher is doing the research for a client group to provide them with knowledge which they need. The clients and the researched can be either different groups of people or the same group. In the third case, the clients are in charge of the research and the researcher is a facilitator; s/he assists the group to conduct their own research on their situation, usually to solve some problem, to evaluate some programme or to bring about some change. Researchers are therefore faced with a number of choices. Do they remain detached and aloof from the social contexts which are being investigated or do they need to become involved in the everyday lives of these people? Is the aim of the research to produce knowledge for its own sake or is it to bring about change? And if it is the latter, how should this be done?

And, finally, social researchers are usually concerned about whether the results of their research will be taken seriously.

What has to be Done to Make Research Objective, Unbiased and Valid?
Issues of objectivity and validity are viewed differently from within the
various approaches to social enquiry, ranging from the specification of
procedures which are claimed to achieve them, to an outright denial that
objectivity is possible and that validity can be independently established.
One typical and common approach adopts the view that there are truths
to be known about the way the natural and social worlds work; regularities
which make up the independently existing reality can be discovered, described and explained by theories, the truth of which can be reliably established. Another approach argues that all knowledge of these worlds is
tentative; we can only approach the truth but never know when we have
discovered it. Existing theories can always be replaced by better theories;
in fact, searching for better theories is the primary aim of science. Our
knowledge is limited by the fact that reality cannot be observed directly,
but only through the concepts and theories we choose to use; change the
concepts and theories and what appears as reality will also change. A more
radical position claims that all knowledge of the world, but particularly of
the social world, is relative in time and space; there are no absolute truths.
The regularities in social life are not universal; they change over time and
can differ across social contexts. However, the most radical position argues
that there is no such thing as objective knowledge, there are only subjective experiences. Researchers can tell a story about some aspect of the
social world, but it is simply *their* story. As this account cannot be repli-
cated, notions of objectivity, bias and validity are irrelevant.

These questions are examined in detail by elaborating, comparing and
evaluating the major approaches to social enquiry which have been developed over the past fifty years. The aim is to provide new researchers with
a comprehensive background to and account of these approaches to
facilitate the choice of an appropriate research strategy, and to provide
experienced researchers with assistance in their critical reflection on current research practices.

Some Basic Concepts

Ontology and Epistemology

Two of the most central concepts in the philosophy of science are *ontology*
and *epistemology*. The root definition of *ontology* is 'the science or study
of being'. For the purposes of the present discussion, *ontology* refers to the
claims or assumptions that a particular approach to social enquiry makes
about the nature of social reality – claims about what exists, what it looks
like, what units make it up and how these units interact with each other.

The root definition of *epistemology* is 'the theory or science of the method
or grounds of knowledge'. Again, in terms of the present discussion,
epistemology refers to the claims or assumptions made about the ways in

which it is possible to gain knowledge of this reality, whatever it is understood to be; claims about how what exists may be known. An *epistemology* is a theory of knowledge; it presents a view and a justification for what can be regarded as knowledge – what can be known, and what criteria such knowledge must satisfy in order to be called knowledge rather than beliefs.

Method and Methodology

Two related concepts must also be distinguished: *methodology* and *method*. There is a tendency in much of the literature to use these concepts interchangeably, to use one when the other is more correct. In particular, *methodology* is frequently used when *method* is more appropriate. Similarly, such phrases as 'the scientific method' are frequently used by philosophers when what they are referring to is *methodology* or even *epistemology*.

Methods of research are the actual techniques or procedures used to gather and analyse data related to some research question or hypothesis. In the social sciences they include engaging people in conversation (ranging from the very formal and structured to the informal and free-flowing), getting people to fill in questionnaires, observing behaviour and examining documents or other records of human activity. *Methodology*, on the other hand, is the analysis of how research should or does proceed. It includes discussions of how theories are generated and tested – what kind of logic is used, what criteria they have to satisfy, what theories look like and how particular theoretical perspectives can be related to particular research problems.

Organization of the Book

Part I elaborates and evaluates the major responses to the first two questions: *What kind of science is social science?* and *Can the methods of the natural sciences be used in the social sciences?* The answers to the second question have been identified as 'Yes', 'No' and 'Yes and No'. Chapter 2 outlines six classical responses: *Positivism* (Yes), *Negativism* (No), *Historicism* (Yes and No), *Critical Rationalism* (Yes and No), *Classical Hermeneutics* (No) and *Interpretivism* (No). These positions have their origins in the nineteenth century and were well developed by the 1950s. In many respects, Positivism represents the first attempt to formulate the scientific method, and its influence persists to the present. The three latter positions are alternative responses to what are regarded as the deficiencies in Positivism. Five contemporary responses are outlined in chapter 3. *Critical Theory* (Yes and No), *Realism* (Yes and No), *Contemporary Hermeneutics* (No), *Structuration Theory* (Yes and No) and *Feminism* (No). While these approaches have links with aspects of the classical approaches, they are reactions to or modifications of them, and they sometimes combine aspects of the classical approaches. Their major contributors are still publishing, *Feminism* being the most recent arrival. These eleven positions are reviewed and their deficiencies discussed in chapter 4.[1]

Part II outlines and reviews the four major research strategies which are associated with eight of the eleven approaches (*Negativism* and *Historicism* are excluded, and *Classical* and *Contemporary Hermeneutics* are combined). The strategies, which contain both a logic of theory construction and a research process, have been labelled as Induction, Deduction, Retroduction and Abduction. Induction is associated with *Positivism*, Deduction with *Critical Rationalism*, Retroduction with *Realism*, and Abduction with *Interpretivism* and *Hermeneutics*. The other approaches use a combination of these strategies. Part III compares the approaches and strategies in terms of a number of themes related to the basic questions set out above.

---

[1] While there are numerous classifications of theoretical perspectives or paradigms in social science, fewer attempts have been made to identify the diversity of approaches to social enquiry. For example, Hughes (1980) works with two categories: positivism and humanism; Guba (1990b) and Schwandt (1990) work with three: positivism/scientific, critical theory/science and constructivism; and Johnson et al. (1984) work with four: empiricism, subjectivism, substantialism and rationalism. The eleven categories of social enquiry being used here overlap with these classifications but are designed to reflect important differences and important recent developments. However, they have been reduced to four research strategies.

Part I
Science and Social Science

2

What Kind of Science is Social Science? Classical Responses

[There] is a controversy which for more than half a century has split not only logicians and methodologists but also social scientists into two schools of thought. One of these holds that the methods of the natural sciences which have brought about such magnificent results are the only ones and that they alone, therefore, have to be applied in their entirety to the study of human affairs ... The other school of thought feels that there is a basic difference in the structure of the social world and the world of nature. This feeling has led to the other extreme, namely the conclusion that the methods of the social sciences are *toto coelo* different from those of the natural sciences ... It has been maintained that the social sciences are ideographic, characterized by individualizing conceptualization and seeking singular assertory propositions, whereas the natural sciences are nomothetic, characterized by generalizing conceptualization and seeking general apodictic propositions. The latter have to deal with constant relations of magnitude which can be measured and can perform experiments, whereas neither measurement nor experiment is practicable in the social sciences. In general, it is held that the natural sciences have to deal with material objects and processes, the social sciences, however, with psychological and intellectual ones and that, therefore, the method of the former consist in explaining, and that of the latter in understanding.

A. Schütz, 'Concept and Theory Formation in the Social Sciences'

Introduction

The controversy which Schütz identified in this quotation has raged for at least a hundred years. While some progress has been made in achieving a better understanding of the nature of the different views, and some proposals for alternative positions to bridge the differences have been offered, the issue of the extent to which social life can be studied in the same way as nature continues to be the central one in the philosophy of social science (Keat and Urry 1975; Bhaskar 1979; Held and Thompson 1989).

In order to answer the question 'Can the methods of the natural sciences be applied to the social sciences?', another question must also be answered: 'What are the methods of the natural sciences?' For the past fifty years there has been as much if not more controversy over this question than there has been over the first one. Many philosophies of science have been proposed and debated centring on issues such as the nature and importance of observation, when observation should occur in the process of developing scientific knowledge, the appropriate form of logic to be used in constructing theories, the role of theories themselves in this process, the structure of theories, and the extent to which scientists work with open minds or are constrained by the beliefs, values and orthodox practices of the community of scientists to which they belong. To answer the first question it will be necessary to deal with the second as well.

It is important to note that the reference to 'methods' in these questions does not refer to the actual *techniques* of observation, data gathering or data analysis, but rather to the logic or *strategy* of enquiry, to the processes by which knowledge is generated and justified. The techniques of data gathering and analysis used in the various disciplines are related to the particular nature of their subject matters. While some techniques may be used in more than one discipline, e.g. the use of particular statistical tests, the study of chemical structures is a very different activity from the study of social structures.

It is not possible to answer the first question with a simple 'Yes' or 'No'. First, more than one method has been claimed to be appropriate in the natural sciences and, secondly, both 'Yes' and 'No' answers have been qualified in various ways. Eleven different answers to the question will be explored, six classical positions in this chapter and five contemporary positions in the next chapter. The first of the classical positions, and the one against which all other positions are reactions, is known as *Positivism* – the only straight 'Yes' answer; it advocates that all sciences, whether natural or social, should use the same method. The second answer is that of *Negativism* – a straight-out 'No'; it claims that a science of the social is impossible. The third answer is 'Yes and No', referred to here as *Historicism*; it advocates a modified form of the method of the natural sciences proposed by Positivism as being appropriate for the social sciences, one in which prediction based on past trends is the primary concern. The fourth answer, another 'Yes and No', is known as *Critical Rationalism*; it also argues for the use of the same methods, but rejects the view of science associated with Positivism in favour of a different method for natural science. The fifth answer, from *Classical Hermeneutics*, is 'No'; it claims that the natural science aim of explanation is not relevant to the social sciences and it is concerned with interpretation, particularly of texts. The sixth, another 'No' answer, is *Interpretivism*; it rejects the methods of the natural sciences as appropriate for the social sciences arguing that, because of the qualitative differences in their subject matters, a different kind of scientific method is required.

This brief overview of the classical positions makes it clear that it is not possible to give a simple answer to the question. A vast and complex array of philosophical positions and arguments will be encountered in the review of these answers. The treatment of them will, of necessity, have to be brief and at times may appear to the professional philosopher to be somewhat superficial. The purpose is to lay the foundations for a consideration of the alternative research strategies that are available to social scientists.

Classical Responses

Positivism

The first answer is a straightforward 'Yes'. It is based on a position known as *Naturalism*, the belief that there can be a *natural* scientific study of people and society, the doctrine known as the 'unity of scientific method'. It is argued that in spite of the differences in subject matter of the various scientific disciplines, both natural and social, the same method or logic of explanation can be used, although each science must elaborate these in a way appropriate to its objects of enquiry (Popper 1961; von Wright 1971; Kolakowski 1972). The philosopher John Stewart Mill (1879) adopted this position as a way of rescuing the social (or moral) sciences from what he regarded as an unsatisfactory state. He believed that all scientific explanations have fundamentally the same logical structure. A more recent philosopher, Karl Popper, adopted a similar position.

> I do not intend to assert that there are no differences whatever between the methods of the theoretical sciences of nature and of society; such differences clearly exist, even between the various natural sciences themselves, as well as between the various social sciences . . . But I agree with Comte and Mill – and many others . . . – that the methods in the two fields are fundamentally the same. (Popper 1961: 130–1)

Popper, as shall be seen, had his particular view of *the* scientific method which differed from that advocated by Mill and the other early supporters of Naturalism. The fact that there are differences in subject matter is not seen to be a problem: 'According to this standpoint, the phenomena of human subjectivity, of volition and will, do not offer any particular barriers to the treatment of social conduct as an "object" on a par with objects in the natural world' (Giddens 1974: 3–4).

In his definition of 'science', Braithwaite has included

> all the natural sciences, physical and biological, and also such parts of psychology and the social sciences (anthropology, sociology, economics) as are concerned with empirical subject-matter . . . This sense of the word 'science' corresponds pretty closely with the most frequent modern use of the word . . . ; it is synonymous with 'natural science' if man [sic] is included with nature. (Braithwaite 1953: 1)

This thesis of Naturalism is a central claim of *Positivism*, a philosophy of the natural sciences which, in its various forms, has been both the dominant doctrine and the object of extensive criticism. In the nineteenth century, Positivism was not merely a philosophy of science; it expressed a more general worldview which lauded the achievements of science. While the term was invented by Comte (1830), one of the founding fathers of sociology, he did not formulate the doctrine.

Numerous attempts have since been made to identify the central tenets of Positivism (see, for example, Abbagano 1967; von Wright 1971; Kolakowski 1972; Giedymin 1975; Hacking 1983; Stockman 1983). In addition to the thesis of the 'unity of method', the following rules or beliefs are generally accepted as characterizing Positivism.

Phenomenalism This rule asserts the uniqueness of experience as the only reliable basis for scientific knowledge. 'We are entitled to record only that which is actually manifested in experience' (Kolakowski 1972: 11). That which is to count as knowledge must be based on experience, on what an observer can perceive by his or her senses. 'The positive tradition gets its character from an insistence on the epistemic primacy of direct observation. The senses give us our sole direct acquaintance with the world, our only source of unvarnished news' (Hollis 1977: 44). This perception must be achieved without the subjective activity of the cognitive process; it must be 'pure experience' with an empty consciousness. Hence, it is a passive model of knowledge. 'An episode of scientific discovery begins with the plain and unembroidered evidence of the senses – with innocent, unprejudiced observation' (Medewar 1969b: 147).

Nominalism The rule of nominalism asserts that any abstract concepts that are used in scientific explanations must also be derived from experience; metaphysical notions about which it is not possible to make any observations, have no legitimate existence except as names or words. As Hindess (1977: 16) has stated it, '[p]ositivism asserts the claims of experience as the ultimate foundation of human knowledge and denies the possibility of meaningful discourse concerning supersensible objects.' For example, the concept of 'God' cannot be regarded as scientific as it is not possible to observe God, and statements such as 'God exists' or 'God does not exist' are meaningless because no observational evidence can have any bearing on them. A development of this rule is the belief that the language used to describe observations must be uncontaminated by any theoretical notions and that the statements in this language can be readily established as true or false by reference to 'reality'. It is a theoretically neutral observation language in which the descriptive terms correspond to real objects. Hence, descriptive terms which do not belong to this privileged language, i.e. theoretical terms which are unobservable, must either be able to be translated into observables or they will be regarded as meaningless.

Atomism The objects of experience, of observation, are regarded as discrete, independent, atomic impressions of events which constitute the ultimate and fundamental elements of the world. In so far as these atomic impressions are formed into generalizations, they do not refer to abstract objects in the world, only regularities among atomic events (Harré 1970).

General Laws Scientific theories are regarded as a set of highly general, law-like statements, and establishing such general laws is the aim of science. These scientific laws summarize observations by specifying simple relations or constant conjunctions between phenomena. Explanations are achieved by subsuming individual cases under appropriate laws. These laws are general in scope in that they cover a broad range of observations and they are universal in form in that they apply, without exception, across time and space: 'Positivism pivots on the Humean theory of causal laws, viz. that laws are or depend upon constant conjunctions of atomistic events or states of affairs, interpreted as the objects of actual or possible experience. This theory itself follows ineluctably from the requirements that knowledge be certain and given-in-experience' (Bhaskar 1979: 158).

Value Judgements and Normative Statements This rule requires a separation of 'facts' and 'values' and denies values as having the status of knowledge: 'we are obliged to reject the assumption of values as characteristics of the world for they are not discoverable in the same way as the only kind of knowledge worthy of the name' (Kolakowski 1972: 17). Giddens has expressed this rule as 'the idea that judgments of value have no empirical content of a sort which renders them accessible to any tests of their "validity" in the light of experience' (1974: 3).

Hacking (1983: 41–57) has identified a similar set of six key ideas which are associated with a positivistic approach to the natural sciences.

1 There is an emphasis on *verification*: the truth or falsity of statements about the world can be settled in some way; they can predict observable states of affairs and are capable of conflicting with observable evidence.
2 *Pro-observation*: what we can see, feel, touch etc. provides the best foundation for non-mathematical knowledge.
3 *Anti-cause*: there is no causality in nature, only constant conjunctions between events, such that events of one kind are followed by events of another kind.
4 *Downplaying explanations*: if all we have are regularities between types of events, then explanation is nothing more than locating an event within a wider-ranging regularity; explanations do not provide deep answers to *why* questions.
5 *Anti-theoretical entities*: given the preceding ideas, unobservable entities may not be offered as causes because reality is what can be observed, and observed regularities are all that can be verified.

6 *Against metaphysics*: the positivist argues that untestable propositions, unobservable entities, causes and deep explanations are derived from metaphysical notions and must be avoided.

According to Halfpenny (1982), it is possible to identify twelve varieties of Positivism. However, for the present purposes, these can be reduced to three (following Outhwaite 1987a). The first brand of Positivism was formulated by Comte as an alternative to theological and metaphysical ways of understanding the world. All scientific knowledge is based on causal laws derived from observation, and all sciences are unified in a hierarchy of related levels, building on mathematics at the lowest level, followed by astronomy, physics, chemistry, biology and, finally, sociology. However, Comte believed in the existence of a social reality independent of the realities of the sciences at lower levels in the hierarchy, and governed by laws that cannot therefore be reduced to the laws of the other sciences; he rejected reductionism.

The second brand of Positivism, known as Logical Positivism, was founded in Vienna in the 1920s. The catch cry of these philosophers was that any concept or proposition that does not correspond to some state-of-affairs, i.e. which cannot be verified by experience, is regarded as meaningless (the 'phenomenalism' rule). At the same time, it is argued that the concepts and propositions of the higher level sciences *can* be reduced to those of the lower ones. In other words, they adopted the reductionist position that the propositions of the social sciences could ultimately be analysed down to those of physics.

The third variety, which was derived from the second and is sometimes referred to as the 'standard view' in the philosophy of science, dominated the English-speaking world after the Second World War. Its fundamental tenet is that all sciences, including the social sciences, are concerned with developing explanations in the form of universal laws or generalizations. Any phenomenon is explained by demonstrating that it is a specific case of some such law. These laws are of the form of 'constant conjunctions' between events, or in the case of the social sciences, statistical correlations or regularities (the 'general law' rule).

At its most general, positivism is a theory of the nature, omni-competence and unity of science. In its most radical shape it stipulates that the only valid kind of (non-analytic)[1] knowledge is scientific, that such knowledge consists in the description of the invariant patterns, the co-existence in space and succession over time, of observable phenomena ... Its naturalistic insistence on the unity of science and scientistic disavowal of any knowledge apart from science induce its aversion to metaphysics, insistence upon a strict value/

---

[1] Analytic statements are true by definition (e.g. 'Black cats are black'), or can be tautological (e.g. 'Either black cats are black or they are not black'). It is self-contradictory to deny either of these kinds of statements. Synthetic knowledge, on the other hand, makes a claim about the world (e.g. 'Black cats are fierce'), and can be denied without self-contradiction.

fact dichotomy and tendency to historicist confidence in the inevitably of scientifically mediated progress. (Bhaskar 1986: 226)

The various brands of Positivism, while differing in some detail, have a particular view of the methods of the natural sciences. Other responses to the question of whether the methods of the natural sciences can be used in the social sciences have not accepted this view. It is therefore useful to distinguish between *Naturalism*, as a positive response to the question, and the specific features that have come to be identified with *Positivism* as a philosophy of science, thus making it possible to adopt a naturalism based on a non-positivist view of science (Keat and Urry 1975: 2).

It was through the work of Comte (1970) and Durkheim (1964) that Positivism was introduced into sociology. Forms of Positivism have dominated sociology, particularly in the decades immediately following the Second World War, and continue to do so today in disciplines such as psychology and economics. In the past fifteen years, Positivism has been the subject of much discussion within sociology (see, for example, Giddens 1974; Fay 1975; Keat and Urry 1975; Adorno et al. 1976; Benton 1977; Hindess 1977; Halfpenny 1982; Bryant 1985). Some examples of how Durkheim advocated the application of the methods of the natural sciences in sociology will be discussed in chapter 5.

Negativism

The proponents of this answer may accept a Positivist view of the natural sciences but argue that the methods of the natural sciences cannot be applied to the social sciences. The arguments for this assertion come in various forms and have been usefully summarized by Popper (1961: 5–34).[2]

1   While the so-called 'laws of nature'[3] are assumed to apply throughout space and time, the regularities in social life are time and space specific. Social uniformities cannot be generalized because they change from one historical period to another and across cultures. The reason for this, it is claimed, is that social uniformities are the result of human activity – they are socially constructed – and can therefore be changed by human activity. 'For social uniformities are not laws of nature, but man-made [sic]; and although they may be said to depend on human nature, they do so because human nature has the power to alter and, perhaps, to control them' (Popper 1961: 7–8).

2   The use of the experimental method is based on the assumption that similar things will happen in similar circumstances. By artificially isolating

---

[2] For similar reviews see Nagel (1961) and Runciman (1969).

[3] These arguments, like much of the popular discussion of the nature of science, assume that the 'laws of nature' are real, that they have an existence independent of the scientist. Popper, however, regarded such laws as the scientist's inventions which are designed to provide an understanding of the natural world.

and controlling the conditions, the influence of one factor on another can be demonstrated with a high level of confidence. Social life, however, is much more complex than natural phenomena and cannot be usefully isolated artificially. In social situations, similar conditions occur only within very limited time periods; history never really repeats itself. Therefore, social conditions can never be precisely repeated and, in any case, in large-scale social experiments, the experimental procedures may artificially eliminate the most important factors and may very well change what is being studied.

3   In the physical sciences (e.g. physics), nothing really new can happen; newness is merely a rearrangement of the elements. In the biological sciences, it is possible for organisms to lose the sense of novelty in experimental situations. Repeating experimental procedures on the same organisms can lead to habitual behaviour; the first application of the procedure changes the possible influence of later applications such that biological newness or novel behaviour can emerge. In other words, organisms learn by experience. However, it is possible to dispose of organisms whose behaviour has been changed by experimental procedures. If societies or social groups are regarded as being like organisms, they too can learn by experience and achieve social newness, but they cannot be disposed of in the same way. This learning becomes part of the group's history.

4   The subject matter of the natural sciences, particularly physics, is much less complicated than the subject matter of the social sciences. Social life presupposes the existence of highly intelligent creatures which have both the capacity and the need for culture. Because they cannot rely on instincts to regulate their activities they have to construct a social world to inhabit, a world of ideas, knowledge, beliefs, values and norms.[4] Therefore, the social sciences face a dual complexity: the impossibility of artificial isolation, and a subject matter that transcends the subject-matters of the natural sciences. Even if social uniformities exist, these complexities may make it impossible to discover them.

5   The theories of the natural sciences are intended to make prediction possible. The form of this prediction (as shall be seen in chapter 5) is that, if certain natural laws apply in a particular circumstance, and certain conditions are met, certain outcomes will follow. However, in the social sciences, a prediction may have an influence on the predicted event. The knowledge of the outcome can change the way people behave, thus producing the possibility of either a self-fulfilling prophesy (Thomas 1928; Merton 1957) or a failed prediction.

6   It follows from the difficulties of making predictions in the social sciences, that there is a complex interaction between the observer and the

---

[4] Popper's development of this point relied on the more limited notion of human psychology and ignored the socially constructed character of social life. For expositions of this latter view, see Berger (1963), Berger and Luckmann (1966), Luckmann (1967), Schutz (1976) and Schutz and Luckmann (1973).

observed which may threaten objectivity. 'The social scientist may be striving to find the truth; but, at the same time, he [sic] must always be exerting a definite influence upon society. The very fact that his pronouncements *do* exert an influence destroys their objectivity' (Popper 1961: 16). Because the social scientist is a member of the category of phenomenon being studied, disinterested detachment may not be possible. Hence, it might be argued, objectivity and the search for truth is impossible in the social sciences; all social research will be contaminated by the values and interests of the researcher.

7   Whereas the natural sciences can work productively in an atomistic manner by regarding its phenomena as consisting of constellations of parts or elements or factors, a social group must be regarded as more than the mere sum of its members, or the sum of the personal relationships existing at any moment in time. Social groups have traditions, institutions, rituals, in short, culture and history. In order to understand and explain social structures and processes it is necessary to treat social groups holistically.

8   The natural sciences, it is argued, aim at causal explanations; the social sciences can only aim at an understanding of meaning and purpose. Therefore,

> [i]n physics events are explained rigorously and quantitatively, and with the aid of mathematical formulae. Sociology tries to understand historical developments in more qualitative terms, for example, in terms of 'national character', or 'spirit of the age'. This is why physics operates with inductive generalisations whereas sociology can only operate with the help of sympathetic imagination. And it is also the reason why physics can arrive at universally valid uniformities, and explain particular events as instances of such uniformities, whereas sociology must be content with the intuitive understanding of unique events, and of the role they play in particular situations, occurring within particular struggles of interests, tendencies, and destinies. (Popper 1961: 20)

9   This use of quantitative analysis and mathematical formulae in the natural sciences is not possible in the social sciences because the concepts found in social theories can only be measured qualitatively, or with a very low level of precision. 'As there is no known way of expressing in quantitative terms the qualities of [social] entities, no quantitative laws can be formulated. Thus, the causal laws of the social sciences, supposing that there are any, must differ widely in character from those of physics, being qualitative rather than quantitative and mathematical' (Popper 1961: 26). This is not to deny that the social sciences may use certain statistical techniques in data analysis, but it is argued that it is not possible to formulate social laws in the precise mathematical terms possible in physics.

This litany of arguments presented by Negativism were not made against social science in general, but were attacks on Naturalism. However, while they are open to debate, they cannot be dismissed lightly. The extent to which they are seen to be a problem depends on the approach to social enquiry adopted. In varying ways, the approaches to social enquiry attempt to resolve those which are considered to be significant. In so far as Negativists are prepared to accept that some form of social research is possible they will limit it to purely descriptive research; explanation and prediction as advocated by Positivism would be considered to be impossible. In this view, social research can produce descriptions of specific events in language that may have specific meanings, using singular statements that assert nothing beyond that event.

It can be argued that the problem of generalizing explanations throughout time and space is not confined to the social sciences. Comparisons which are made with positional astronomy, for example, neglect the fact that this area of the natural sciences is the exception rather than the rule. Predictions made in the natural sciences, even by means of well-known physical laws, occur only within certain artificial and idealized conditions, such as in a perfect vacuum. 'With the less exact sciences, such as meteorology, prediction is notoriously hazardous, while with living systems (not to say sub-atomic physics) we are seldom dealing with anything better than probabilities' (Richards 1983: 86–87). Whether these sciences will be able to improve their predictive capacity in the future is an open question. However, the influence of culture and history is regarded by the advocates of some approaches as making impossible the kind of predictions claimed by Positivism. But this does not rule out the possibility of social *science*, it just makes for a different kind of science.

On the problem of using experiments in the social sciences, Popper (1961: 93–97) has contended that the argument rests on a lack of understanding of the experimental method used in physics. Of course, without knowing a great deal about a particular phenomenon, it is difficult to describe what would constitute similar conditions, and what kind and degree of similarity is relevant. Similarly, it may be difficult to establish what degree and type of experimental controls are necessary. These problems are present in both the natural and social sciences and, according to Popper, can only be resolved by experimentation. While the physicist may be in a better position than the social scientist to cope with these problems, either because social phenomena are more complex than natural phenomena, or because physics has a longer history, according to Popper, there is nothing fundamentally different between the two fields in their potential to conduct experiments.

It is worth noting, however, that many areas of the natural sciences, for example, astronomy, have developed without being able to use experimental manipulation, and in some areas of modern science, such as geology and evolutionary biology, there is little scope for it.

Hence those areas of human social enquiry in which opportunities for controlled experiments are rare, cannot be disqualified from the ranks of science on this account alone. In any event there are some areas, notably social psychology, where experiments indistinguishable in design from those of the natural sciences are routinely performed, while economists make extensive use of idealized models which may be analysed mathematically in much the same way as in physics and physiology. Finally, the 'field investigations', in many social sciences, do not differ in any significant way from those in, say, botany or entomology. (Richards 1983: 86)

It has been argued that the possibility of social researchers allowing their values and prejudices to influence the research process – such as the choice of what is studied, how it is studied, what is regarded as acceptable evidence, how it is collected and how the results are interpreted – makes it difficult to achieve objectivity as understood in Positivism. Whether complete objectivity is possible, or even approachable, is a complex issue which will be taken up later. While such issues may appear to be less serious in the natural sciences, they are nevertheless present. Some of those who believe that value-free social science is not possible have suggested that social scientists should state their values and attitudes as fully and honestly as possible to help others to be aware of possible influences and, hence, how the research results should be interpreted. However, while this may be desirable, it may still be difficult to establish the effects of a social scientist's values and attitudes on the research process and outcomes. Another radical solution has been to abandon the idea of a value-free or objective social science, to treat social phenomena as essentially subjective and to maximize the subjective involvement of the researcher.

It is clear that there are some particular problems which make it difficult to model the social sciences on the natural sciences, but it is also clear that the natural sciences are not without their own problems. Whether the conclusion is that social science is not really possible will depend on how these difficulties are viewed, what responses are made and, more particularly, what kind of social science is considered to be appropriate.

Historicism

In part, Historicism is a response to some of the problems raised by Negativism about the possibility of social science. The central claim is that as there are fundamental differences between the natural and social sciences, only some of the methods of the natural sciences can be applied in the social sciences. In particular, it is the issue of generalization that is considered to separate the two realms. According to Historicism, historical and cultural relativity makes most of the methods of the natural sciences inapplicable in the social sciences (Popper 1961: 5–6).

In spite of this, Historicism accepts that there are two common elements in the methods of the natural and social sciences. Both methods are theoretical and empirical; they are concerned to explain and predict events through the use of theories, and they rely on observation both to identify these events and to accept or reject any theory. By observing the patterns or trends in the past, Historicism claims that predictions can be made about future trends.

It is the success of fields such as positional astronomy, with its capacity to predict astronomical phenomena such as eclipses and the paths of comets, that has encouraged Historicism to argue that social science can predict future events such as revolutions. It is acknowledged that social predictions may lack the detail and precision of natural science predictions but their vagueness is compensated for by their scope and significance. Historicism is interested in large-scale forecasts, not short-term predictions (Popper 1961: 36–7).

Historicism aims at developing laws of historical development, laws that link up the successive historical periods, laws of process and change rather than uniformities. The experimental method is not appropriate for testing such laws. The observation of future events is the only way to establish the validity of such historical laws; the testing must be left to history. Historicism therefore claims that the discipline of sociology is theoretical history. 'Sociology thus becomes, to the historicist, an attempt to solve the old problem of foretelling the future; not so much the future of the individual as that of groups, and of the human race' (Popper 1961: 42). Thus, while Historicism rejects the capacity of the social sciences to develop universal laws through the use of methods such as the experiment, it claims that through the establishment of laws of historical development it is possible to predict the future course of history.

Popper (1961) has attacked four of the arguments on which Historicism is based: the holistic approach to social theories and social change; the character of historical laws; the variability of experimental conditions; and, the relativity of generalizations. As the last two have been dealt with in the preceding section, only the first two will be discussed here.

As an alternative to Historicism's holistic approach to social theories and social change, Popper adopted what he called 'piecemeal engineering' or a 'piecemeal tinkering' approach to scientific investigation (1961: 67). This is a step by step process used to understand any phenomenon and to avoid unwanted consequences; it involves monitoring what has been achieved against what was expected. It is necessary to avoid conducting experiments or proposing social change of such complexity and scope that it is impossible to understand the processes which are occurring; it may develop in unmanageable or undesirable directions. For this reason, Popper objected to 'utopian engineering' which attempts a complete reconstruction of a society in terms of a set of ideals. He preferred the process of learning by trial and error under conditions in which the errors are manageable.

Popper (1961: 97–104) has argued that while it is possible that a particular theory will be found to be time and place specific, even in the natural sciences, it is an important postulate of the scientific method to search for theories which are general. For,

[i]f we were to admit laws that are themselves subject to change, change could never be explained by laws. It would be the admission that change is

simply miraculous. And it would be the end of scientific progress; for if unexpected observations were made, there would be no need to revise our theories: the *ad hoc* hypothesis that the laws have changed would 'explain' everything. (Popper, 1961: 103)

Popper was critical of the central historicist doctrine regarding the claim that the task of social science is to develop laws of historical development, laws of evolution of society which can be used to foretell its future. He argued that this claim is based on the false notion that evolutionary 'theories' include universal laws. Such propositions, however, are particular historical statements.

[T]he search for the law of the 'unvarying order' in evolution cannot possibly fall within the scope of scientific method, whether in biology or in sociology ... The evolution of life on earth, or of human society, is a unique historical process. Such a process, we may assume, proceeds in accordance with all kinds of casual laws, for example, the laws of mechanics, of chemistry, of heredity and segregation, of natural selection, etc. Its description, however, in not a law, but only a singular historical statement. Universal laws make assertions concerning some unvarying order ... But we cannot hope to test a universal hypothesis nor to find a natural law acceptable to science if we are forever confined to the observation of one unique process. Nor can the observation of one unique process help us to foresee its future development. (Popper, 1961: 108–9)

He went on to argue that while history may sometimes repeat itself in certain ways, this does not mean that any apparent repetition or cycle will continue to occur in the future. 'The idea of the movement of society itself – the idea that society, like a physical body, can move as a whole along a certain path, and in a certain direction – is merely a holistic confusion' (Popper, 1961: 114). It is the case that social change may have certain trends or tendencies, but such trends are not universal laws. Trends may persist for hundreds of years but may change at any time in the future. 'There is little doubt that the habit of confusing trends with laws ... inspired the central doctrines of evolutionism and historicism – the doctrines of the inexorable laws of biological evolution and the irreversible laws of motion of society' (Popper, 1961: 116). Popper objected to the kind of logic that is used to generalize from trends in the past to future states of affairs (see chapter 5).

Popper's attack on Historicism is an attack on Marx's claims that the revolutions throughout recorded history reveal a consistent trend in which oppressors are overthrown by the oppressed. Marx used this trend to predict the outcome of the class struggle in our time, in which the bourgeoisie would be overthrown by the proletariat and, in this case, such struggles would cease and a classless society would be created. In the process, Popper has provided arguments for a different view of science which is referred to here as Critical Rationalism.

Critical Rationalism

Critical Rationalism adopts the position that the natural and social sciences differ in their content but not in the logical form of their methods. However, it rejects the Positivist position in favour of a different logic of explanation based on a critical method of trial and error in which theories are tested against 'reality'. This approach is commonly known as the 'method of hypothesis'.

The early foundations of this approach were laid by the English mathematician and theologian, William Whewell (1794–1866), in his monumental work on *The Philosophy of the Inductive Sciences* (1847). Whereas Bacon's view of science had been based on what he believed it should be, Whewell examined how scientists actually carry out their activities. Whewell's view of science was based on his own work as a scientist, not primarily as a philosopher. It has been argued that 'Whewell's exposition of the classical hypothetico-deductive theory of science is probably the most masterful one written before the philosophy of science became a full-bodied discipline in the twentieth century' (Butts 1973: 57).

Whewell was a contemporary of Mill and debated the nature of induction with him. He was critical of Mill's view that scientific knowledge consists of forming generalizations from a number of particular observations, and he challenged the view that observations can be made without preconceptions. He rejected the idea that generalizing from observations is the universally appropriate scientific method and argued that hypotheses must be invented at an early stage in scientific research in order to account for what is observed. For him, observations do not make much sense until they have been organised by some 'conception', an organizing idea, supplied by the researcher. The researcher's task is to find appropriate 'conceptions by which facts are bound together'. He called these 'conceptions' *colligations*. These fundamental ideas cannot be deduced from observations; they cannot be seen in the facts because 'all facts involve ideas unconsciously'. Facts are bound together by a new thought, by 'an act of the mind'. In other words, hypotheses must be applied to bring some order to data.

These 'conceptions' involve the use of new concepts or phrases which have not been applied to these 'facts' previously. In the case of Kepler it was *elliptical orbit*, and for Newton it was *gravitate*. However, Whewell was not able to offer rules for producing these 'conceptions', nor did he believe that the process could be taught. Rather it requires 'inventive talent'; it is a matter of guessing several conceptions and then selecting the right one. He shifted the source of explanations from observations to constructions in the mind of the scientist that will account for observed phenomena.

To hit upon the right conception is a difficult step; and when this step is once made, the facts assume a different aspect from what they had before: that done, they are seen in a new point of view; and the catching this point of view is a special mental operation, requiring special endowments and habits of thought. Before this, the facts are seen as detached, separate, lawless; afterwards, they are seen as connected, simple, regular; as parts of one general fact, and thereby possessing innumerable new relations before unseen. (Whewell quoted in Brody and Capaldi 1968: 137)

Not all such 'conceptions' produce good theories. However, Whewell thought that it was impossible to doubt the truth of a hypothesis if it fits the facts well. In spite of this kind of self-validation, he was prepared to put hypotheses to the test by making predictions and appropriate observations. It is in this latter view of science that Whewell anticipated Popper's approach.[5] Popper was not particularly interested in the notion of hypotheses being organizing ideas; rather, he was concerned with the view of science in which hypotheses, or conjectures, were produced as tentative answers to a research problem and were then tested.

Popper, the founding father of *Critical Rationalism*, first published his ideas in German in 1934, in *The Logic of Scientific Discovery* (translated into English in 1959); a number of other works since then also set out his ideas (1961, 1972, 1976, 1979). While not a member of the Vienna circle, Popper had a close intellectual contact with it. He shared with this tradition the view that scientific knowledge, imperfect though it may be, is the most certain and reliable knowledge available to human beings. However, he was critical of Positivism, particularly Logical Positivism, and was at pains to distance himself from it. He rejected the idea that observations are the foundation of scientific theories and he recognized the important historical role played by metaphysical ideas in the formation of scientific theories.

Popper's philosophy of science depends on an ontology which views nature as consisting of certain essential uniformities. If nature is organized this way, it follows that there will be universal statements which are true because they correspond to these 'facts' of nature. But, according to Popper, in spite of the belief that science proceeds from observation to theory, to imagine that we can start with pure observation, as the Positivists have claimed, without anything in the nature of a theory, is absurd. Observations are always selective and occur within a frame of reference or a 'horizon of expectations'. Rather than wait for regularities to impose themselves on us from our observations, we must actively impose regularities upon the world. We must jump to conclusions, although these may be discarded later if observations show that they are wrong. It is a process of trial and error, of conjecture and refutation (Popper 1972).

Popper developed his philosophy of science in response to Hume's earlier argument that generalizing from past observations cannot be logically justified. Hume had suggested that the idea we have of cause and effect comes from having experienced many instances of constant conjunctions

[5] For a detailed discussion of Whewell's work see Butts (1968, 1973).

in the past. This led him to ask two related questions, one about general-ising from experience, and the other about the belief in the uniformity of nature; whether '*instances of which we have had no experience, must re-semble those, of which we have had experience*' and whether '*the course of nature continues always uniformly the same*' (Hume 1888: 89). On the first he concluded that '*even after the observation of the frequent or constant conjunction of objects, we have no reason to draw any inference concerning any object beyond those of which we have had experience*' (Hume 1888: 139), and on the second, 'that the supposition, *that the future resembles the past*, is not founded on arguments of any kind, but is deriv'd entirely from habit, by which we are determin'd to expect for the future the same train of objects, to which we have been accustom'd' (1888: 134). Popper had no disagreement with Hume's argument that there are no logical grounds for using past experience to establish causal laws, but he was dissatisfied with his view that the tendency we have to accept this is the result of custom or habit. He was concerned that holding an expectation that regularities are everywhere may lead us to attempt to find them even when there are none. These expectations may lead to dogmatic attitudes and an unwill-ingness to give up a belief in a particular regularity.

Hence, Popper concluded that it is up to the scientist to invent regular-ities in the form of theories, but these theories must then be tested by making appropriate observations; the attitude must be critical rather than dogmatic.

> For the dogmatic attitude is clearly related to the tendency to *verify* our laws and schemata by seeking to apply them and to confirm them, even to the point of neglecting refutations, whereas the critical attitude is one of readi-ness to change them – to test them; to refute them; to *falsify* them, if pos-sible. This suggests that we may identify the critical attitude with the scientific attitude, and the dogmatic attitude with the one which we have described as pseudo-scientific. (Popper 1972: 50)

The theories produced by this process are passed on, not as dogmas, but with the injunction that they be further improved.

This critical attitude makes use of both verbal argument and observa-tion; observation is used in the interest of argument.

> [T]he role of logical argument, of deductive logical reasoning, remains all-important for the critical approach; not because it allows us to prove our theories, or to infer them from observation statements, but because only by pure deductive reasoning is it possible for us to discover what our theories imply, and thus to criticize them effectively. Criticism ... is an attempt to find the weak spots in a theory, and these, as a rule, can be found only in the more remote logical consequences which can be derived from it. It is here that purely logical reasoning plays an important part in science. (Popper 1972: 51)

The question of whether theories or observations come first was not a problem for Popper.

It is quite true that any particular hypothesis we choose will have been preceded by observations – the observations, for example, which it is designed to explain. But these observations, in their turn, presupposed the adoption of a frame of reference: a frame of expectations: a frame of theories. If they are significant, if they created a need for explanation and thus gave rise to the invention of a hypothesis, it was because they could not be explained within the old theoretical framework, the old horizon of expectations. There is no danger here of an infinite regress. (Popper 1972: 47)

Critical Rationalism, as expounded by Popper, is a search for truths about the world. However, he argued that we can never hope actually to establish whether theories are in fact true; all we can hope to do is to eliminate those which are false. Science aims to get as near the truth as possible by a process of rational criticism in which theories are tested against descriptions of observed states of affairs. These theories are either rejected or provisionally accepted, and are then subjected to further tests. We never know when we have produced a true theory; all we have are those theories which have, for the present, survived this critical testing process. For Popper, 'truth' means 'correspondence with the facts', and 'facts' are descriptions of observed states of affairs.

For reasons similar to those that motivated the Logical Positivists to want to demarcate science from metaphysics, one of Popper's major concerns was to develop a secure criteria for demarcating science from pseudoscience. Science is separated from other forms of knowledge by the fact that its theories are capable of being exposed to rigorous empirical testing and therefore to the possibility of being falsified. Marx's theory of history (Historicism) and Freud's psychoanalysis were regarded by him as non-scientific theories. Psychoanalysis can explain everything an individual can do or experience, while in the case of Marx's theory it may be less a matter of whether the theory can be falsified than of it having been falsified and still being retained. The adherents of the theory may reject what might be regarded as falsifying evidence by constantly modifying the theory. 'Once your eyes were thus opened you saw confirming instances everywhere; the world was full of verifications of the theory. Whatever happened always confirmed it' (Popper 1972: 35). Because all observations can be explained or excused by such theories, no observation can challenge them. Therefore, according to Popper, as the theories cannot be falsified, they do not have scientific status. He did not intend to show that non-science was meaningless; rather, that if metaphysical notions were included in theories, the testing process would soon establish whether they had any scientific status. Hence, the Positivist distinction between theoretical and observation statements is rejected, as is the possibility of establishing the truth of a theory.

In addressing the methods of the social sciences in one of his later publications, Popper summarized what he called his main thesis.

(a) The method of the social sciences, like that of the natural sciences, consists in trying out tentative solutions to certain problems: the problems from which our investigations start, and those which turn up during our investigation. Solutions are proposed and criticised. If a proposed solution is not open to pertinent criticism, then it is excluded as unscientific, although perhaps only temporarily.

(b) If the attempted solution is open to pertinent criticism, then we attempt to refute it; for all criticism consists of attempts at refutation.

(c) If an attempted solution is refuted through our criticism we make another attempt.

(d) If it withstands criticism, we accept it temporarily; and we accept it, above all, as worthy of being further discussed and criticised.

(e) Thus the method of science is one of tentative attempts to solve our problems; by conjectures which are controlled by severe criticism. It is a consciously critical development of the method of 'trial and error'.

(f) The so-called objectivity of science lies in the objectivity of the critical method. This means, above all, that no theory is beyond attack by criticism; and further, that the main instrument of logical criticism – the logical contradiction – is objective. (Popper 1976: 89–90)

The differences between the methods advocated by Positivism and Critical Rationalism, and how they translate into strategies of social research, will be elaborated in chapter 5.

Classical Hermeneutics

Of all the responses to be considered here, *Hermeneutics* is the most diverse and complex, and the least well understood by social scientists. 'Hermeneutic' literally means making the obscure plain but is generally translated as 'to interpret'.[6] For the most part, hermeneutics has been concerned with interpreting texts. However, the relevance of hermeneutics to contemporary social science lies in the possibility of regarding as texts the records made of social life, and in the application of the approaches that have been established to interpret them.

Hermeneutics emerged in the seventeenth century in Germany and referred, initially, to the principles of biblical interpretation developed by Protestant groups to provide clergy with manuals for scriptural exegesis. However, textual exegesis and theories of interpretation, in religious, literary and legal fields, date back to antiquity. In time, the English usage of the word referred to non-biblical interpretation, particularly of texts that are obscure or symbolic, in order to get at hidden meaning. The advent of

---

[6] The following outline of the hermeneutic tradition is based mainly on Palmer (1969), Outhwaite (1975), Makkreel (1975), Linge (1976), Rickman (1976, 1979, 1988), Bauman (1978), Thompson (1981a,b), Betanzos (1988) and Gadamer (1989).

rationalism in the eighteenth century led to the Bible being interpreted to make it relevant to 'enlightened rational' people. Its mythical elements were purged and, by natural reason, great moral truths were extracted from the historical context in which they were hidden (an activity known as *philological hermeneutics*). Hence, the aim of early hermeneutics was the understanding of texts written in radically different situations.

The next stage, developed by Schleiermacher, provided the foundation for modern hermeneutics. Because he saw hermeneutics as a science for understanding any utterance in language, hermeneutics moved from a concern with the analysis of texts from the past to the problem of how a member of one culture grasps the experiences of a member of another culture, or how a person from one historical period understands life in another historical period. It became the study of understanding itself, of the conditions of dialogue (this became known as *general hermeneutics*).

For Schleiermacher, understanding has two dimensions: grammatical interpretation, which corresponds to the linguistic aspect of understanding and which sets the boundaries within which thought operates; and psychological interpretation, which attempts to recreate the creative act which produced the text or social activity. Psychological interpretation involves placing oneself within the mind of the author or the social actor in order to know what was known by this person as s/he wrote the text or prepared for and engaged in some social act. It is the art of re-experiencing the mental processes of the author of a text or the conversation of a social actor; it is the reverse of the process which produced the text or conversation as it starts with the finished expression or activity and goes back to the mental activity by which it was produced. It consists of a laborious process of endeavouring to construct the life context in which the activity has taken place and in which it makes sense. This process is known as the *hermeneutic circle*, of endeavouring to grasp the unknown whole in order to understand the known parts.

> We understand the meaning of an individual word by seeing it in reference to the whole of the sentence; and reciprocally, the sentence's meaning as a whole is dependent on the meaning of individual words. By extension, an individual concept derives its meaning from a context or horizon within which it stands; yet the horizon is made up of the very elements to which it gives meaning. By dialectical interaction between the whole and the part, each gives the other meaning; understanding is circular. (Palmer 1969: 87)

Since communication is a dialogical relationship, the hermeneutic circle assumes a community of meaning shared by the speaker (or author) and the hearer (or reader). However, evidence of these shared meanings consists of largely incomprehensible fragments of elements in the 'conversation'. The task is to piece together these bits and pieces in order to reconstruct the system of shared meanings.

> The circle starts from the divination of the totality to which the confronted element belongs; if the guess is correct, the element in question reveals part of the meaning, which in turn gives us the lead toward a better, fuller, more specific reconstruction of totality. The process goes on, in ever wider circles, until we are satisfied that the residue of opacity still left in our object does not bar us from appropriating its meaning. (Bauman 1978: 31)

The grammatical approach to interpretation uses a comparative method and proceeds from the general to the particular. The psychological approach is intuitive and uses both the comparative method and the 'divinatory' method. In the latter, the interpreter transforms him/herself into the author to grasp the mental processes involved. Although these two approaches have equal status, they cannot be practised at the same time: in considering the common language, the writer is forgotten; in understanding the author, the language is forgotten.

> The first interpretation is called 'objective', since it is concerned with linguistic characteristics distinct from the author, but also 'negative', since it merely indicates the limits of understanding; its critical value bears only upon errors in the meaning of words. The second interpretation is called 'technical' [and through it] the proper task of hermeneutics is accomplished ... What must be reached is the subjectivity of the one who speaks, the language being forgotten. Here language becomes an instrument at the service of individuality. This interpretation is called 'positive', because it reaches the act of thought which produced the discourse. (Ricoeur in Thompson 1981b: 47)

Ultimately, the aim in understanding the author or social actor from the psychological point of view is to gain access to what is meant in the text or in the social activity.

This process of interpretation is considerably more laborious and difficult for the interpreter than is the activity of understanding in which participants in a 'conversation' need to engage. Much of this latter understanding is taken-for-granted and is drawn on without reflection. However, as Schleiermacher has argued, the interpreter, as an outsider, is in a better position than the author to grasp and describe 'the totality'.

From its background in scriptural and other textual interpretation, hermeneutics came to be seen as the core discipline which provided a foundation for understanding all great expressions of human life, cultural and physical. The instigator of this transition was Dilthey (1833–1911) who referred to this range of concerns as the 'human studies' or the 'human sciences' (*Geisteswissenschaften*). Dilthey argued that the study of human conduct should be based on the method of understanding (*verstehen*) to grasp the subjective consciousness of the participants, while the study of natural phenomena should seek causal explanation (*erklären*). He rejected the methods of the natural sciences as being appropriate for the human sciences and addressed his work to the question: how is objectivity possible in the human sciences? He set out to demonstrate the methods, approaches and categories, applicable in all the humans sciences, which would guarantee objectivity and validity. Whether he produced a satisfactory answer to the question is a matter of some debate but he is regarded by some as the most important philosopher in the second half of the nineteenth century.

In his early work, Dilthey hoped that the foundation of the human sciences would be based on descriptive psychology, an empirical account of consciousness devoid of concerns with causal explanation. He believed that psychology could provide a foundation for the other social sciences in the same way as mathematics underlies the natural sciences. All human products, including culture, were seen to be derived from mental life. However, he later came to realize the limits of this position and turned to Husserl's phenomenology, particularly his doctrine of *intentionality* of consciousness, for the foundation. Subsequently, he became convinced that this did not go far enough or deep enough. Finally, he moved from a focus on the mental life of individuals to understanding based on socially produced systems of meaning.

> In his last years, then, Dilthey seems to have modified his earlier central interest in psychology substantially, first under the influence of attacks on it by Ebbinghaus and the neo-Kantians, then under the powerful influence of Husserl's phenomenological approach and his theory of intentionality, and finally under the influence of his hermeneutical approach to understanding not only individual men but also cultural systems and organizations that have acquired an 'objectified' form in history. (Betanzos 1988: 28)

He came to stress the role of social context and what he called 'objective mind' – objectifications or externalizations of the human mind, or the 'mind-created world' – which are sedimented in history, in what social scientists now call culture.

> Every single human expression represents something which is common to many and therefore part of the realm of objective mind. Every word or sentence, every gesture or form of politeness, every work of art and every historical deed are only understandable because the person expressing himself [sic] and the person who understands him are connected by something they have in common; the individual always experiences, thinks, acts, and also understands, in this common sphere. (Dilthey, quoted in Outhwaite 1975: 26–7)

Dilthey now argued that phenomena must be situated in the larger wholes from which they derive their meaning; parts acquire significance from the whole and the whole is given its meaning by the parts. 'The emphasis shifts from the empathetic penetration or reconstruction of other people's mental processes to the hermeneutic interpretation of cultural products and conceptual structures' (Outhwaite 1975: 26).

Dilthey insisted that the foundation for understanding human beings is in life itself, not in rational speculation or metaphysical theories. Life, by which he meant the human world – social, historical reality – provides us with the concepts and categories we need to produce this understanding. He was critical of the approaches to human understanding of philosophers, such as Locke, Hume and Kant, because there was 'no real blood flowing in the veins' of their human subjects, 'only the diluted juices of reason as mere mental activity'. He regarded the core of life as being instinct, feeling, passion and thought. Thought can be about life and can articulate and explain it, but the most fundamental form of human experience is *lived experience (Eelebnis)*, first-hand, primordial, unreflective experience. Life, or lived experience, is a series of acts in which willing, feeling, thinking, imaginative and creative human beings interact with the physical environment and with other human beings and, in the process, create their world. This lived experience can only be understood through its expressions – gestures, facial expressions, informal rules of behaviour, works of art, buildings, tools, literature, poetry, drama, laws, social institutions – such as religion and cultural systems – which come to posses an independent existence of their own. These 'objectifications of life', or residues of our thoughts in cultural achievements and physical things, can be understood through an inner process of *verstehen*, of hermeneutic understanding.

> [W]e understand [*verstehen*] ourselves and others only because we introduce our own lived experience of life into every kind of expression of our own life and that of others. Thus the combination of lived experience, expression, and understanding [*Erleben, Ausdruck, und Verstehen*] is the specific process whereby mankind [sic] exists for us as an object of the human sciences. Hence the human sciences are grounded in this connection of life, expression, and understanding. (Dilthey, quoted in Betanzos 1988: 24)

The dual process of discovering taken-for-granted meanings from their externalized products, and understanding the products in terms of the meanings on which they are based, is what Schleiermacher had earlier referred to as the *hermeneutic circle*. Dilthey continued to assert the view that objective understanding must be the ultimate aim of the human sciences even if they use this circular method of understanding.

The capacity of another person, or a professional observer, to understand human products is, according to Dilthey, based on a belief that all human beings have something in common. However, he accepted the possibility that human 'expressions' of one group may be unintelligible to members of another group; they may be so foreign that they cannot be understood. On the other hand, they may be so familiar that they do not require interpretation. 'Interpretation would be impossible if the expressions of life were totally alien. It would be unnecessary if there was nothing alien in them. [Hermeneutics] thus lies between these two extreme opposites. It is required wherever there is something alien that the art of understanding has to assimilate' (Dilthey, quoted in Habermas 1972: 164).

Many scholars have contributed to the development of hermeneutics. Two other early contributors will be discussed here because of their methodological relevance, Husserl and Heidegger. Heidegger was influenced by Dilthey but also by the phenomenological method of his mentor, Husserl. Heidegger, in turn, has helped to lay the foundation for one branch of contemporary hermeneutics.

Husserl was instrumental in establishing a parallel intellectual tradition to hermeneutics known as *phenomenology*. He set himself the task of developing a method that would achieve pure understanding, liberated from the relativism of historical and social entanglements. This was the method of phenomenological reduction in which consciousness is freed from presuppositions and thus is able to grasp meaning in its true essence. '[C]onsciousness liberated from the world will be capable of grasping the true meaning; not the contingent meaning, meaning as it happens to be seen – but meaning in its true, necessary essence' (Bauman 1978: 111). Husserl wished to establish truth independently of what people in sociohistorical situations happen to think it is. He argued that in everyday life, in what he called the 'natural attitude', people naïvely accept their world as self-evident; they complacently refrain from questioning or doubting it. Only an exceptional person is able to break out of this natural attitude, to bracket absolutely everything which such an attitude requires us to assume. What is required is nothing less than transcendental *epoche*, of suspending belief.

> The act of *epoche*, so Husserl tells us, differs essentially from supposedly similar operations accomplished by philosophers of the past. It does not mean denying the world in the style of sophist, nor questioning its existence in the style of sceptics. *Epoche* means simply a methodological limitation which allows us to make only such judgments as do not depend for their validity on a spatio-temporal world ... Epoche and transcendental reduction, the 'suspension' of everything empirical, historically transient and culture-bound, are the operations which have to be performed for this direct insight to become possible. As all the 'empirically given' data are to be disposed of on the way, they cannot be employed as steps leading to the final accomplishment: the capture of meaning. (Bauman 1978: 119, 123)

This desire for a path to pure truth, uncontaminated by taken-for-granted ideas, beliefs and prejudices, and unrestricted by the limits of personal knowledge and experience, is not new. What is new in Husserl is the belief that it is possible for a human being to exist in a state of pure consciousness, consciousness free from any earthly attachments, and thus be able to discover the essence of things. It is an act of faith, and a state that can only be imagined in a negative way – as emptiness. However, as Bauman has pointed out, to bracket the world away and leave the empirical individual 'would be like installing burglar alarms on the door but leaving the thief inside the house' (1978: 121). He was also critical of the elitism in Husserl's position, the claim that pure consciousness is a feat that only a few can accomplish.

What Heidegger found attractive in Husserl's work was the notion of a preconceptual method of grasping phenomena. Like Dilthey, he also wanted to establish a method that would reveal life in terms of itself. However, Heidegger saw this new method differently from Husserl. In fact, he turned Husserl's position on its head. Husserl had demanded that we must stand back from, or radically disengage ourselves from, our involvement in our everyday world in order to free our consciousness to grasp the truth. Instead, for Heidegger, understanding is a mode of being and can and must be grasped by ordinary people; it is the foundation of human existence. 'Heidegger's hopes are lodged with a worldly existence uncontaminated by false philosophy, rather than with a consciousness unpolluted by existence' (Bauman 1978: 149). 'Whereas Husserl had approached it with an idea of bringing into view the functioning of consciousness as transcendental subjectivity, Heidegger saw in it the vital medium of man's [sic] historical being-in-the-world' (Palmer 1969: 125). The difference in their views may be related to the fact that Husserl was trained in mathematics and Heidegger in theology.

The central idea in Heidegger's work is that understanding is a mode of being rather than a mode of knowledge, an ontological problem rather than an epistemological problem. It is not about how we establish knowledge; it is about how human beings exist in the world. Understanding is the basis of being human.

For Heidegger, understanding is embedded in the fabric of social relationships and interpretation is simply making this understanding explicit in language. In this everyday world the need for understanding only occurs when the world does not function properly; understanding occurs when something goes wrong. 'I start looking for words when existence reveals to me its rough edges; I need words to patch up the cracks in my world ... [W]e can easily do without it [understanding]. Or rather, we could, if the world functioned smoothly and without interruption' (Bauman 1978: 156, 159). Therefore, understanding is an achievement within the reach of all human beings. 'Understanding is, in fact, our fate, against which we can fight, but from which we cannot escape' (Bauman 1978: 166). This understanding consists of seeing possibilities, of opening oneself up to both the future and the past.

The implications of Heidegger's position, which he clearly recognized, is that history is viewed, as it were, from the inside not the outside; there is no understanding of history outside of history. As Heidegger has put it: 'Interpretation is never a presuppositionless grasping of something in advance.' To assume that what is 'really there' is self-evident is to fail to recognize the taken-for-granted presuppositions on which such assumed self-evidence rests. All understanding is temporal; it is not possible for any human being to step outside history or their social world. Hence, Heidegger moved away from both Dilthey and Husserl.

To recapitulate, early hermeneutics arose in order to overcome a lack of understanding of texts; the aim was to discover what the text means. Schleiermacher shifted the emphasis away from texts to an understanding of how members of one culture or historical period grasp the experiences of a member of another culture or historical period. He argued for a method of psychological interpretation, of re-experiencing the mental processes of the author of a text or speaker in a dialogue. This involved the use of the *hermeneutic circle* to piece together the fragments of meaning that are available; it is the process of grasping the unknown whole from the fragmented parts and using this in order to understand any part. Dilthey then shifted the emphasis again to the establishment of a universal methodology for the human sciences, one which would be every bit as rigorous and objective as the methods of the natural sciences. He moved from psychological interpretation to the socially produced systems of meaning, from introspective psychology to sociological reflection, from the reconstruction of mental processes to the interpretation of externalized cultural products. Lived experience provides the concepts and categories for this understanding. For both Schleiermacher and Dilthey, as an interpreter's prejudices would inevitably distort his/her understanding, it is necessary to extricate oneself from entanglement in a sociohistorical context. Whereas Husserl wished to establish the path to pure consciousness, and hence to pure truth, by bracketing the natural attitude, Heidegger regarded understanding as being fundamental to human existence and, therefore, the task of ordinary people. He argued that there is no understanding outside of history; human beings cannot step outside of their social world or the historical context in which they live. Prejudgements shaped by our culture are the only tools we have.

> Dilthey ... never ceased to be fascinated by the ideal of objective understanding of history, i.e. understanding which itself would not be historical; he earnestly sought a vantage-point above or outside human existence, from which history could be seen as an object of objective study ... [However] Dilthey could only offer the end of history as this point from which true understanding would become a possibility. Husserl can be seen as a philosopher who has drawn logical conclusions from the failure of historical hermeneutics to offer solid foundations for objective understanding: he assumed that objective understanding can be reached only outside and in spite of history, by reason, which by its own effort lifts itself above its existential historical limitations. Heidegger's is the opposite solution of Dilthey's dilemma. There is no understanding outside history; understanding is tradition engaged in an endless conservation with itself and its own recapitulation ... The end of history, instead of revealing the true meaning of the past, would mean the end of understanding: understanding is possible only as an unfinished, future-oriented activity. Far from being unfortunate constraints imposed upon understanding, prejudgements shaped by tradition are the only tools with which understanding can be attained. (Bauman 1978: 170)

Bauman (1990) has characterized these two hermeneutic traditions as being concerned with either legislative reason or interpretive reason. Schleiermacher and Dilthey form the base of the former, and Heidegger, and later Gadamer (see chapter 3), established the latter. Schleiermacher was concerned with a method for establishing true meanings and avoiding false meanings. He regarded the interpreter as being able to provide a better understanding than could the author of the text. In his earlier work, Dilthey argued that interpretations would get nearer the truth over time as succeeding generations of intellectuals benefited from successive stages in the widening of cognitive horizons. He claimed that superior cultures produce superior interpreters. Both authors were claiming the path to true interpretations. Heidegger, on the other hand, could see no escape for interpreters from their location in space and time. Interpretation is not the preserve of the expert; it is part of everyday life, or at least of those occasions when understanding is required. Rather than being a search for truth, it is the opening up of possibilities.

Interpretivism

Interpretivism had its origins in the intellectual traditions of *hermeneutics* and *phenomenology*. Various terms have been used to identify this approach, such as anti-naturalist, anti-positivist or post-positivist. Its central tenet is that there is a fundamental difference between the subject matters of the natural and social sciences. The study of natural phenomena requires the scientist to invent concepts and theories to describe and explain; the scientist has to study nature, as it were, from the outside. Through the use of theories, the natural scientist makes choices about what is relevant to the problem under investigation. The study of social phenomena, on the other hand, requires an understanding of the social world which people have constructed and which they reproduce through their continuing activities. However, people are constantly involved in interpreting their world – social situations, other people's behaviour, their own behaviour, and natural and humanly created objects. They develop meanings for their activities together, and they have ideas about what is relevant for making sense of these activities. In short, the social world is already interpreted before the social scientist arrives.

> The difference between the social and natural world is that the latter does not constitute itself as 'meaningful': the meanings it has are produced by men [sic] in the course of their practical life, and as a consequence of their endeavours to understand or explain it for themselves. Social life – of which these endeavours are a part – on the other hand, is *produced* by its component actors precisely in terms of their active constitution and reconstitution of frames of meaning whereby they organise their experiences. (Giddens 1974: 79)

The contributors to Interpretivism who have been selected for consideration have their roots in German intellectual traditions and in British ordinary language philosophy: Weber (1864–1920), Schütz (1899–1959) and Winch (1926–). While the publications of the latter two spill over into the contemporary period, their work has been regarded as pioneering and has become the inspiration for many contemporary writers.

While Weber followed in the hermeneutic tradition, he was also highly critical of it. He was concerned with establishing causal explanations with the result that his work is a blend of the Interpretive and Positivist approaches. Weber's fundamental methodological concern was with the conditions of and limits to establishing the validity of interpretive understanding. Like Dilthey, he set himself the task of devising an objective way of understanding the essentially subjective subject matter of sociology, of establishing an objective science of the subjective. It has been through the translation of his work that the term *verstehen* has become well known among English-speaking social scientists.

The major statement of Weber's position can be found in the passages in which he defined sociology and its methodological foundations (Weber 1962, 1964; Runciman 1977). He defined sociology as 'a science which attempts the interpretive understanding of social action in order thereby to arrive at a causal explanation of its course and effects' (Weber 1964: 88). This interpretive understanding is directed towards the subjective states of mind of social actors and the meanings which they have used as they engage in particular social action. However, understanding for Weber 'is not the subtle intuitive sympathy which philosophers favour – but intellectual, analytical and predictive explanation of action' (Sahay 1971: 68).

Weber distinguished between *action* and *social action*. *Action* refers to 'all human behaviour when and in so far as the acting individual attaches a subjective meaning to it' (1964: 88). 'By "social" action is meant an action in which the meaning intended by the agent or agents involve a relation to *another* person's behaviour and in which that relation determines the way in which the action proceeds' (Runciman 1977: 7). Therefore, for action to be regarded as social and to be of interest to the social scientist, the actor must attach subjective meaning to it and it must be directed towards the activities of other people. 'Social action, which includes both failure to act and passive acquiescence, may be oriented to the past, present, or expected future behaviour of others . . . The "others" may be individual persons, and may be known to the actor as such, or may constitute an indefinite plurality and may be entirely unknown as individuals' (Weber 1964: 112). This definition allows for the possibility of non-social overt action directed towards an inanimate object, such cases lying outside the interest of the social scientist.[7] According to Weber, subjective

[7] It is important to recognize that Weber's concept of *action* is not a new term for behaviour. Action is behaviour and motives brought together: behaviour is observed and motives are inferred.

meanings may be of three kinds: they may refer to the actual intended meanings used by a social actor; to the average or approximate meanings used by a number of social actors; or, they may be thought of as typical meanings attributed to a hypothetical social actor (1964: 96).

Drawing on Dilthey, Weber distinguished between four modes of understanding: two broad types – *rational* understanding and *empathetic* or appreciative understanding – and two versions of the rational type – *direct* and *motivational* understanding. 'In the sphere of action things are rationally evident chiefly when we attain a completely clear intellectual grasp of the action-elements in their intended context of meaning. Emphathetic or appreciative accuracy is attained when, through sympathetic participation, we can adequately grasp the emotional content in which the action took place' (Weber 1964: 90–1). *Direct* understanding of a human expression or activity is like grasping the meaning of a sentence, a thought, or a mathematical formula. It is an immediate, unambiguous, matter-of-fact kind of understanding which occurs in everyday situations and which does not require knowledge of a wider context. *Motivational* understanding of social action, on the other hand, is concerned with means and ends; it is the choice of a means to achieving some goal.

It was with this motivational form of rational action that Weber was primarily concerned. He regarded human action which lacks this rational character as being unintelligible. The statistical patterns produced by quantitative data, such as the relationship between educational attainment and occupational status, are not understandable on their own. Not only must the relevant action which links the two components of the relationship be specified, but the meaning that is attached to this action must also be identified. 'Statistical uniformities constitute understandable types of action ... and thus constitute "sociological generalizations", only when they can be regarded as manifestations of the understandable subjective meaning of a course of social action' (Weber 1964: 100).

Weber's approach is clearly illustrated in his research on *The Protestant Ethic and the Spirit of Capitalism* (1958). He became fascinated by a statistical correlation between occupation and religion, in particular, the different occupations of Protestant and Catholics.

> A glance at the occupational statistics of any country of mixed religious composition brings to light with remarkable frequency ... the fact that business leaders and owners of capital, as well as the higher grades of skilled labour, and even more the higher technically and commercially trained personnel of modern enterprises, are overwhelmingly Protestant. (Weber 1958: 35)

While Weber recognized that these differences might be explained in part by historical circumstances, such as the advantages of inherited wealth and the educational opportunities it affords, he argued that the explanation must be sought in the intrinsic character of the religious beliefs of

Protestants and Catholics. In looking for different kinds of motivation, he focused on differences in the meaning given to work. These differences, in turn, were seen to be derived from differences in theology. In short, the Calvinist doctrine of predestination (that God has already determined who will go to heaven and no amount of penitence or good works will alter this) created a problem of how to find out whether you have been chosen. The ability to live a pure, honest, non-indulgent life was seen to be a clue and this was accompanied by a view of work as a 'calling', as a way of serving, even worshipping God. The result of hard work and frugality gave the early Protestants the motivation and resources to both stimulate and take advantage of the capitalist economic revolution. This approach to work came to be known as the *Protestant work ethic*. However, in Catholicism, a 'calling' was to a specifically religious life and work was regarded as necessary for survival but not religious in character. According to Weber, all of the other major world religions lacked this meaning and hence motivation for work. Therefore, the explanation for the statistical correlation was to be found in the differences in religious beliefs which resulted in different meanings for work.

Weber defined a motive as 'a complex of subjective meaning which seems to the actor himself or to the observer an adequate ground for the conduct in question' (Weber 1964: 98). He acknowledged that motives can be both rational and non-rational, they can be formulated to give action the character of being a means to some end, or they can be associated with emotional (affectual) states. Only in the case of rational motives did he consider that it was possible to formulate sociological explanations.

For an explanation to be 'adequate on the level of meaning' it needs to identify what he called 'typical complexes of meaning' which are associated with 'coherent courses of conduct'. On the other hand, the causal adequacy of a sequence of events entails the probability that it will always occur in the same way in the future, i.e. that the components of the sequence have usually occurred together and can be expected to do so in the future.

> If adequacy in respect to meaning is lacking, then no matter how high the degree of uniformity and how precisely its probability can be numerically determined, it is still an incomprehensible statistical probability, whether dealing with overt or subjective processes. On the other hand, even the most perfect adequacy on the level of meaning has causal significance from a sociological point of view only in so far as there is some kind of proof for the existence of a probability that action in fact normally takes the course which has been held to be meaningful. (Weber 1964: 99–100)

Weber regarded meaningful interpretations as plausible hypotheses which need to be tested. As experimentation is generally not available in the social sciences, he recommended the use of the comparative method in which experimental conditions are sought in natural situations. If this is not possible, he suggested that the researcher will have to resort to an 'imaginary experiment' 'which consists in thinking away certain elements of a chain of motivation and working out the course of action which would then probably ensue, thus arriving at a causal judgment' (1964: 97).

While Weber's methodology is founded on meaningful social action, he regarded this as only one aspect of the sociologist's concerns. The discussion of his concept of sociology is only preparatory to his discussion of social relationships. He defined social relationships as 'the situation where two or more persons are engaged in conduct wherein each takes account of the behavior of the other in a meaningful way and is therefore oriented in these terms' (Weber 1962: 63). Weber was not primarily concerned with the actor's own subjective meaning but, rather, with the meaning of the situation for a constructed hypothetical actor. He was more particularly concerned with the effect on human behaviour not simply of meaning but of meaningful social relations. His ultimate concern was with large-scale uniformities.

While he was influenced by Hermeneutics, Weber dealt with different issues; he wished to understand and explain social action and social relationships rather than the interpretation of texts. Even although his own research dealt mainly with historical data, he adopted a sociological rather than a historical approach. He saw sociology as being concerned with general concepts and generalized uniformities, whereas he saw history dealing with individual actions (1962: 51).

In developing his version of *verstehen*, he gradually disengaged himself from hermeneutics by developing a view of understanding based on typical motives. He transformed the subjectivity of *verstehen* into understanding based on the construction of rational models of social action.

> Weber's struggle was not about forcing a sociology thoroughly dedicated to objectivism to pay a little more attention to subjectivity and subjectively held values. On the contrary, his was the long and exhausting battle for the emancipation of social science from the relativism in which it floundered, burdened as it was with its idealist and German-hermeneutical legacy. (Bauman 1978: 87)

An aspect of Weber's approach, which has caused later sociologists some difficulties, was his willingness to treat as equivalent the meanings which the social actor attributes to his/her actions and the meanings an observer regards as adequate. This is not surprising given the origins of the hermeneutic tradition in the interpretation of ancient texts. However, his concerns were different from those of this tradition in that he considered that:

> understanding involves the interpretive grasp of the meaning present in one of the following contexts: (a) as in the historical approach, the actual intended meaning for concrete individual action; or (b) as in cases of sociological mass phenomena the average of, or an approximation to, the actual

intended meaning; or (c) the meaning appropriate to a scientifically formulated pure type (an ideal type) of a common phenomenon. (Weber 1964: 96)

Hence, he was not particularly interested in the specific meanings social actors give to their actions but with approximations and abstractions. In any case, as he did not wish to confine himself to either contemporary or micro-situations he was forced to deal with the observer's interpretations. Nevertheless, he regarded such interpretations only as hypotheses to be tested. His work on the Protestant ethic dealt with the typical meaning given to work by the early Calvinists, not with the meaning given by Calvin himself or any one of his followers.

Weber's desire to link statistical uniformities with *verstehen* has led to a variety of interpretations of his version of Interpretivism. Positivists who have paid attention to his work have tended to regard the *verstehen* component as simply a potential source of hypotheses, while Interpretivists have tended to ignore his concern with statistical uniformities and causal explanation.

> Weber seems to have gone too far in trying to meet the claims of positive science and hence landed himself in a position far less easily defensible than would have been the case had he stuck to arguing that there was some relationship between the logic of *verstehen* and the logic of scientific proof. What he does is try to relate *verstehen* to a specific kind of scientific proof based upon the demonstration of probabilities of a statistically determinable kind. This might have had the effect of giving sociology a certain respectability in scientific circles, but in the event the position was untenable and most of Weber's successors have therefore been forced to abandon either his concern with meaning or his tendencies towards scientific positivism. Neither of these positions does Weber justice and what is overlooked is that the whole argument about the two types of explanation is intended to lead into a discussion about truly sociological concepts (i.e. concepts which refer not merely to the meaning of action but to social relations and structures of social relations). (Rex 1971: 24)

As Weber never pursued methodological issues beyond the requirements of his own substantive work, he operated with many tacit assumptions and some of his concepts were not well developed. These aspects of Weber's work have been taken up sympathetically by Schütz (1963a,b, 1970, 1976), for whose work Weber and Husserl provided the foundations. Like Weber, he considered that 'the most serious question which the methodology of the social sciences has to answer is: How is it possible to form objective concepts and objectively verifiable theory of subjective meaning-structures?' (Schütz 1963a: 246), and he regarded the meanings and interpretations that people give to their actions and situations as being the distinguishing feature of social phenomena. Social reality consists of the

> cultural objects and social institutions into which we all are born, within which we have to find our bearings, and with which we have to come to

terms. From the outset, we, the actors on the social scene, experience the world we live in as a world both of nature and of culture, not as a private but as an intersubjective one, that is, a world common to all of us, either actually given or potentially accessible to everyone; and this involves inter-communication and language. (Schütz 1963a: 236)

This is a world of taken-for-granted meanings and interpretations which both facilitate and structure social relationships.

A consequence of holding this view of social reality is that Interpretive social science requires a very different approach to that of the natural sciences.

It is up to the natural scientist to determine which sector of the universe of nature, which facts and events therein, and which aspects of such facts and events are ... relevant to their specific purpose ... Relevance is not inherent in nature as such, it is the result of the selective and interpretive activity of man [sic] within nature or observing nature. The facts, the data, and events with which the natural scientist has to deal are just facts, data, and events within his [sic] observational field but this field does not 'mean' anything to the molecules, atoms, and electrons therein ... But the facts, events, and data before the social scientist are an entirely different structure. His [sic] observational field, the social world, is not essentially structureless. It has a particular meaning and relevance structure for the human beings living, thinking, and acting therein. They have preselected and preinterpreted this world by a series of common-sense constructs of the reality of daily life, and it is these thought objects which determine their behavior, define the goal of their action, the means available for attaining them – in brief, which help them to find their bearings within their natural and socio-cultural environ-ment and to come to terms with it. (Schütz 1963b: 305)

From the outset, Schütz's aim was to put Weber's sociology on a firm foundation. In pursuing this task, he not only elaborated the concept of action, but also offered a methodology of ideal types (1963a,b). He argued that, in assuming that the concept of the meaningful act is the basic and irreducible component of social phenomena, Weber failed, among other things, to distinguish between the meaning the social actor *works with* while action is taking place, the meaning the social actor *attributes to* a completed act or to some future act, and the meaning the sociologist *attributes* to the action. In the first case, the meaning worked with during the act itself, and the context in which it occurs, is usually taken for granted. In the second case, the meaning attributed will be in terms of the social actor's goals. In the third case, the context of meaning will be that of the observer, not the social actor. Weber appeared to assume that the latter is an adequate basis for arriving at the social actor's attributed meaning and that there will be no disputes between actors, or between actors and observers, about the meaning of a completed or future act.

Schütz has provided the foundation for a methodological bridge be-tween the meaning social actors attribute and the meaning the social scientists must attribute in order to produce an adequate theory. According to Schütz, social life is possible, in both face-to-face and more anonymous situations, to the extent that social actors use typifications of both persons and courses of action. The particular typifications used by social actors will be related to their biographically and situationally determined system of interests and relevances, and are socially transmitted, constructed and refined by a process of trial and error (1963a: 243).

In intimate face-to-face situations it may be possible for social actors to grasp fragments of the subjective meaning that other actors bestow on their actions. However, according to Schütz, in these situations, and more particularly in anonymous situations, subjective meanings – motives, goals, choices, plans – can only be experienced in their typicality (1963a: 244). It is from these typifications that social theories must be constructed.

> Now, this same social world which we immediately experience as meaningful is also meaningful from the standpoint of the social scientist. But the context of meaning in which he [sic] interprets this world is that of systematizing scrutiny rather than that of living experience. His data, however, are the already constituted meanings of active participants in the social world. It is to these already meaningful data that his scientific concepts must ultimately refer: to the meaningful acts of individual men and women, to their everyday experiences of one another, to their understanding of one another's meanings, and to their initiation of new meaningful behavior of their own. He will be concerned, furthermore, with the concepts people have of the meaning of their own and other's behavior and the concepts they have of the meaning of artefacts of all kinds. (Schütz 1976: 10)

Schütz has added to the discussion of the role of *verstehen* in the social sciences by distinguishing three uses of the concept. First, it refers to the epistemological problem of how understanding is possible (Gadamer's problem); second, it refers to a method peculiar to the social sciences (Dilthey's problem); but, thirdly, it refers to the experiential form in which social actors deal with the social world (Heidegger's problem). In this latter sense, it is the process by which people negotiate their way in their everyday social situations, how they discover the taken-for-granted meanings that are operating.

> *Verstehen* is, thus, primarily not a method used by the social scientist, but the particular experiential form in which common-sense thinking takes cognizance of the social cultural world. It has nothing to do with introspection; it is a result of processes of learning or acculturation in the same way as the common-sense experience of the so-called natural world. *Verstehen is*, moreover, by no means a private affair of the observer which cannot be controlled by the experiences of other observers ... Moreover, predictions based on *Verstehen* are continuously made in common-sense thinking with high success. (Schütz 1963a: 239)

Schütz argued that *verstehen* is not 'subjective' in the sense that understanding the motives of another person's action 'depends upon the private, uncontrollable, and unverifiable intuition of the observer or refers to his [sic] private value system' (1963a: 240). Rather, it is 'subjective' because its aim is to discover what a social actor 'means' by his/her actions in contrast to the meaning this action has for other social actors in the situation or for an outside observer.

Another tradition of Interpretive social science was developed in Britain by Winch (1958) under the influence of the later philosophy of Wittgenstein. Winch wanted to draw a clear distinction between the natural and social sciences while at the same time arguing for an essential identity between the social sciences and philosophy. He was one of the first to drawn on British ordinary language philosophy as a basis for explicating what is meant by 'social' and, in the process, his arguments drew heavily on Wittgenstein's concepts of 'language-game' and 'form of life'.

At a time when Positivism and Critical Rationalism ruled supreme in the social sciences in the English-speaking world, Winch argued that basing social science on natural science was a mistake because understanding society is both conceptually and logically different from understanding nature (Winch 1958: 72, 94, 119). The difference between society and nature is not just that the former is more complicated than the latter, as was claimed by Mill (1879).

> Now though human reactions are very much more complex than those of other beings, they are not *just* very much more complex. For what is, from one point of view, a change in the degree of complexity is, from another point of view, a difference in kind: the concepts which apply to the more complex behaviour are logically different from those we apply to the less complex. (Winch 1958: 72)

He rejected attempts to understand human activity based on physiological states, general dispositions or causal explanations, in favour of 'reasons' for acting in a particular way.[8]

While there is some debate about whether Winch accepted a Positivist view of the natural sciences (see, for example, Keat 1971; Stockman 1983), he certainly claimed that there is a radical difference between the natural and social sciences. Following Wittgenstein's view of language as rule-following within a 'form of life' or culture, Winch argued that social behaviour is to be understood as rule-following behaviour and not as causally regular behaviour. Whereas the natural sciences are concerned with establishing causal sequences, the social sciences are concerned with understanding the meaning of human conduct in terms of rule-following. To understand what someone is doing it is necessary to grasp the rule being followed. These rules are not private; they are shared and maintained by

[8] See Turner (1980) for a useful review and critique of Winch's position.

people in a social context and are embodied in the behaviour of other people. A person's actions are intelligible to others to the extent that they are following accepted standards of what is appropriate in that social context. The presence of social regularities is used as evidence that some rule is operating, whether or not people are consciously aware of it. Hence, Winch linked the notion of meaningful action to rule-following. '[A]ll behaviour which is meaningful (therefore, all specifically human behaviour) is *ipso facto* rule-governed' (1958: 52). Rules therefore provide both the reasons and the motives for the behaviour, and learning these rules 'belongs to the process of learning to live as a social being' (1958: 83).

Winch was critical of Weber's distinction between 'action' and 'social action', between action which is merely meaningful and that which is both meaningful and social. He regarded this distinction as being incompatible with his position; 'all meaningful behaviour must be social, since it can be meaningful only if governed by rules, and rules presuppose a social setting' (1958: 116). Winch took Weber's notion of meaningful social action and translated it into Wittgenstein's notion of rule-following against a background of interpersonal agreements on criteria.

Winch posed, and endeavoured to answer, a fundamental epistemological question. What is the relationship between 'the world' and the language in which we try to describe 'the world'? (1958: 120). He argued that language determines what will count as 'the world'.

> Our idea of what belongs to the realm of reality is given for us in the language that we use. The concepts we have settle for us the form of the experience we have of the world ... [However] when we speak of the world we are speaking of what we in fact mean by the expression 'the world': there is no way of getting outside the concepts in terms of which we think of the world ... The world *is* for us what is presented through those concepts. That is not to say that our concepts may not change; but when they do, that means that our concept of the world has changed too. (Winch 1958: 15)

This position led Winch to argue that language and social activity are inextricably bound together. '[O]ur language and our social relations are just two different sides of the same coin. To give an account of the meaning of a word is to describe how it is used; and to describe how it is used is to describe the social intercourse into which it enters' (1958: 123). Further, he argued that 'the social relations between men [sic] and the ideas which men's actions embody are really the same thing considered from different points of view' (1958: 121). In other words, the 'social reality' of social relationships is embedded in the concepts that are used by participants in social contexts to talk about their 'world'. He was determined to show 'that social relations really exist only in and through the ideas which are current in society; or alternatively, that social relations fall in the same logical category as do relations between ideas' (1958: 133).

Review

Many arguments have been presented to support the case that a science of human behaviour and social life is not possible. Most of them derive from a view that any social uniformities are not the result of the same processes that produce regularities in physical or biological phenomena. They are seen to be the result of actions and decisions of human beings and can, therefore, be changed. It is claimed that not only do general laws of social life not exist but that even if they did their complexity, and the inappropriateness of experimental or mathematical procedures for their investigation, make it impossible to discover them. And even if they did exist and could be discovered, predictions based on them are likely to be confounded by the capacity of human beings to take such information into account in their actions.

Such arguments have not deterred the Positivists, the Critical Rationalists or the Interpretivists from providing answers to the question of whether the natural and social sciences should share the same methods. However, their approaches differ dramatically in terms of whether they accept the Negativist arguments and, if so, how they deal with them. A broad spectrum of answers has been offered, ranging from a dogmatic 'Yes' to a definite 'No'. However, answers to this question presuppose a view of what constitutes the methods of the natural sciences and, for many decades, one particular view prevailed.

> The central debate within the philosophy of the social sciences has concerned the methodological unity of natural and social sciences. However, the way in which this debate has been conducted is fundamentally misconceived. This is because it has been viewed primarily in terms of the relevance of one particular conception of science, that of positivism, to the study of social phenomena. But ... there are a number of different conceptions of science and ... it is erroneous to discuss the methodological unity issue simply in terms of one particular characterisation of the natural sciences. (Keat and Urry 1975: 1)

Two such views of the natural sciences have been discussed in this chapter. Naturalism argues for the 'unity of method', but does so on the basis of a Positivistic view of science. Positivism regards reality as discrete events that can be observed by the human senses. The only knowledge of this reality that is acceptable is that which is derived from experience, the recording of the 'unembroidered evidence of the senses'. The language used to describe this knowledge consists of concepts which correspond to real objects and the truth of statements in this language can be determined by observation, which are uncontaminated by any theoretical notions. It is assumed that there is order in this reality which can be summarized in terms of the constant conjunctions between observed events or objects. These regularities, which are considered to apply across time and space, constitute general laws but not causes; explanations are achieved by demonstrating that any regularity is a specific case of some more general law. Positivism, but particularly the version known as Logical Positivism, rejects all theoretical or metaphysical notions that are not derived from experience. In the same way, value judgements are excluded from scientific knowledge as their validity cannot be tested by experience. That which cannot be verified by experience is meaningless.

The second view, Critical Rationalism, has supported Naturalism but has rejected many features of Positivism; it has advocated a very different view of the methods of the natural sciences. While adopting the assumption that there are uniformities in nature that can be discovered and described, it rejects the idea that 'pure' observation is possible. Observations are always made within a frame of reference, with certain expectations in mind. Therefore, generalizing from a limited set of 'impure' observations is not a satisfactory basis for scientific theories. Observations may furnish evidence of regularities that need to be explained, but the process of explanation must begin with a tentative theory, an idea that could account for what has been observed. Such a conjecture must then be subjected to critical examination and rigorous testing against 'reality'. Observations need to be made to collect data relevant to the theory. If these data are not consistent with the theory, the theory must be rejected, or at least modified and retested. If the data are consistent with the theory it can be provisionally accepted; it is corroborated. However, no theory is ever proved; its truth can never be established conclusively. The best that can be done is to eliminate false theories; corroborated theories will be used until such time as better theories are developed and tested.

These two views of science may share a common ontology but they adopt fundamentally different epistemologies. They both believe in the existence of an 'external' reality which is ordered, but they differ in the role that observation plays in discovering this order and in how the order is explained. Positivism views uncritically the activity of observing and the possibility of establishing the truth of a theory, whereas Critical Rationalism accepts the inherent limitations of observations and the impossibility of knowing whether a theory is true. Positivism places its faith in 'objective' procedures to arrive at the truth, while Critical Rationalism, as its name implies, is sceptical and rigorous in its evaluation of any theory that is proposed. The logics of their procedures are fundamentally different as are their products. Positivism produces descriptions of regularities which form a hierarchy of generality; lower level 'conjunctions' are explained as being specific cases of higher level regularities. Critical Rationalism, on the other hand, is interested in causal explanation which is regarded as a set of related and satisfactorily tested hypotheses. (The nature of these theories will be elaborated in chapter 5.)

Those founders of hermeneutics who were interested in establishing the social sciences with the same legitimacy and reputation as the natural sciences, rejected as inappropriate the concern of the natural sciences with explanation. Rather, they were interested in the understanding of human activities that can be obtained from the interpretation of the meanings which underlie these activities. The methods of the natural sciences (and for early hermeneutics this was the Positivist approach) were therefore considered to be inappropriate for the study of human activities. From the beginning, the problem of how an interpreter from a particular time and culture could grasp the experiences of members of another culture, particularly from another historical period, was regarded as being fundamental. One approach was to try to reconstruct the mental activity of the author of a text or social activity, another was to reflect on the objectified expression and residues of cultural achievements. Both activities involve a process of constructing the whole meaning from the available fragments and then using the evolving whole to understand the parts, a process known as the *hermeneutic circle*.

A second fundamental issue which came to divide the hermeneutic tradition concerned the possibility of producing 'objective' knowledge from these activities, an understanding freed from the limitations of the social and historical location of the observer. The aspiration that human beings could exist in a state of pure consciousness gave way to a fully blown recognition that this is not only impossible but that it is also undesirable. The social world should be understood on its own terms in the same manner as its participants do, from the inside as it were, not from some neutral outside position occupied by an expert.

Hermeneutics and phenomenology provided the foundations for the Interpretivist view of the relationship between the natural and social sciences. This approach agreed that the natural scientist has to study nature from the outside and, therefore, at least in the Critical Rationalist view, has to invent suitable concepts and theories to describe and explain this reality. However, for the Interpretivist, social reality is the product of its inhabitants; it is a world which is already interpreted by the meanings which participants produce and reproduce as a necessary part of their everyday activities together. Hence, because of this fundamental difference in the subject matters of the natural and social sciences, different methods are required. The founders of this approach followed the branch of hermeneutics which sought to establish an objective science of the subjective with the aim of producing verifiable knowledge of the meanings which constitute the social world. The attention focused on the nature of meaningful social action, its role in understanding patterns in social life, and how this meaning can be assessed. Rather than trying to establish the actual meaning that a social actor gave to a particular social action, Interpretivists considered it is necessary to work at a higher level of generality. Social regularities can be understood, perhaps explained, by constructing models of typical meanings used by typical social actors engaged in typical courses of action in typical situations. Such models constitute tentative hypotheses to be tested. Only social action which is rational in character, i.e. which is consciously selected as a means to some goal, is considered to be understandable.

The question of whose meanings are used to construct these ideal types has been a matter of some dispute. Can the observer's point of view be used to attribute likely meanings or must they be taken from the social actor's point of view? The later contributors to Interpretivism raised the question of the relationship between the concepts and meanings of social actors and the concepts and meanings used in social theories, and argued that the latter must be derived from the former. Language came to be seen as the medium of social interaction and everyday concepts as structuring social reality. This everyday reality is paramount; it is argued that it is the social actor's not the social investigator's point of view that is the basis of any accounts of social life.

There are, therefore, three major classical positions which offer fundamentally different answers to the question of the relationship between the methods of the natural and social sciences. The Positivist approach, which emerged out of the philosophical discussions that accompanied the establishment of the natural sciences, made no distinction. Likewise, for Critical Rationalism, although this approach was based on a very different conception of the methods of the natural sciences. And running parallel to the emergence of Positivism was the negative responses of Hermeneutics and Interpretivism. While they did not necessarily challenge either of the Positivist or Critical Rationalist conceptions of the methods of natural sciences, they rejected them in favour of radically different methods for the social sciences. Chapter 3 explores more recent responses to the question, responses which largely reject Positivism and Critical Rationalism and incorporate aspects of Classical Hermeneutics and Interpretivism.

Further Reading

Key References

Bauman, Z. 1978. *Hermeneutics and Social Science.*
Bryant, C.G.A. 1985. *Positivism in Social Theory and Research*
Halfpenny, P. 1982. *Positivism and Sociology: Explaining Social Life.*
Hindess, B. 1977. *Philosophy and Methodology in the Social Sciences.*
Keat, R. and Urry, J. 1975. *Social Theory as Science.*
—— 1982. *Social Theory as Science*, 2nd edn.
Outhwaite, W. 1975. *Understanding Social Life: The Method Called Verstehen.*
Popper, K.R. 1959. *The Logic of Scientific Discovery.*
—— 1961. *The Poverty of Historicism.*
—— 1972. *Conjectures and Refutations.*
Schütz, A. 1963a. 'Concept and Theory Formation in the Social Sciences'.
—— 1963b. 'Common-sense and Scientific Interpretation of Human Action'.
—— 1976. *The Phenomenology of the Social World.*
Weber, M. 1964. *The Theory of Social and Economic Organization.*
Winch, P. 1958. *The Idea of Social Science and its Relation to Philosophy.*

General References

Adorno, T.W. et al. 1976. *The Positivist Dispute in German Sociology*.
Bauman, Z. 1990. 'Philosophical Affinities of Postmodern Sociology'.
Bernstein, R.J. 1976. *Restructuring Social and Political Theory*.
Betanzos, R.J. 1988. 'Introduction'.
Bhaskar, R. 1979. *The Possibility of Naturalism*.
Fay, B. 1975. *Social Theory and Political Practice*.
—— 1987. *Critical Social Science: Liberation and its Limits*.
Giddens, A. 1974. *Positivism and Sociology*.
Hacking, I. 1983. *Representing and Intervening*.
Harré, R. 1960. *An Introduction to the Logic of the Sciences*.
—— 1972. *The Philosophy of Science: An Introductory Survey*.
Hempel, C.E. 1966. *Philosophy of Natural Science*.
O'Hear, A. 1989. *An Introduction to the Philosophy of Science*.
Palmer, R.E. 1969. *Hermeneutics: Interpretation Theory in Schleiermacher, Dilthey, Heidegger, and Gadamer*.
Popper, K.R. 1976. 'The Logic of the Social Sciences'.
—— 1979. *Objective Knowledge: An Evolutionary Approach*.
Stockman, N. 1983. *Antipositivist Theories of the Sciences*.
Thomas, D. 1979. *Naturalism and Social Science*.
Tudor, A. 1982. *Beyond Empiricism: Philosophy of Science in Sociology*.
Weber, M. 1958. *Basic Concepts in Sociology*.
—— 1962. *The Protestant Ethic and the Spirit of Capitalism*.
Winch, P. 1964. 'Understanding a Primitive Society'.
Wolff, K.H. 1984. *Alfred Schütz: Appraisals and Developments*.

3

What Kind of Science is Social Science? Contemporary Responses

Introduction

Five contemporary responses to the key question, 'Can the methods of the natural sciences be used in the social sciences?', are reviewed in this chapter. All five responses are critical of or entirely reject both *Positivism* and *Critical Rationalism* and, to varying degrees, use or build on *Classical Hermeneutics* and/or *Interpretivism*. The first of these responses, *Critical Theory*, is a 'Yes and No' response; it argues for a combination of methods for the social sciences, including some aspects of *Positivism* and *Interpretivism*, and adds an emphasis on human emancipation. The second response, *Realism*, is another 'Yes and No' response. In recognizing the qualitative differences in subject matters between the natural and social sciences, it also adopts aspects of *Interpretivism*, but argues for principles of enquiry different from those contained in any of the other responses, principles which are claimed to be common to both areas of science. The third response, *Contemporary Hermeneutics*, is another definite 'No'; it develops the concerns of *Classical Hermeneutics* in directions which take it further away from *Positivism* and *Critical Rationalism* than any of the other responses. The fourth response, and the last of the 'Yes and No' responses, is *Structuration Theory*; it provides a synthesis of aspects of many theoretical and philosophical traditions, with a strong foundation in *Contemporary Hermeneutics* and *Interpretivism*. While its concerns are more ontological than epistemological, it provides the foundation for a research strategy that transcends many of the deficiencies in earlier approaches. And, finally, another 'No' response from the emerging approach of *Feminism*. While it includes some issues absent in the other approaches – for example, a concern about the masculine nature of science and the consequences for knowledge of women being viewed as an oppressed class

– it grapples with many of the same issues. It shares some features of *Interpretivism*, *Critical Theory* and *Structuration Theory* and, in its present developing state, includes a variety of views. These contemporary responses are much more complex than most of the classical responses and contain a high degree of internal diversity.

Contemporary Responses

Critical Theory

Critical Theory, developed by the Frankfurt School in Germany in the 1930s, builds on German intellectual traditions. Following the Second World War, during which its founders moved to the United States, the School became popular outside Germany, particularly in the late 1960s. It is founded on the idea that *reason* is the highest potentiality of human beings and that, through its use, it is possible to criticize and challenge the nature of existing societies. The early Critical Theorists, particularly Horkheimer and Marcuse, regarded reason as a 'critical tribunal' which is based on the values of freedom and pleasure. They saw human beings as free, autonomous agents who are able to create and control their own lives as long as their society lacks any form of alienation. They regarded capitalist society as fundamentally irrational in that it failed to satisfy existing wants and produced false wants and needs. Hence, the writings of the early Critical Theorists were largely directed towards presenting a particular view of human beings and offering a critique of capitalism.

At the same time, Critical Theorists were opposed to Positivism, particularly Logical Positivism, mainly because it denied the intelligibility of the concept of reason. According to the Logical Positivists, as reason is not derived from experience it falls outside the realm of scientific knowledge. Hence, for Critical Theorists, Positivism supports the status quo because it rules out the possibility of a society based on this critical capacity (Keat and Urry 1975: 220).

The views of Critical Theory on the relationship between the natural and social sciences discussed here will be restricted to those of its leading contemporary exponent, Jürgen Habermas. With his intellectual roots in Hermeneutics, Habermas, like the Interpretivists, claimed that the subject matters of the natural and social sciences are fundamentally different. Critical Theory does not support the 'unity of method' principle of Naturalism; there is a fundamental difference in the modes of experience used by the two fields. Habermas (1970, 1972) described the natural sciences as using 'sense experience', and the social and cultural or hermeneutic sciences as using 'communicative experience'. The former is based on direct observation and the latter on the understanding of meaning derived from communication with the social actors.

He argued that no system of basic concepts comparable to that established [in natural science] for the investigation of moving bodies and observable events was in principle possible in the study of society. This is because societies are differently constituted as objects of possible knowledge. They form a network of intentional actions; and statements about intentional actions are not reducible to statements about observable events. The investigator must gain access to his [sic] data through an understanding of meanings. (Connerton 1976: 35)

Following Husserl, Habermas rejected the 'objectivist illusion' of Positivism, according to which the world is conceived as a universe of facts independent of the 'observer' whose task is to describe them, and he accepted the same premise as Interpretivism that social and cultural reality is already pre-interpreted by the participants as a cultural symbolic meaning system which can be changed over time. Therefore, the process for understanding this socially constructed reality is 'dialogic'; it allows individuals to communicate about their experience within a shared framework of cultural meanings. Alternatively, in the natural sciences the process is 'monologic'; the technical manipulation by the researcher of some aspect of nature. In the latter, the researcher is a 'disengaged observer' who stands in a subject-to-object relationship to the subject matter while, in the former, the researcher is a 'reflective partner' whose relationship is that of subject to co-participant (Stockman 1983: 143–4, 152).

The 'objectivist illusion' involves regarding the objects that are 'perceived' by means of theoretical constructs as things that actually exist, that are real. There is a failure to recognize that knowledge of the seemingly objective world of facts is really based on the assumptions about the nature of reality that are embedded in the common-sense and frequently taken-for-granted thinking of everyday life. Hence, once this illusion was recognized, Habermas considered that it was possible to identify the fundamental interests which underpin the procedural rules of any science.

One of the central concepts in Habermas's understanding of knowledge is that of 'interest' or, more correctly translated, 'cognitive interests' or 'knowledge-constitutive interests'. These interests, he argued, determine what counts as the objects of knowledge, the categories relevant to what is taken to be knowledge, as well as the procedures for discovering and justifying knowledge. Interests are fundamental because they relate to the conditions which make the continuation of human life possible (Bernstein 1976: 192).

Habermas (1972: 301–17) classified the processes of scientific enquiry into three categories, each of which produces its own form of knowledge: they are distinguished according to their underlying interests, their anthropologically rooted strategies for interpreting life experiences, and their means of social organization. The first form of knowledge is derived from the *empirical–analytic* sciences (including the natural sciences and economics, sociology and political science) which are interested in technically exploitable knowledge, in prediction and control, and thus with increasing the possibility of human domination over nature and social relations; human social existence is based on work (the ways in which individuals control and manipulate their environment in order to survive). The second form of knowledge is derived from the *historical–hermeneutic* sciences and is based on practical interests in the communicative understanding between individuals and within and between social groups, with the interpretive understanding of linguistic communication in everyday discourse, and with the understanding of traditions and their artistic and literary products; human social existence is based on interaction (ordinary language communication). The third form of knowledge is derived from *critical theory*, involving self-reflection, and is based on an emancipatory interest in achieving rational autonomy of action freed from domination; human social existence is based on power (asymmetrical relations of constraint and dependency) (Habermas 1972).

This scheme can be represented as follows (based on Giddens 1977b: 140).

Type of science	Underlying interests	Aspects of social existence
Empirical–analytic	Prediction and control	Work (instrumental action)
Historical–hermeneutic	Understanding	Interaction (language)
Critical theory	Emancipation	Power

The distinction between 'work' and 'interaction' is critical to this scheme. Individuals are seen to shape and determine themselves both through work and through communicative action and language.

By 'work' ... I understand either instrumental action or rational choice or their conjunction. Instrumental action is governed by *technical rules* based on empirical knowledge. In every case they imply conditional predictions about observable events, physical and social. These predictions can prove correct or incorrect. The conduct of rational choice is governed by *strategies* based on analytic knowledge. They imply deductions from preference rules (value systems) and decision procedures; these propositions are either correctly or incorrectly deduced ... But while instrumental action organizes means that are appropriate or inappropriate according to criteria of an effective control of reality, strategic action depends only on the correct evaluation of possible alternative choices, which results from calculations supplemented by values and maxims. By 'interaction', on the other hand, I understand *communicative action*, symbolic interaction. It is governed by binding *consensual norms*, which define reciprocal expectations about behavior and which must be understood and recognized by at least two acting subjects. Social norms are enforced through sanctions. Their meaning is objectified in ordinary language communication. While the validity of technical rules and strategies depends on that of empirically true or analytically correct propositions, the validity of social norms is grounded only in the intersubjectivity of the mutual understanding of intentions and secured by the general recognition of obligations. (Habermas 1971: 91–2)

For Habermas, it is not only important to recognize the need for both the *empirical–analytic* sciences and the *historical–hermeneutic* sciences, but also to recognize the differences between them.[1]

The first two forms of knowledge reflect the traditional division between the natural sciences (*Naturwissenschaften*) and the humanities (*Giesteswissenschaften*), while the third form is new. However, the distinction between the *empirical–analytic* sciences and the *historical–hermeneutic* sciences is not intended to correspond to differences in subject matter. Human beings can be studied as part of nature, as in biology, or as social actors. Rather, the distinction is concerned with the interests of the researcher and, hence, with the way reality is viewed. The *empirical–analytic* sciences are concerned with bodies in motion, with events and processes which can be explained causally, while the *historical–hermeneutic* sciences deal with speaking and acting subjects whose utterances and actions can be understood (McCarthy 1984: 70).

This distinction also appears to run parallel to the long-established contrast in German social thought between 'explanation' and 'understanding', the former being associated with the natural sciences and the latter with the social and cultural sciences (Bottomore 1984: 57–58). However, Habermas argued that Critical Theory involves all three forms of knowledge and is therefore not identical with *self-reflection*. It includes: interpretive understanding of systems of belief and modes of communication using the methods of historical–hermeneutic science; the critical evaluation of these; and the investigation of their causes by the methods of empirical–analytic science.

Within the social sciences, Habermas distinguished between the hermeneutic or cultural sciences, and the 'systematic' social sciences, such as sociology. The latter, he argued, may have to draw on the methods of empirical–analytic science in order to study relatively stable and widespread empirical regularities in social life, even if these regularities are historically specific. They may have to draw on methods other than hermeneutic ones. In addition, as cultural traditions serve as ideologies, it may be necessary for *emancipatory* science to draw on both the other two forms of knowledge.

In his later work, Habermas realized that his theory of cognitive interests needed further development. In order to provide a foundation for *emancipatory* science, he had to find a way of establishing the claims of a 'critical' theory; he had to find a way of establishing the truth of the critique. This was achieved by developing a 'consensus theory of truth', as against Positivism's correspondence theory of truth. In brief, he argued that truth claims can ultimately be decided only through critical discussion,

---

[1] For summaries of Habermas's theory of cognitive interests, see Keat and Urry (1975: 223–4), Giddens (1977b: 137–41), Held (1980: 255–6), Thompson (1981a: 82–4), Bubner (1982: 46), and Outhwaite (1987a: 81). For critical reviews, see Bernstein (1976: 173–225) and McCarthy (1984: 53–91).

through the achievement of a 'rational consensus', not through an appeal to evidence gained by observation. For such a consensus to be regarded as perfectly rational, it must be possible to demonstrate that any rational, competent person would come to the same conclusion if they were free of all constraints or distorting influences, whether their source was open domination, conscious strategic behaviour or the more subtle barriers to communication deriving from self-deception. Such a set of ideal circumstances he called 'an ideal speech situation'. Even if such a situation is impossible to achieve, it is nevertheless assumed or anticipated in all discourse. All participants is such a discourse must not only have the same chance to speak but they must also be free to question and refute claims of other speakers. Any such discourse is based on the assumption that what a speaker says is understandable and true, and that the claims made are sincere and appropriate for the speaker to make. It is deviation from these assumptions that leads to 'distorted communication'. Hence, truth involves the promise of reaching a consensus. Critical Theory claims to be grounded in a normative standard that is not arbitrary but is inherent in the very structure of social action and language (Held 1980: 256).

Critical theory is critical of the natural sciences because, as a result of their dependence on technical rationality (or instrumental reason), and their success in the domination of nature, they and technology have become an important new source of authority and power in society. In order to be emancipated from the domination of technical rationality the social theorist must enable people to understand their situation in the social world to help them become emancipated through being competent communicators.

The broad view of Positivism with which Critical Theorists have worked has made it possible for Habermas to accept some of the features of Positivism while at the same time rejecting others. For example, he rejected Positivism's ideas about causal laws as universal truths in favour of the view that they have a practical function. They can be the basis for action, the results of which can be assessed and fed back into their improvement. 'Causal laws are thus to be seen as recipes for producing effects, recipes which nature itself follows to produce its own effects and which people can discover to produce the effects they desire' (Stockman 1983: 67).

A modified version of Critical Theory has been developed by Fay (1975) as an alternative to both Positivism and Interpretivism. He gave his version three main features. First, as it is based in the felt needs and sufferings of a group of people, it is necessary to understand the world from their point of view. Secondly, his Critical Theory recognizes that many of the actions people perform are caused by conditions over which they have no control and which are not based on conscious knowledge and choice. Therefore, it is necessary to try to discover the 'quasi-causal and functional laws of social behaviour' that operate in particular contexts. Thirdly, there is a recognition that social theory is interconnected with social practice such that the truth or falsity of a theory is partially determined by whether it can be translated into action, i.e. if an adequate understanding has been achieved of people's felt needs and experienced privations, and of the structural conflicts and inherent contradictions which cause them, and this leads to action which overcomes them, then the theory must have some validity. This is usually referred to as the 'pragmatic view of truth'. Thus, not only is the theory grounded in the self-understanding of the social actors, but it must be possible to translate it into their language in order for them to be able to change their self-understanding and act on the theory.

[A] critical theory is clearly rooted in concrete social experience, for it is one which is explicitly conceived with the practical intention of overcoming felt dissatisfaction. Consequently, it names the people for whom it is directed; it analyses their suffering; it offers enlightenment to them about what their real needs and wants are; it demonstrates to them in what way their ideas about themselves are false, and at the same time extracts from these false ideas implicit truths about them; it points to those inherently contradictory social conditions which both engendered specific needs and make it impossible for them to be satisfied; it reveals the mechanisms in terms of which this process of repression operates; and, in the light of changing social conditions which it describes, it offers a mode of activity by which they can intervene in and change the social processes which are thwarting them. A critical theory arises out of the problems of everyday life, and is constructed with an eye towards solving them ... [T]he claims of such a theory can only be validated partially in terms of the responses that the social actors themselves have to the theory. This is to say that whether it indeed offers a way out of an untenable situation (and is therefore a true theory) is partially determined by whether those for whom it is written recognise it as a way out and act on its principles. (Fay 1975: 109–10)

More recently, Fay (1987) has argued that a fully developed critical social science consists of a complex of four different theories which comprise ten sub-theories.

I   *A theory of false consciousness* which
    1 demonstrates the ways in which the self-understandings of a group of people are false ... or incoherent ... or both ... ;
    2 explains how the members of this group came to have these self-understandings, and how they are maintained;
    3 contrasts them with an alternative self-understanding, showing how this alternative is superior.
II   *A theory of crisis* which
    4 spells out what a social crisis is;
    5 indicates how a particular society is in such a crisis ... ;
    6 provides an historical account of the development of this crisis partly in terms of the false consciousness of the members of the group and partly in terms of the structural bases of the society.
III *A theory of education* which
    7 offers an account of the conditions necessary and sufficient for the sort of enlightenment envisioned by the theory;

8 shows that given the current social situation these conditions are satisfied.

IV *A theory of transformative action* which

9 isolates those aspects of a society which must be altered if the social crisis is to be resolved and the dissatisfactions of its members lessened;

10 details a plan of action indicating the people who are to be the 'carriers' of the anticipated social transformation and at least some general idea of how they might do this. (Fay 1987: 31–2)

These theories must not only be consistent with one another but must also be systematically related such that the elements of one theory or sub-theory is employed, where appropriate, in the other theories or sub-theories. Fay argued that Habermas's theory of late capitalism covers all the components of this scheme except for sub-theories 8 and 10. This gap in Habermas's work has been one of the most frequent criticisms, i.e. that his theories are academic and utopian and have little bearing on political life (Fay 1987: 33).

Realism

Realism offers a 'Yes' answer but rejects the Positivist view of science in favour of an alternative. Realists believe that they have unearthed the only scientific principles that are capable of capturing the nature of reality. For the social sciences to be scientific they must adopt these same principles. At the same time, because Realism adopts the Interpretive position that there are fundamental differences between natural and social phenomena, it does not insist on an identity of method. Rather, it is concerned with developing methods appropriate to the particular subject matter of the social sciences, methods based on realist principles. Realism tries to reflect scientific practice, while at the same time avoiding its fatal flaws (Harré 1986).

According to Realism, science is concerned with what kinds of things there are and how these things behave. It is concerned with a reality that is claimed to exist and act even if it has not yet been observed, and this reality has a life of its own apart from the activities of science (Bhaskar 1986: 5). Realism claims that the entities, states or processes described by theories really do exist. 'Protons, photons, fields of force, and black holes are as real as toe-nails, turbines, eddies in the stream, and volcanoes' (Hacking 1983: 21). It also claims that theories are either true or false; science aims at the truth about how the world behaves.

Realist elements in philosophies of science are not new; what is relatively new is the elaboration of realist philosophies of social science which provide an alternative answer to the key question. There are two major strands of Realism in the social sciences: one in which Harré has applied his realist theory of the natural sciences to social psychology; and another in which

Bhaskar, Keat and Urry, and Benton have developed various versions of a realist social science to accommodate Marxist structuralism. Bhaskar, like Harré, also drew on his realist theory of the natural sciences.

Bhaskar rejected most of the arguments of Negativism and insisted that social *science* is possible. However, while the methods of the natural and social sciences share common principles, their procedures will differ because of the differences in their subject matters. '[T]he human sciences can be sciences *in exactly the same sense*, though *not in exactly the same way*, as the natural ones' (Bhaskar 1979: 203). He argued for a qualified anti-positivist naturalism. Because the subject matter of the social sciences cannot be reduced to the subject matter of the natural sciences (for example, human behaviour cannot be reduced to biochemical reactions), there are qualitative differences between them. Hence, social objects cannot be studied in the same way as natural objects, but they can be studied 'scientifically' as *social* objects (Bhaskar 1979: 26–7). 'Thus it is obvious that one can no more set out to experimentally identify (or non-vacuously simulate) the causes of the French revolution than one can contemplate interviewing a gene' (Bhaskar 1979: 30, n. 40).

Realism adopts an anti-positivist position while accepting the Interpretive view that social reality is pre-interpreted, that society is both *produced* and *reproduced* by its members and is therefore both a *condition* and an *outcome* of their activity; the social sciences have a subject–subject relationship to their subject matter rather than a subject–object one characteristic of the natural sciences. However, while sharing Positivism's desire for producing causal explanations and Interpretivism's views on the nature of social reality, Realism argues for a view of science that is very different from either of these approaches.

Bhaskar's (1978) aim was to provide a comprehensive alternative to Positivism, paying particular attention to its view of causal laws as constant conjunctions. He argued that there is a distinction between a causal law and a pattern of events. A constant conjunction must be backed by a theory which provides an explanation of the link between the two events, a theory which provides a conception or picture of the mechanism or structure at work. These mechanisms are nothing more than the tendencies or powers that things have to act in a particular way. The capacity of a thing to exercise its powers, or the likelihood that it does, will depend on the circumstances which may be favourable or unfavourable (Harré 1970: 277–8). Therefore, Realism is ultimately a search for generative mechanisms.

Bhaskar argued that 'if science is to be possible the world must consist of enduring and transfactually active mechanisms' (1975: 20). It is therefore necessary to assume that such mechanisms are independent of the events which they generate such that they may be out of phase with the actual pattern of events. It is also necessary to assume that events can occur independently of them being experienced.

The combined tendencies of these structures and mechanisms *may* generate events that in turn *may* be observed, but the events take place whether or not there is anyone around to observe them, and the tendencies of the underlying structures of reality remain the same even when they counteract each other in such a way as to produce no (directly or indirectly) observable change in reality. (Outhwaite 1983a: 321–2)

Hence, Bhaskar proposed that experiences, events and mechanisms constitute three overlapping domains of reality; the domains of the *empirical*, the *actual* and the *real*. The *empirical* domain consists of events which can be observed, the *actual* domain consists of events whether or not they are observed, and the *real* domain consists of the structures and mechanisms which produce these events (see table 1).

Table 1 Domains of reality

	Domain of empirical	Domain of actual	Domain of real
Experiences	✓	✓	✓
Events		✓	✓
Mechanisms			✓

Source: adapted from Bhaskar 1975: 56.

According to Harré, the first stage in the process of Realist science is to produce critical descriptions of non-random patterns by 'exploration' – to extend what is known by common observation – and by 'experiment' to check critically the authenticity of what is thought to be known. In carrying out exploration, a scientist may have some idea about the direction in which to go but no very clear idea of what to expect. This critical descriptive phase is referred to as *empirical studies* and is followed by *theoretical studies* which are concerned with producing a rational explanation of the non-random patterns found in empirical studies. This is achieved by identifying the causal or generative mechanisms which produce the patterns. It is possible, however, that phenomena which appear to have no pattern might be produced by a variety of different and unconnected mechanisms (Harré and Secord 1972: 69–71).

Harré has summarized his realist approach to the natural sciences as consisting of three key assumptions.

1 Some theoretical terms refer to hypothetical entities.
2 Some hypothetical entities are candidates for existence – some could be real things, qualities, and processes in the world.
3 Some candidates for existence are real – it can be demonstrated that they exist. (Harré 1972: 91)

Hence, because causal mechanisms are, in general, different in kind from the phenomena that they explain, these mechanisms can become the subject for further scientific study. The explanation of their principles of operation requires the formulation of new models, and so on (Harré 1970: 261). Bhaskar has summarized Realism in much the same way.

> [W]e have in science a three-phase schema of development, in which in a continuing dialectic, science identifies a phenomenon (or range of phenomena), constructs explanations for it and empirically tests its explanations, leading to the identification of the generative mechanisms at work, which now becomes the phenomenon to be explained, and so on. On this view of science its essence lies in the move at any one level from manifest phenomena to the structures that generate them. (Bhaskar 1978: 4)

Bhaskar's approach consists of five principles (Outhwaite 1987a: 45–6).

1 A distinction is made between *transitive* and *intransitive* objects of science. Transitive objects are the concepts, theories and models which are developed to understand and explain some aspects of reality, and intransitive objects are the real entities and their relations that make up the natural and social worlds.
2 Reality is stratified into three levels or domains: the empirical, the actual and the real. The *empirical* domain consists of the events that can be observed (the area on which Positivists concentrate), the *actual* domain consists of events whether they are observed or not, and the *real* domain consists of the structures and process that make up reality and which produce events.
3 Causal relations are regarded as powers or *tendencies* of things which interact with other tendencies such that an observable event may or may not be produced, and may or may not be observed. Social laws need not be universal; they need only represent recognized tendencies. This view contrasts with the Positivist view in which causal laws are regarded as universal constant conjunctions between events.
4 In the domain of the real, definitions of concepts are regarded as *real definitions*, i.e. statements about the basic nature of some entity or structure. These are neither summaries of what is observed nor stipulations that a term should be used in a particular way.
5 Explanatory *mechanisms* in the domain of the real are postulated and the task of research is to try to demonstrate their existence.

Harré has argued that creative model building, and the identification of powers and natures, should be an essential part of the methods of the social sciences just as they are in the natural sciences.

> [T]he human and natural sciences should in fact employ the same methods, and ... much of the disappointment one must feel with the progress of the human sciences in the Twentieth Century derives from their imitating a false

picture of the natural sciences, in particular the picture delineated by positivists. (Harré and Secord 1972: 82)

These methods, and their application in the social sciences, will be elaborated in chapter 6.

Bhaskar (1983, 1986) has added an emancipatory component to his version of Realism. He has argued that social science is non-neutral in a double sense. 'It consists of a *practical intervention* in social life, and it *logically entails* value judgments' (Bhaskar 1983: 275–6). He was critical of the view that social actors' interpretations or accounts must be regarded as incorrigible, i.e. as not being open to correction by an outside expert, that these interpretations are all that is necessary for social knowledge, or that such knowledge is rooted in them. He has argued that, in adopting such an Interpretive (or Hermeneutic) foundation for Realism,

> it is important to distinguish the meaning of an act (or utterance) from the agent's intention in performing it. The meaning of an act is a social fact which, to the extent that the act is intentional, is utilized by the actor in the production of his performance. But the reason that the act is performed by the agent is a fact about the person which cannot be read off or deduced from its social meaning. (Bhaskar 1983: 292)

In this argument, Bhaskar has distinguished between meanings of actions which are necessarily social in character (presumably because they are intersubjective), and beliefs about, or reasons (motives) given for actions, which are personal. He considered it to be important to distinguish the knowledge (meanings) used in action from the beliefs (motives) that prompt or rationalize it. It follows from this that if a social scientist has an adequate theory to show that a particular belief is false (that it is illusory, inadequate or misleading), and why such a belief is believed, then it is possible to offer a critique of such a belief, and mandatory to suggest action which might be rationally directed to removing or transforming this false belief (Bhaskar 1983: 298). There is clearly some overlap between this position and those advocated by Habermas and Fay, and, as shall be seen, by Rex and Giddens; all have sympathy with Marx's notion of false consciousness.

While the views of Realism advocated by Harré and Bhaskar have a great deal in common, they also differ in fundamental ways, in particular, in their view of social reality and how it can be known. Harré has argued for an interpretive social psychology, while Bhaskar has adopted a more structuralist or materialist ontology. Harré wished to maintain a separation between reasons and causes, arguing that 'reason explanations' are the analogue in the social sciences of the 'mechanism explanations' of the natural sciences. However, they both agree that social science is a search for the fundamental structures and mechanisms of social life.

Contemporary Hermeneutics

The review of *Classical Hermeneutics* in chapter 2 revealed two polarized positions which divide on the claim of whether or not objective interpretation is possible. One, based on the work of Schleiermacher and Dilthey, looked to hermeneutics for general methodological principles of interpretation. It endeavoured to establish an objective understanding of history and social life above and outside human existence. The other, based on the work of Heidegger, regarded hermeneutics as a philosophical exploration of the nature and requirements for all understanding and regarded objectively valid interpretation as being impossible. It claimed that there is no understanding outside history and culture; understanding is an integral part of everyday human existence and is therefore the task of ordinary people, not experts. These traditions have persisted, the latter being developed by Gadamer and Ricoeur, and the former by Betti.

Gadamer was not particularly interested in the further development of hermeneutic methods for the social sciences, nor was he specifically concerned with the interpretation of texts. Rather, his interest was in all human experience of the world and what is common to all modes of understanding. '[T]he way that we experience one another, the way that we experience historical traditions, the way that we experience the natural givenness of our existence and of our world, constitutes a truly hermeneutic universe' (Gadamer 1989: xiv). He wished to focus on the process of understanding itself, and did so by addressing three questions. How is 'understanding' possible? What kinds of knowledge can 'understanding' produce? What is the status of this knowledge? This agenda he regarded as philosophical rather than methodological.

The key to understanding for Gadamer is the grasping of the 'historical tradition', a way of understanding and seeing the world at a particular time and in a particular place within which, for example, a text is written. It involves adopting an attitude which allows a text to speak to us, while at the same time recognizing that the tradition in which the text is located may have to be 'discovered' from other sources. For Gadamer, hermeneutics goes beyond the analysis of a text on its own terms to the location of it in its historical context. The aim is to 'hear' beyond the mere words.

> Interpretation . . . does not refer to the sense intended, but to the sense that is hidden and has to be revealed. Thus every text not only presents an intelligible meaning but, in many respects, needs to be revealed. . . . [The historian] will always go back behind them and the meaning they express to enquire into the reality of which they are the involuntary expression . . . They, like everything else, need explication, ie to be understood not only in terms of what they say, but of what they bear witness to. (Gadamer 1989: 300–1)

When viewed in the context of disciplines such as anthropology and sociology, 'historical tradition' can be translated as 'culture' or 'worldview', and 'texts' as records of conversations between social participants or with a researcher. Gadamer's position would require us to look beyond what is said to what is being taken for granted while it is being said, to the everyday meaning of both the language used and the situations in which the conversations occur.

Another important feature of Gadamer's approach is the recognition that the process of understanding the products of other traditions or cultures cannot be detached from the culture in which the interpreter is located. He was critical of Dilthey's attempt to produce an 'objective' interpretation of human conduct. Rather, the task of the interpreter is to engage a text (a historical or contemporary social event) in dialogue with the aim of understanding the question of which it is an answer (Gadamer 1989: 334). However, to reconstruct the question, the interpreter will need to go beyond the original historical 'horizon' to include his/her own 'horizon'.

A text or historical act must be approached from within the interpreter's horizon of meaning, and this horizon will be broadened as it is fused with that of the act or text. The process of understanding involves a 'fusion of horizons' in which the interpreter's own horizon of meaning is altered as a result of the hermeneutical conversation with the other horizon through the dialectic of question and answer. The interpreter engages the text in dialogue, a process that transforms both the text and the interpreter. 'It is true that a text does not speak to us in the same way as does another person. We, who are attempting to understand, must ourselves make it speak' (Gadamer 1989: 340). However, making the text speak is not an arbitrary process; it is guided by the search for the question which it answers. The anticipation of an answer by the interpreter presumes that some historical consciousness has been achieved as has an attitude of openness to the tradition entailed in the text. The interpreter is not trying to discover what the text 'really means' by approaching it with an unprejudiced open mind; s/he is not so much a knower as an experiencer for whom the other tradition opens itself.

For Gadamer, hermeneutics is about bridging the gap between our familiar world and the meaning that resides in an alien world. '*Understanding is not reconstruction but mediation* . . . [It] remains essentially a mediation or translation of the past meaning into the present situation . . . [It] is an event, a movement of history itself in which neither interpreter nor text can be thought of as autonomous parts' (Linge 1976: xvi). Collision with another horizon can make the interpreter aware of his/her own deep-seated assumptions, of her/his own prejudices or horizon of meaning, of which s/he may have remained unaware; taken-for-granted assumptions can be brought to critical self-consciousness and genuine understanding can become possible. The interpreter does not simply read what is there in the text.

> Rather, all reading involves application, so that a person reading a text is himself [sic] part of the meaning he apprehends. He belongs to the text that

he is reading . . . He can, indeed he must, accept the fact that future generations will understand differently what he has read in the text. And what is
true for every reader is also true for the historian. The historian is concerned
with the whole of historical tradition, which he has to combine with his own
present existence if he wants to understand it and which in this way he keeps
open for the future. (Gadamer 1989: 304)

Gadamer argued that understanding what another person says is not a
matter of 'getting inside' his/her head and reliving her/his experiences. As
language is the universal medium of understanding, understanding is about
the translation of languages. However, 'every translation is at the same
time an interpretation' (Gadamer 1989: 346). Every conversation presupposes that the two speakers speak the same language and understand what
each other says. But the hermeneutic conversation is usually between different languages, ranging from what we normally regard as 'foreign' languages, through to differences due to changes in a language over time or
to variations in dialect. The hermeneutic task is not the correct mastery of
another language but the mediation between different languages. Thus,
understanding as the fusion of horizons occurs through language; language
allows the mediation, the interpenetration and transformation of past and
present. Whether it be a conversation between two persons, or between an
interpreter and a text, a common language must be created.

In the same way as people belong to groups, they also belong to language and history; they participate in them. 'Because of our belongingness
to language and because of the belongingness of the text to language, a
common horizon becomes possible . . . The belongingness to, or participation in, language as the medium of our experience of the world . . . is the
real ground of the hermeneutical experience' (Palmer 1969: 208). Language,
after all, is the game of interpretation that we are all engaged in every day.
Thus, language allows us not only to understand a particular experience,
but also the world in which the experience occurs. Gadamer argued that
even from the world of our own language we can grasp the world of
another language.

Our own language world, this world in which we live, is not a tight enclosure
that hinders the knowing of things as they are; rather, it encompasses basi-
cally everything which our insight is able to broaden and lift up. Certainly
one tradition sees the world differently from another. Historical worlds in
the course of history have differed from each other and from today. At the
same time, however, the world is always a human, and this means a lin-
guistically created, world which is presented in whatever heritage it may be.
(Gadamer 1960; quoted in Palmer 1969: 207)

Therefore, as language has a universal function of providing human beings
with a world of shared understanding, and hermeneutics is linguistic in
nature, hermeneutics itself also has universal significance.

Kilminster has summarized Gadamer's view of hermeneutics.

> For Gadamer, understanding is not a special method of *Verstehen* but an ontological condition of humankind. In the interpretation of texts written in different periods, it is impossible to eliminate the prejudices or preunderstandings that we bring to them, because we cannot escape the tradition from which we enter into the subject matter of the text. Both the interpreter and the tradition being investigated through the text contain their own 'horizon' in Gadamer's terms, so the task of hermeneutic inquiry is a circular one of integrating one's own horizon with that of the tradition concerned in a 'fusion of horizons'. This is an unending process whereby we test out our preunderstandings, so changing our understanding of the past and ourselves in a continuous process. (Kilminster 1991: 104)

Betti (1962), the Italian historian of law, drew on the work of Schleiermacher and Dilthey and argued that interpretation is a reconstruction of the meaning the author intended. While he did not exclude subjectivity from human interpretation, he argued that the interpreter must be able to penetrate the foreign subjectivity which is embodied in the text being studied. Texts are regarded as having their own autonomy and as having something to say to us that is independent of our act of understanding. The study of history should leave aside the present standpoint of the historian and return to objectivity.

In contrast, Gadamer regarded the search for objective historical knowledge as 'an illusion of objectifying thinking'. 'To speak of "objectively valid interpretations" is naïve, he asserted, since to do so assumes that it is possible to understand from some standpoint outside of history' (Palmer 1969: 46). In response to Betti's criticisms, Gadamer argued that he was interested in ontology, not epistemology, with establishing what all ways of understanding have in common rather than being concerned with problems of method.

> We are confronted with two very different conceptions of the scope and purpose of hermeneutics, the methods and kinds of thinking appropriate to it, and the essential character of the discipline as a field of study. With two very different definitions, resting on different philosophical foundations, the two thinkers formulate hermeneutics to fulfil very different purposes. Betti, following Dilthey in quest of a foundation discipline for the *Geisteswissenschaften*, looks for what is practical and useful to the interpreter. He wants norms to distinguish right from wrong interpretations, one type of interpretation from another. Gadamer, following Heidegger, asks such questions as: What is the ontological character of understanding? What kind of encounter with Being is involved in the hermeneutical process? How does tradition, the transmitted past, enter into and shape the act of understanding an historical text? (Palmer 1969: 59)

The basic issue which divides these two positions, of whether objectivity is possible, is particularly troublesome for social researchers and has surfaced in the work of many contributors to the Hermeneutic and Interpretive approaches to social science.

Ricoeur, a French philosopher writing mainly in the 1960s and 1970s, further developed the hermeneutics of Heidegger and Gadamer. His contribution emerged gradually during his career and culminated in the formulation of a semantics of discourse which provides the foundation for a general theory of interpretation centred on the concept of the text. In addition to providing answers to several philosophical problems, his theory of interpretation offers solutions to a number of controversies in the methodology of the social sciences (Thompson 1981a: 70).

Like Weber, Ricoeur assumed that the central concern of the social sciences is with meaningful social action. He argued that such social action shares the essential features of texts and can therefore be included under a general theory of interpretation. He defined a text as any discourse fixed in writing. While this discourse could have been spoken, the written form takes the place of speech; speech could have occurred in the situation which the text identifies. The reader takes the place of the other person in the dialogue, just as writing takes the place of speaking and the speaker. However, unlike Gadamer, Ricoeur argued that it is not possible to say that reading is a dialogue with the author, as the relation of the reader to the text is different from that between two speakers in a dialogue.

> Dialogue is an exchange of question and answer; there is no exchange of this sort between the writer and the reader. The writer does not respond to the reader. Rather, the book divides the act of writing and the act of reading into two sides, between which there is no communication. The reader is absent from the act of writing; the writer is absent from the act of reading. The text thus produces a double eclipse of the reader and the writer. It thereby replaces the relation of dialogue, which directly connects the voice of one to the hearing of the other. (Ricoeur 1981a: 146–7)

Ricoeur argued that language has no subject – nobody speaks; it is outside of time and it has no world. Discourse, on the other hand, is an event in time in which something happens when someone speaks; it refers to a world which it claims to describe, express or represent and it is addressed to another person. In spoken discourse the participants are socially situated and their dialogue is about something in *their* world but, in the case of a text, the author and the reader do not share a common world. Therefore, this 'leaves the text, as it were, "in the air", outside or without a world' (Ricoeur 1981a: 148). It creates a distance from spoken discourse.

Ricoeur suggested a number of ways in which this 'distanciation' occurs. Putting discourse in writing severs the meaning of what is said from the intentions of the speaking subject; the meaning of an utterance stands in its own right. In spoken discourse the intention of the speaker and the meaning of what is said frequently overlap, but the meaning of the text no longer coincides with the meaning intended by the author. In spoken discourse the speaker addresses a hearer, while written discourse is addressed to a unknown audience and to anyone who can read. 'The text thus "decontextualises" itself from its socio-historical conditions of production, opening itself to an unlimited series of readings' (Thompson 1981a: 52). Further, the text is not limited in terms of its frame of reference as is the case in spoken discourse.

A consequence of these distanciations is that several interpretations of a text are possible and, according to Ricoeur, they will not have equal status. If they are in conflict, the problem is how to choose between them. Ricoeur concluded that the problem of finding the right understanding cannot be solved by searching for the alleged intention of the author; the author's intentions have no privileged role. How then can the problem be resolved? '[T]he elimination of inferior interpretations is not an empirical matter of verification and proof, but a rational process of argumentation and debate' (Thompson 1981a: 59, 53).

For Ricoeur, to read is to join the discourse of the text with the discourse of the reader. Because of its open character, the text is renewed in the process and interpretation is achieved. This is accompanied by the self-interpretation of the reader through 'appropriation', making one's own what was initially alien – the convergence of the horizons of the writer and the reader. Appropriation is the process by which the revelation of new 'forms of life' (Wittgenstein), or 'modes of being' (Heidegger), give the reader new capacities of knowing her/himself. Appropriation is not a kind of possession, or taking hold of; it is a moment of dispossession of the narcissistic *ego*; the text gives a *self* to the *ego* (Ricoeur 1981b: 192–3). In short, appropriation is the recovery of that which is at work within the text.

This view of the text allowed Ricoeur to develop an alternative view of the opposition between explanation and understanding to that crystallized by Dilthey and addressed by Weber. He rejected Dilthey's view of hermeneutics as the attempt to reproduce the creative process which produced a text and claimed that this view was inconsistent with Dilthey's other concern to achieve an objective logic of interpretation. Instead, he argued that his distinction between speech and the text allows for two possibilities: as readers we can regard a text as having no author and no world, and explain it in terms of its internal relations, its structure; or we can treat the text as recorded speech and interpret it. In the first case, the text is regarded as language (*langue*) and is treated according to the explanatory rules of linguistics, while in the second case it is treated as speech (*parole*) and is interpreted. 'These two possibilities both belong to reading, and reading is the dialectic of these two attitudes' (Ricoeur 1981a: 152), but it is the second attitude that is the real aim of reading.

Ricoeur believed that this distinction provided a way of combining explanation and understanding. The analysis of the structure of language as a closed system provides a form of explanation, while a depth interpretation of the text as speech provides understanding. He argued that understanding cannot be reduced to structural analysis; understanding requires a different attitude towards the text which is not concerned with what might be hidden in it but is concerned with what it is pointing to.

Thompson regarded Ricoeur's proposal to conceive of action as a text as unsatisfactory. For example, he suggested that Ricoeur failed to provide a clear and convincing defence of the notion that the meaning of an action may be detached from the event of its performance. 'For the meaning of an action is linked to its description, and how one describes an action is deeply affected by circumstantial considerations' (Thompson 1981a: 127). He rejected Ricoeur's claim that participants in social action have no particular privilege when it comes to interpreting their actions.

> For it is precisely because contemporaries do have a privileged position that there are methodological problems concerning the relation between the everyday descriptions of lay actors and the theoretical accounts of external observers, and concerning the relation between the latter accounts and the subsequent courses of action pursued by reflective and informed agents in the social world. Lay actors may not have the first word in the interpretation of their action, but they do, in a fundamental epistemological sense, have the final word. To conceive of action as a text in accordance with Ricoeur's hermeneutical discourse is to eliminate such problems by a premature piece of conceptual legislation. (Thompson 1981a: 127)

While Ricoeur was aware of the limitations of a theory of action that ignored social structures, Thompson has argued that he failed to provide an adequate account of the relation between action and social structure. As in any philosophy of social science with an interpretive foundation or bias, Ricoeur tended to 'reduce the results of the empirical disciplines to diagnostic indications of hidden realms of subjectivity, rather than regarding them as evidence for the determination of objective social conditions' (Thompson 1981a: 129).

Structuration Theory

Structuration Theory is the concept used to identify a contemporary approach to social theory and methodology advocated by Anthony Giddens. However, 'Structuration theory is not intended to be a theory "of" anything, in the sense of advancing generalizations about social reality' (Giddens 1991: 204). It is, rather, an attempt to reconstruct some of the basic premises of social analysis, particularly an ontological framework for the study of human social activities. Giddens has used the term 'social theory' to cover issues he considered to be the concern of all the social sciences. 'These issues are to do with the nature of human action and the acting self; with how interaction should be conceptualized and its relation to institutions; and with grasping the practical connotations of social analysis' (1984: xvi–xvii).

In his numerous publications, Giddens has identified the two most critical theoretical dilemmas in the social sciences today and he has proposed ways of moving beyond them. The first dilemma is the issue under discussion in this and the previous chapter: the relation between the natural and social sciences. The second dilemma concerns the relation between the individual and society, between 'agency' (or action) and 'structure', between deterministic and voluntarist theories of human behaviour.

On the first dilemma, Giddens has presented arguments for the development of a 'hermeneutically informed social theory' to fill the gap created by the dissolution of the 'orthodox consensus' which dominated sociology in the 1950s and 1960s. The intellectual strands of this consensus can be traced back well into the nineteenth century and culminated in the Positivistic view of the natural and social sciences, and a functionalist view of social theory. He has pointed out that the collapse of the orthodox consensus has highlighted the common theoretical concerns of a whole range of social sciences, extending from literary criticism to the philosophy of science.

As a background to his views on the way social science needs to be redesigned, Giddens made a number of points about the relationship between the natural and social sciences, and between Positivistic and Interpretive social science. For the most part, his arguments on these issues are against the views of Merton (1957), a supporter of the 'orthodox consensus', on the nature of sociology and the logic of sociological explanation. For example, whereas Merton saw sociology as an immature natural science, Giddens has argued that the social sciences are not relative newcomers. 'Social science is as old as natural science is; both can be dated back to the post-Renaissance period in Europe, as recognisably "modern" in form' (Giddens 1979: 241). While their developments have been uneven, the social sciences are not at a rudimentary stage along the path already successfully travelled by the natural sciences; they are not some kind of inferior copy of the natural sciences.

> The social sciences share with natural science a respect for logical clarity in the formulation of theories and for disciplined empirical investigation. But social science is not a battered tramp steamer chugging along vainly in the wake of the sleek cruiser of the natural sciences. In large degree the two simply sail on different oceans, however much they might share certain common navigational procedures. There are thus profound differences between the social and natural sciences, but they do not concern the presence or absence of interpretation as such. (Giddens 1987: 18)

Giddens' critique of the orthodox consensus in social science dealt with the nature of social laws, with the role of ordinary language, with the relationship between revelatory and critical views of social science, with the distinction between description and explanation, and with the need for an adequate theory of action. First, the issue of the differences between laws in the natural and social sciences. It is now well established that no amount of accumulated data will determine which of two competing theories will be accepted or rejected (known as the principle of the underdetermination of theories by facts). The level of underdetermination is most social sciences is likely to be higher than in most of the natural sciences. The reasons for this include 'difficulties of replication of observations, the relative lack of possibilities for experimentation, and the paucity of "cases" for comparative analysis with regard to theories concerned with total societies' (1979: 243). Then there is the fundamental difference in the logical form of the laws in the natural and social sciences. In the natural sciences laws are usually regarded as being immutable, given the operation of certain boundary conditions. This is not the case in the social sciences where generalizations are restricted by time and space. This is because the 'boundary conditions involved with laws in the social sciences include as a basic element the knowledge that actors, in a given institutional context, have about the circumstances of their actions' (1979: 244). This knowledge can change, including under the influence of knowledge of the laws themselves. The orthodox consensus had sociology pursuing laws of the same logical form as those assumed to apply in the natural sciences.

Secondly, the orthodox consensus also accepted the traditional view of language as a medium for describing the world. In this view, the basic features of language have a one-to-one relationship with objects in the real world; language is regarded as providing pictures of corresponding aspects of reality. However, description is only one of the things that language can do; it is also a medium of social life and is therefore a central element in all the activities in which social actors engage. 'Since the orthodox consensus accepted the traditionally-established view of language, those working with it dismissed the relation between ordinary language – the language employed in the course of day-to-day conduct – and the technical meta-languages of social science as of no particular interest or importance' (1979: 245–6). Further, they preferred the precision they believed to be possible in a discipline-based language in preference to the vague and imprecise language of everyday life. But the relationship between lay language and technical language is a central problem in the social sciences. Giddens' position is that all social science is parasitic upon lay concepts (1987: 19).

The third feature of the orthodox consensus was its reliance on a revelatory view of science in which it is seen to demystify common-sense beliefs about the natural world by offering more profound explanations than are available in everyday knowledge. Social science based on this principle has frequently been criticized by lay people as 'telling us what we already know in a language that we cannot understand'. Giddens has rejected this revelatory view of social science and has taken the lay critique of social science seriously.

Fourthly, Giddens (1987: 18) also rejected the opposition between explanation (*erklären*) and understanding (*verstehen*) which has been used to differentiate the natural and social sciences. Rather, he considered that the process of rethinking social theory in terms of a different view of the character of human social activity must be accompanied by a rethinking of the logical form of natural science. It is no longer appropriate to advocate a hermeneutic foundation for the social sciences and still retain a positivistic view of the natural sciences as, he claimed, Dilthey, Winch and Habermas had done. The natural and the social sciences

> *are not entirely separate endeavours, but feed from a pool of common problems.* For just as it has become apparent that hermeneutic questions are integral to a philosophical understanding of natural science, so the limitations of conceptions of the social sciences that exclude causal analysis have become equally evident. We cannot treat the natural and social sciences as *two independently constituted forms of intellectual endeavour*, whose characteristics can be separately determined, and which then subsequently can be brought together and compared. Philosophers and practitioners of sociology must remain attentive to the progress of natural sciences; but any philosophy of natural science in turn presupposes a definite stance towards problems of social theory. (Giddens 1979: 259)[2]

In his reconstruction of social theory and methodology, Giddens has drawn heavily on Gadamer's version of hermeneutics, particularly the idea of understanding being based on the 'fusion of horizons'. But, unlike Gadamer, he has viewed hermeneutics as providing a basis for explanation and he was anxious to avoid problems of relativism. While he argued that various branches of hermeneutics and Interpretivism have made useful contributions to the clarification of the logic and method of the social sciences, he identified three problems that have to be resolved in order to transcend the limitations of Interpretivism: the concept of 'action' – and the corresponding notions of intention, reason and motive – need to be clarified; the theory of action needs to be connected to the analysis of the properties of institutional structures; and an appropriate logic of social-scientific method needs to be developed. In addition, one of the strengths of the 'orthodox consensus', its primary concern with the unanticipated conditions and the unintended consequences of this social action, needs to be incorporated.

What distinguishes Giddens' theory from the orthodox consensus is his insistence that the production and reproduction of society is a skilled accomplishment of social actors. It is 'brought about by the active constituting skills of its members', 'but they do so as historically located actors, and not under conditions of their own choosing.' This production of society by its members 'draws upon resources, and depends upon conditions, of which they are unaware or which they perceive only dimly' (1976a: 157, 161). Therefore, it is necessary to 'complement the idea of the production of social life with that of the *social reproduction* of structures' (1976a: 126–7).

---

[2] Keat and Urry (1975) and Giddens (1977a) have argued that the natural sciences are also concerned with 'understanding' or 'interpretation' in so far as communication occurs between members of natural-scientific communities. However, this use of 'understanding' with reference to such scientific communities is misleading as the relationship between the members of these communities and their objects of study are monologic, not dialogic. These objects cannot participate in the relationship scientists have with them (Stockman 1983: 210–11).

Out of these complementary ideas Giddens developed the central theorem of Structuration Theory, the *duality of structure*. 'By the *duality of structure* I mean that social structures are both constituted *by* human agency, and yet at the same time are the very *medium* of this constitution' (1976a: 121).

> One way to illustrate this idea is by taking an example from language. The structural properties of language, as qualities of a community of language speakers (e.g. syntactical rules) are drawn upon by a speaker in the production of a sentence. But the very act of speaking that sentence contributes to the reproduction of those syntactical rules as enduring properties of the language. The concept of the duality of structure, I believe, is basic to any account of social reproduction, and has no functionalist overtones at all. (Giddens 1981: 19)

Social structures are both the conditions and the consequences of social interaction; they are the rules and resources social actors draw on as they engage each other in interaction, not patterns of social relationships. They are not external to the social actor; they exist in memory traces and are embodied in social practices. This view is very different from that adopted by the structuralist traditions of social science.

> Giddens's key conceptual innovation in this regard is to argue that we should cease to conceive of 'structure' as a kind of framework, like girders of a building or the skeleton of a body, and that we should conceptualize it instead as the 'rules and resources' which are implemented in interaction. In interacting with one another, individuals draw on the rules and resources which comprise structure, in much the same way as an individual draws on the rules of grammar in uttering a well-formed speech act. Like the rules of grammar, structure is both 'enabling' and 'constraining': it enables us to act as well as delimiting the courses of possible action. By focussing on the generative character of rules and resources, we can see that structure is both constitutive of everyday action and, at the same time, reproduced by that action. (Held and Thompson 1989: 3–4)

In summary, Structuration Theory is an attempt to establish a bridge between the concerns of some traditions of social theory with the experiences of social actors, and the concerns of other traditions with the existence of forms of social totalities, between 'agency' and 'structure'. It requires a theory of the human agent, an account of the conditions and consequences of social action, and an interpretation of 'structure' as dealing with both conditions and consequences (Giddens 1979: 49). It dispenses with the notion of 'function' as used in the orthodox consensus and is based on the view that dualities such as 'subject' and 'object', or 'action' and 'structure', need to be reconceptualized under the concept of *duality of structure*.

Giddens regarded social actors as being both capable and knowledgeable. The former refers to the fact that social actors, in any phase in a given sequence of conduct, could have acted differently, even though they may generally act out of habit. The latter refers to what social actors know about their social situation and the conditions of their activity within it. Social actors are viewed as having the capacity reflexively to monitor interaction as it happens and the setting within which it occurs. At the same time, they can give reasons for (or rationalize) their actions. However, these accounts may not correspond to the mutual knowledge tacitly employed by them in the production of social encounters. They may not be able to articulate this knowledge, and they may have other unconscious motives (1979: 56–9). Hence, Giddens has distinguished between the reasons given for an action and the motives which may have produced it.

> If reasons refer to the grounds of action, motives refer to the wants which prompt it. However, motivation is not as directly bound up with the continuity of action as are its reflexive monitoring or rationalization. Motivation refers to potential for action rather than to the mode in which action is chronically carried on by the agent. Motives tend to have a direct purchase on action only in relatively unusual circumstances, situations which in some way break with the routine. For the most part motives supply overall plans or programmes . . . within which a range of conduct is enacted. Much of our day-to-day conduct is not directly motivated. (Giddens 1984: 6)

This is due to the fact that motives tend to be unconscious. Giddens has proposed four layers to consciousness and action: reflexive monitoring (using discursive consciousness); rationalization of action (giving reasons); practical consciousness (which may be tacit and cannot be readily articulated); and, unconscious motivation (repressed semiotic impulses of which the social actor is usually not aware).

Giddens also stressed the need to acknowledge, as social theory has not done previously, that social existence occurs in time and space. 'The basic domain of study of the social sciences, according to the theory of structuration, is neither the experience of the individual actor, nor the existence of any form of societal totality, but social practices ordered across space and time' (1984: 2).

There are numerous implications of Structuration Theory for the context and conduct of social research. Giddens has proposed that social research can occur at four related levels.

1 Hermeneutic elucidation of frames of meaning.
2 Investigation of context and form of practical consciousness.
3 Identification of bounds of knowledgeability.
4 Specification of institutional orders.

Level 1 involves the use of the double hermeneutic or, in Schütz's terms, the description of first-order constructs and the generation of second-order constructs from them. Researchers who favour quantitative methods may either ignore this level altogether, or regard it as purely descriptive. However, it can be both explanatory and generalizing when it has to do with answering why-questions about the mutual intelligibility of divergent frames of meaning (1984: 328). At level 2, various investigations at level 1 across a variety of contexts, within a society or between societies, can be compared and generalizations established about common elements of a range of types of practical consciousness, including efforts to probe unconscious meanings. Level 3 focuses on the limits of social actors' knowledgeability in the shifting context of space and time. This includes the study of unintended consequences and unacknowledged conditions of action. Level 4 deals with the conditions of social and system integration through the identification of the main institutional components of social systems, be they total societies or other smaller of larger systems (1984: 328–9).

Giddens has suggested that levels 1 and 2 are usually associated with qualitative methods, and levels 3 and 4 with quantitative methods, reflecting also the division between 'micro' and 'macro' analysis. However, he argued that this division is a methodological residue of the dualism of structure and action, and can be overcome by recognizing the duality of structure. These levels of research are intended to reinforce the significance of the duality of structure. It is possible to focus research attention at one extreme largely to the exclusion of the other, but this must be regarded simply as a methodological device.

Finally, Giddens has provided some guidelines for orienting social research. First, all social research is necessarily 'anthropological' or ethnographic due to the double hermeneutic. As a result, literary style is important for the ethnographic descriptions which aim to describe a social world to those who are unfamiliar with it. Social scientists are communicators who mediate between frames of meaning using the same sources of description (mutual knowledge) as novelists or other fiction writers. 'Thick description' may be necessary in some types of research, especially of the ethnographic kind, but it is not necessary 'where the activities studied have generalized characteristics familiar to those to whom the "findings" are made available, and where the main concern of the research is with institutional analysis, in which actors are treated in large aggregates or as "typical" in certain respects' (1984: 285).

Secondly, social research must be 'sensitive to the complex skills which actors have in co-ordinating the contexts of their day-to-day behaviour. In institutional analysis these skills may be more or less bracketed out, but it is essential to remember that such bracketing is wholly methodological' (1984: 285). The usual mistake in this latter analysis is to allow a methodological device to determine the way reality is regarded. To the extent that social life is predictable, this predictability is made to happen by social actors. 'If the study of unintended consequences and unacknowledged conditions of action is a major part of social research, we should never the less stress that such consequences and conditions are always to be interpreted within the flow of intentional conduct' (1984: 285).

Thirdly, the social researcher needs to be sensitive to the time–space constitution of social life. This means that social scientists can no longer 'let historians be specialists in time and geographers specialists in space . . . Analysing the time–space co-ordination of social activities means studying the contextual features of locales through which actors move in their daily paths and the regionalization of locales stretching away across time–space' (1984: 286).

While Giddens regarded social theory as inevitably critical theory, he did not wish to defend a version of Marxism, or to align himself with Critical Theory. Rather, he adopted the humanistic position similar to that advocated by Berger (1963) that sociology has the potential to unmask the pretensions and propaganda by which people cloak their relations with each other and can, thereby, empower people to take charge of their own lives. Giddens regarded sociology as an inherently critical discipline in its capacity to undermine ideology and the capacity of dominant groups to have their view of the world accepted as reality. 'To regard social agents as "knowledgeable" and "capable" is not just a matter of the analysis of action; it is also an implicitly political stance' (1982: 16). However, the capacity of the theories and findings of the social sciences to be of value to policy-makers is limited by the fact that, unlike natural science, the social sciences are involved in a subject–subject relation to their objects of study. While the natural scientists and technologists can use their theories and findings to alter the reality they study, they normally do so at the time and in the manner of their choosing. However, once social scientific knowledge is made public, it has the capacity to have an influence on social life through being filtered by social actors into their day-to-day activities.

> This is a large part of the reason why the social sciences might appear to provide much less information of value to policy-makers than do the natural sciences. The social sciences necessarily draw upon a great deal that is already known to the members of the societies they investigate, and supply theories, concepts and findings which become thrust back into the world they describe. The 'gaps' which can be made to appear between the specialist conceptual apparatus and the findings of social sciences and the knowledgeable practices incorporated into social life are very much less clear than in natural science. Viewed from a 'technological' standpoint, the practical contributions of the social sciences seem, and are, restricted. However, seen in terms of being filtered into the world they analyse, the practical ramifications of the social sciences have been, and are, very profound indeed. (Giddens 1984: 354)

To conclude this section, an approach very similar to that developed by Giddens is briefly outlined. In spite of his detailed critique of both Ricoeur and Habermas, Thompson has drawn heavily on their work to produce what he has labelled as *Critical Hermeneutics*, 'a critically and rationally justified theory for the interpretation of human action' (Thompson 1981a: 4). Using ordinary language philosophy as a backdrop, he has also high-lighted the deficiencies of this tradition, in particular, the tendency to treat language as the basic component of the social world, to the neglect of phenomena which lie beyond the linguistic realm, and to reject the con-

cept of explanation from social enquiry. He found Ricoeur and Habermas
to be counterbalances to these tendencies.

It is possible to summarise Thompson's approach as follows:

1 Explanation in the social sciences is derived from the relation between action and structure.
2 Action and structure are linked through the medium of institutions –
   'specific constellations of social relations and material resources'.
3 'Institutions are characterised by a variety of schemata which define
   the parameters of permissible action.'
4 'Such schemata are transmitted through trial and error, imitation
   and concerted calculation' and enable social actors to negotiate the
   routine and novel circumstances of everyday life.
5 These schemata manifest themselves in the desires, attitudes, beliefs
   and values of the social actors.
6 'Institutional schemata do not specify the course of action to be pursued in every foreseeable situation, but merely provide general principles for the creative production of particular acts.'
7 Social action is produced by neither motives (social actors' grounds
   for performing an action) or causes (the antecedent conditions which
   compel a social actor to act), but by 'schematic generation' in which
   'the accumulated conventions of the past impinge upon the actor and
   govern the creative production of the future.'
8 The concept of schematic generation transcends the dilemma of freedom and necessity; 'schemata generate action in a way which is not
   deterministic, establishing flexible boundaries for the negotiation of
   unanticipated situations.'
9 Social actors may 'reflect upon and transform such schemata in
   accordance with their collective interests'.
10 Social structure consists of 'a series of elements and their interrelations, which conjointly define the conditions for the persistence of a
   social formation and the limits for the variation of its constituent
   institutions'.
11 These elements are necessary for the continuation of a particular social
   formation and specify the limits by which certain social institutions
   can be altered; it is their 'social structuration'.
12 While the specification of the meaning of action is a practical accomplishment of lay actors in everyday life, meaning is neither exhausted
   or determined by lay actors' accounts of what they are doing.
13 The elucidation of meaning 'may be facilitated by the reconstruction
   of the schemata which generate action, and by the clarification of the
   elements which structurate institutions'.
14 Critique and self-reflection in the social sciences must not only be
   directed to false consciousness about institutional and structural
   arrangements, but also to the institutional and structural arrangements
   themselves (Thompson 1981a: 174–9).

Feminism

Feminism's answer to the key question is in the negative and overlaps with aspects of Hermeneutics, Interpretivism and Critical Theory. While feminists may not wish to renounce the aims of science to 'describe, explain, and understand the regularities, underlying causal tendencies, and meanings of the natural and social worlds' (Harding 1986: 10), they have been critical of the view of the natural and social worlds, and the methods of the dominant approaches in the natural and social sciences. The core feminist criticism is that all science is based on a masculine way of viewing the world; it is androcentric. It omits or distorts women's experiences (Oakley 1974; Smart 1976; Stanley and Wise 1983). The argument has been presented as follows.

> What counts as knowledge must be grounded on experience. Human experience differs according to the kinds of activities and social relations in which humans engage. Women's experience systematically differs from the male experience upon which knowledge claims have been grounded. Thus the experience on which the prevailing claims to social and natural knowledge are founded is, first of all, only partial human experience only partially understood: namely, masculine experience as understood by men. However, when this experience is presumed to be gender-free – when the male experience is taken to be the human experience – the resulting theories, concepts, methodologies, inquiry goals and knowledge-claims distort human social life and human thought. (Harding and Hintikka 1983b: x)

Feminist critiques of androcentric science have ranged from liberal to radical (Keller 1987; Harding 1986). At the liberal end of the continuum, the charge concerns unfair employment practices which has led to most scientists being men: the sciences have attracted and retained more men than women; and men dominate the positions of leadership and power in scientific organizations. This is a political criticism and does not challenge traditional conceptions of science. The next, slightly more radical criticism, concerns the bias in the choice and definition of research problems; male definitions of problems and male forms of explanation have dominated allegedly value-neutral and objective science. This is particularly the case in the health sciences where, it is argued, biological technologies have been used in the service of sexist (as well as racist, homophobic and classist) social projects. The third criticism claims that there is bias in the design and interpretation of experiments. An example cited is that rats used in animal learning experiments are always male.[3] Claims are also made that the interpretation of observations and experiments can also be biased, particularly in the social sciences. A fourth criticism relates to a series of rigid dualisms (such as objective/subjective, reason/emotion, mind/body, fact/value, public/private, individual/collective, self/other) which have been

---

[3] For a detailed critique of androcentrism in psychology, see Sherif (1987).

perpetuated and used to distinguish between 'fundamental' masculine and feminine characteristics. And, finally, the most radical criticism is to question the assumptions of objectivity and rationality that underlie science.

Over the past thirty years, Feminism has challenged the notion of neutrality in science by addressing the areas of psychiatry and mental health, childbirth, contraception and abortion. These arguments have included concerns that women lack access to the benefits of science, that research does not take women's problems seriously and that science has contributed to women's oppression. It is argued that medical knowledge serves male interests and legitimates inequalities between the sexes. By exposing the ideological nature of medical science, as misrepresenting the reality of women's health and illness and as serving the interests of the medical profession, feminists have sought to reclaim control of their bodies from the profession (Dugdale 1990).

> Many feminist theorists have argued that women have different conceptions of the basic constituents of reality, different assumptions about their own relationships to the natural world, different views of the importance and connectedness of other people, more ready access to their own emotions and feelings, and distinct ways of assessing moral responsibility, based on a context of human relationships rather than abstract rights of isolated individuals. (Fee 1986: 47)

It has been suggested that the preconditions of a feminist science would be

> one in which no rigid boundary separates the subject of knowledge (the knower) and the natural object of that knowledge; where the subject/object split is not used to legitimize the domination of nature; where nature itself is conceptualized as active rather than passive, a dynamic complex totality requiring human cooperation and understanding rather than a dead mechanism, requiring only manipulation and control. In such feminist imaginings, the scientist is not seen as an impersonal authority standing outside and above nature and human concerns, but simply a person whose thoughts and feelings, logical capacities, and intuitions are all relevant and involved in the process of discovery. Such scientists would actively seek ways of negotiating the distances now established between knowledge and its uses, between thought and feeling, between objectivity and subjectivity, between expert and nonexpert, and would seek to use knowledge as a tool of liberation rather than domination. (Fee 1986: 47)

The issue of the impact on women of the many dualisms which have dominated Western thought, and have pervaded everyday life, is a recurring theme in feminist writings (in addition to Harding 1986, see, for example, Glennon 1979, 1983; Fee 1981, 1986; Harstock 1983; Salleh 1984; and Rose 1986). Glennon has placed this theme at the centre of women's oppression, with the 'masculine/feminine' dualism being but one more variation. The media portray women as emotional, passionate and intuitive, but also illogical and fickle, while men are seen to be rational, analytical and productive, but also insensitive and impersonal. Mothers are viewed as providing expressive relationships with children, while fathers are left with instrumental relationships. The danger here, argued Glennon, is that, by accepting these features of modern life as law-like, we remove possible alternatives from our consciousness.

Glennon has identified four ideal types of feminism: *instrumentalism*, which proposes that humans are at their most authentic when they are rational, productive and individualistic, and that the expressive and private spheres must be eliminated; *expressivism*, the opposite to instrumentalism, which elevates the emotional, expressive, spontaneous and communal to a superior rather than inferior position; *polarism*, which posits essential differences between males and females and proclaims that individuals must find their true gender essence rather than adopt what passes for femaleness and maleness in sexist society; and, *synthesism*, which assumes that all human beings are a mixture of masculine and feminine qualities. In the latter,

> the ideal human is a dialectical fusion of reason and emotion and that any division of self into roles is dehumanising. It [synthesism] advocates the total reorganization of society to eliminate division of labor as we know it, requiring change of both females and males, each having to integrate within the orientation that was thought of as the preserve of the 'opposite' sex. (Glennon 1983: 263–4)

Millman and Kanter (1975) have presented (and Harding 1986 has reviewed) an early feminist critique of the social sciences in which problematic assumptions that have directed sociological research have been identified.

1 Important areas of social enquiry have been overlooked. For example, by emphasizing a Weberian means/end model of motivation, the role of emotion in social life has largely been ignored.
2 Sociology has focused on the visible, dramatic, public and official spheres of social life largely to the exclusion of the invisible, less dramatic, private and informal spheres. This tends to make invisible the ways in which women have gained informal power and has hidden the informal systems of sponsorship and patronage that facilitate career paths for men.
3 There is a tendency to assume a 'single society' and to ignore the possibility that men and women may inhabit different social worlds, in spite of living in the same physical location (Bernard 1973). Women are likely to have different and broader views about what constitutes social interaction, and to regard much of what men count as nature as being part of culture.
4 In several areas of research, gender is not taken into account and analysed as a possible explanatory variable.

5   Social science frequently explains the status quo rather than exploring alternatives for a more just and humane society.

6   The use of certain methods, particularly quantitative, can prevent the discovery of information that may be crucial for understanding the phenomenon under consideration. The preference for dealing with variables, as is the case with quantitative methods, rather than people, as in qualitative methods, may be related to a masculine need to manipulate and control, and an inability to relate to all types of people in an empathetic way, particularly in relatively unstructured and ambiguous natural situations.

Recognition of the androcentric features of science has led feminists to search for an appropriate epistemology for both the natural and social sciences. Harding (1987c: 182–4) has identified two main responses to this problem; *feminist empiricism* and the *feminist standpoint*. *Feminist empiricism* has challenged three related aspects of traditional empiricism (incorporated in Positivism and Critical Rationalism).

> First, it questions the assumption that the social identity of the observer is irrelevant to the 'goodness' of the results of research, asserting that the androcentricism of science is both highly visible and damaging ... It argues that women *as a social group* are more likely than men *as a social group* to select problems for inquiry that do not distort human social experience. Second, feminist empiricism questions the potency of science's methodological and sociological norms to eliminate androcentric biases; the norms themselves appear to be biased insofar as they have been incapable of detecting androcentricism. Third, it challenges the belief that science must be protected from politics. It argues that *some* politics – the politics of movements for emancipatory social change – can increase the objectivity of science. (Harding 1986: 162)

Feminist empiricism has argued that the deficiencies in the existing dominant forms of science – the masculine bias in problem formulation, concepts, theories, methods of enquiry and interpretation of results – can be overcome by a rigorous adherence to the rules of (this kind of) scientific method; it is 'bad science' which is responsible for these biases in research.

Unfortunately, while feminist empiricism undercuts the assumptions of traditional science, it appears to be internally inconsistent. As Feminism is a political movement, feminist researchers clearly have strong commitments to bring about a particular kind of society. Science, however, is supposed to be value-neutral and dispassionate; the norms of science are intended to eliminate or at least control the goals, interests and values of the researcher. The fact that feminist empiricism has argued that women (or feminists, either men or women) as a group are more likely to produce objective results than men (or non-feminists) as a group, tends to undermine their central claim that adherence to scientific rules is the solution. Ultimately, the problem with this solution is that it is left with the inherent deficiencies of these historically dominant forms of natural science and the 'orthodox consensus' in the social sciences.

The *feminist standpoint* offers a different view on how politicized research can produce preferable research results. It builds a distinctive feminist science on the social experiences of women and gives women, or feminists, a privileged position in their ability to understand the social world. It also claims to overcome the dualisms characteristic of Western thought. The feminist standpoint is based, particularly, on Hegel, Marx and Freud, and focuses on the consequences of the experiences of women in the division of labour, including production and reproduction, and the differential experiences of boys and girls in their relationships to their mothers in the sexual division of labour in child rearing (Smith 1974, 1979; Flax 1983; Harstock 1983; Rose 1983)[4]. 'Women and men . . . grow up with personalities affected by different boundary experiences, differently constructed and experienced inner and outer worlds, and preoccupations with different relational issues' (Harstock 1983: 295). It is argued that 'men's dominant position in social life results in partial and perverse understandings, whereas women's subjugated position provides the possibility of more complete and less perverse understandings' (Harding 1986: 26). In the same way that Marx argued that the proletariat potentially has a superior capacity to know the world, derived from their particular subjugated experiences, feminists have argued that there is a feminine standpoint on the world which is 'a morally and scientifically preferable grounding for our interpretations and explanations of nature and social life' (Harding 1986: 26).

Standpoint feminists like Rose and Keller have argued that the androcentric character of science is not inevitable; rather than rejecting science entirely, or trying to achieve the hopeless task of neutralizing it, women can reconstitute it. According to Rose, it is the division of labour which has been responsible for the distortion of science; the alienating effects of the division between mental and manual labour in the production of things has led to a concern to unite hand and brain. It is now necessary to recognize caring labour as being critical in the production of people; the heart now has to be included. 'Bringing caring labor and the knowledge that stems from participation in it to the analysis becomes critical for the transformative program equally within science and within society' (Rose 1983: 90).

Keller (1978, 1987) has suggested that the concern with rationality, objectivity and technical tinkering, characteristic of the dominant view of science, is a consequence of the precariousness male infants experience in developing their identity as they distance themselves from their mothers. She has regarded these masculine traits as potentially pathological. It is therefore necessary to reconceptualize objectivity as a dialectical process

---

[4] The work of these four contributors to the feminist standpoint has been reviewed by Harding (1986).

which breaks down the objectivity/subjectivity dualism; it also requires the application of critical reflection to scientific activities.

Keller has defined objectivity as 'the pursuit of a maximally authentic, and hence maximally reliable, understanding of the world around oneself' (1985: 116). She has distinguished two types of objectivity, 'dynamic' and 'static'.

> Dynamic objectivity aims at a form of knowledge that grants to the world around us its independent integrity but does so in a way that remains cognizant of, indeed relies on, our connectivity with that world. In this, dynamic objectivity is not unlike empathy, a form of knowledge of other persons that draws explicitly on the commonality of feelings and experiences in order to enrich one's understanding of another in his or her own right. By contrast, I call static objectivity the pursuit of knowledge that begins with the severance of subject from object rather than aiming at the disentanglement of one from the other. For both static and dynamic objectivity, the ambition appears the same, but the starting assumptions one makes about the nature of the pursuit bear critically on the outcome . . . Dynamic objectivity is thus a pursuit of knowledge that makes use of subjective experience . . . in the interests of a more effective objectivity. (Keller 1985: 117)

Salleh has captured the essence of this different approach to objectivity.

> An empathic, cyclic, *reflexive logic* is supposed, without incisive categorical boundaries between the knowing subject-in-process, object, and its representation. The artificial dualisms of masculine and feminine, history and nature, signifier and signified would be replaced by a *metabolism* of the subject and field . . . [F]or a new 'definition' [of objectivity] is offered [involving] . . . a communion with the object rather than its penetration by the diverse agency of instrumental reason. (Salleh 1984: 33)

While standpoint feminism may avoid the problems of feminist empiricism, it has its own difficulties. According to Dugdale (1990), it leaves uncontested the dualisms which structure sexual differences and current scientific practices. Rose (1986) has acknowledged that this continues to be a problem but has suggested that the tensions within these dualisms can provide a creative framework for struggle. However, Harding has argued that it is not possible to establish *a* feminist method as women's social experiences are cross-cut by class, race and culture. A single standpoint could only be achieved by the undesirable dominance of a group with one combination of these experiences. Therefore, as it is not possible to transcend the boundaries of class, race and culture, there must be many feminisms. However, there is 'a feminist perspective on science that shows the ways in which gender-based dominance relations have been programmed into the production, scope, and structure of natural knowledge, distorting the content, meaning, and uses of that knowledge' (Fee 1986: 54). Perhaps, as Fee has suggested, a truly feminist science will only be possible when society is fully transformed by the feminist project.

As is the case with the other approaches to social enquiry, these two feminist approaches to science, feminist empiricism and standpoint feminism, are likely to appeal to different audiences. Feminists who have had a strong commitment to the traditional views of science are likely to subscribe to feminist empiricism, while those who have a commitment to either some form of Marxism, or who accept contemporary philosophies of science, are likely to adopt standpoint feminism. According to Harding, the tensions between and within these two positions suggest that they are transitional epistemologies in a transitional culture, and this may be a virtue.

> Perhaps sciences and epistemologies should always be in tension with each other: if the grounds for accepting knowledge claims are in perfect fit with the claims advanced, we should worry about what kinds of knowledge are being suppressed, subjugated, sent underground. After all, it is just such a hegemonous science/epistemology to which feminist scholars object. (Harding 1987c: 187)

Rather than trying to create *a* feminist method for the social sciences, Harding (1987b: 7–9) has argued that the best feminist analysis has three distinctive characteristics. First, to counter the fact that social science has traditionally dealt with questions that are problematic within the social experiences characteristic of men, feminist researchers have insisted that their research must be based on women's experiences as a source of research problems, hypotheses and evidence. Secondly, as traditional social research has been for men, feminist research must be designed for women, to deal with what *they* regard as problematic from their experiences. Thirdly, in recognition that the cultural background of the researcher is part of the evidence that enters into the results of the research, the researcher must place her/himself in the same critical plane as the subject matter. This feature of good feminist research avoids the 'objectivist' stance that attempts to have the researcher appear as an invisible, autonomous voice of authority. 'Introducing this "subjective" element into the analysis in fact increases the objectivity of the research and decreases the "objectivism" which hides this kind of evidence from the public' (Harding 1987b: 9).

The issue of the relationship between the natural and social sciences has taken on a distinctive character in the work of Harding. The common practice of regarding physics as the paradigm of science has created difficulty for Feminism because of its androcentric characteristics. Harding has proposed that 'a critical and self-reflective social science should be the model for all science' (1986: 44). Physics should be regarded as a special case: its subject matter is much less complex than that of biology and the social sciences; its concepts, hypotheses and theories all involve interpretation; it is becoming increasingly atypical in its capacity to exclude intentional and learned behaviour in its subject matter; and it has no capacity to deal with 'irrational' behaviour and belief, a requirement in the social sciences. Harding wanted to make the social sciences the 'queen of the sciences' using Feminism as the paradigm. Of course, by turning the everyday view of the relationship between the sciences on its head, she was able to argue from a position of strength rather than having to defend a 'less mature' form of science.

Dorothy Smith, a very influential Feminist sociologist, has provided a critique of the male-dominated 'orthodox consensus' in American sociology. In addition to relying heavily on Schütz, her work has drawn on and adapted Marxian-based theories of class conflict. The outcome is a sociology akin to Habermas's Critical Theory, classified by Harding as standpoint feminist.

Smith objected to a sociology which uses conceptual procedures, models and methods which discard everyday experiences of the world as a source of reliable information in the name of objectivity. The nature of the social world itself, how it can be known, and the relation between it and the researcher, are not questioned. The state of the discipline, as Smith experienced it during her graduate studies in California, confronted women sociologists with a contradiction between what it required and their experience of the world. The ideology of the ruling class was seen to dominate and control the social consciousness of the society in general, as well as sociology. Women, both as members of the society and as academics, had no alternative mode to understand their experiences. The Weberian model of rational social action, in which choices are seen to be made between means to some end, is foreign to the experiences of most women. These experiences 'tend to show a loose, episodic structure that reflects the way their lives are organized and determined externally to them' (Smith 1979: 152).

From her analysis of the discipline, Smith argued that it is not possible to have objective knowledge which is independent of the social location of the researcher. The socially constructed world must be known from within; it is never possible to stand outside it. Smith did not intend by this argument to suggest that what is required is for the sociologist to explore her/his inner experiences, or any other approach in which self is the sole focus and object. Rather, the *society* is discovered from within by the sociologist paying attention to her/his direct experience of this social world, using her own tacit knowledge. However, she 'aims not at a reiteration of what she already (tacitly) knows, but at an exploration through that of what passes beyond it and is deeply implicated in how it is' (Smith 1974: 11–12). It is also necessary to recognize that other people have other experiences and may live in different social worlds; the researcher is separated from the world as it is experienced by those being studied. A compelling example from her own experience illustrates her contentions.

Riding a train not long ago in Ontario I saw a family of Indians, woman, man, and three children standing together on a spur above a river watching the train go by. There was (for me) that moment – the train, those five people seen on the other side of the glass. I saw first that I could tell this incident as it was, but that telling as a description built in my position and my interpretations. I have called them a family; I have said they were watching the train. My understanding has already subsumed theirs. Everything may have been quite other for them. My description is privileged to stand as what actually happened, because theirs is not heard in the contexts in which I may speak. If we begin from the world as we actually experience it, it is at least possible to see that we are located and that what we know of the other is conditional upon that location as part of a relation comprehending the other's location also. There are and must be different experiences of the world and different bases of experience. We must not do away with them by taking advantage of our privileged speaking to construct a sociological version which we then impose upon them as their reality. We may not rewrite the other's world or impose upon it a conceptual framework which extracts from it what fits with ours. Our conceptual procedures should be capable of explicating and analyzing the properties of their experienced world rather than administering it. Their reality, their varieties of experience must be an unconditional datum. (Smith 1974: 12)

In proposing that social research should begin with everyday experiences, Smith did not wish to suggest 'that sociology can be done without knowing how to do it and that we can approach our work with a naïve consciousness. Indeed, I believe sociology to be rather more difficult than it has been made to seem' (Smith 1979: 174). What she wished to argue against was the dominant view that the everyday world is unformed and unorganized, and that a conceptual framework is necessary to select, assemble and order observations.

Smith recognized that it was necessary for the researcher to go beyond both his/her own experiences and those of the people being studied. There is a larger context in which these experiences are located.

Once she becomes aware of how her world is put together as a practical everyday matter and of how her relations are shaped by its concrete conditions (even in so simple a matter as that she is sitting in the train and it travels, but those people standing on the spur do not) the sociologist is led into the discovery that she cannot understand the nature of her experienced world by staying within its ordinary boundaries of assumption and knowledge. To account for that moment on the train and for the relation between the two experiences (or more) and the two positions from which those experiences begin involves positing a total socio-economic order 'in back' of that moment. The coming together which makes the observation possible as well as how we were separated and drawn apart as well as how I now make use of that here – these properties are determined elsewhere than in that relation itself. (Smith 1974: 12)

Smith has acknowledged that the analysis of these experiences and the everyday knowledge will not reveal the social order which lies behind it.

No amount of observation of face-to-face relations, no amount of analysis of commonsense knowledge of everyday life, will take us beyond our essential ignorance of how it is put together. Our direct experience of it constitutes it (if we will) as a problem, but it does not offer any answers (Smith 1974: 13).

The role of the sociologist is to explicate for members of a society the social organization which lies hidden behind the world of their experiences. It is at this point that Smith specifically incorporated elements of Realism in conjunction with elements of Interpretivism, Marxism and Critical Theory. 'The structures which underlie and generate the characteristics of our directly experienced world are social structures and bring us into unseen relations with others' (1974: 13).

Lengermann and Niebrugge-Brantley (1988: 432) have summarized the position of which Smith's views are an exemplar.

People understand and act toward reality from the vantage point of their structurally patterned situations. Because this fact extends even to the sociologist, certainty about the truth becomes a suspect and elusive condition. That certainty can only be achieved if sociologists: (1) seek their facts at the points of intersection between the understandings of the world held by differently situated and often oppositionally related groups; (2) stay focused not only on these different accounts but on the situated vantage points from which they arise; (3) remain sensitive to the situationality of their own professional efforts to know the world; (4) remain sensitive to the differences in perception that people may have about the requirements of their structural locations; (5) stay modest about their 'certainty' and recognize its processual basis, its precarious state, and the permeability of all their concepts; and (6) stay constantly aware of and attempt to compensate for the ways that structural inequalities weight different groups' accounts of social reality.

Review

It is evident that these five contemporary responses to the question of the relationship between the methods of the natural and social sciences are much more complex than the classical ones, and are not necessarily internally coherent. However, they are all critical of both Positivist and Critical Rationalist approaches, although they may still allow some place for a component of such approaches within a multifarious scheme.

The Critical Theory of Habermas supports the view that as the subject matters of the natural and social sciences are fundamentally different the principle of the 'unity of method' must be rejected. In common with Interpretivism and Structuration Theory, Habermas accepted the preinterpreted nature of social reality and its methodological implications. The natural sciences can only use observation but the social sciences can use communication. However, he rejected the possibility of 'objective' observation in the natural sciences, arguing that the assumptions embedded in both theoretical constructs and common-sense thinking determine what will be regarded as reality rather than producing knowledge of it directly; 'cognitive interests' can influence what is produced as knowledge.

For Habermas, scientific enquiry falls into three categories based on different interests: the *empirical–analytic* sciences which are interested in technical control over nature and social relations; the *historical–hermeneutic* sciences which are based on practical interests of communicative understanding; and *critical theory* which has an emancipatory interest in human autonomy. While the first is characteristic of the natural sciences, it has also been applied to social life. In fact, Habermas argued that all three need to be used in the social sciences. Systems of belief and modes of communication need to be interpreted by historical–hermeneutic methods and evaluated against an ideal speech situation. Empirical–analytic methods are used to study stable and widespread social regularities and to determine the (practical rather than universal) causes of these beliefs and modes of communication. Critical Theory, based on a rational consensus of what constitutes ideal forms of human communication, can then be used to specify what constitutes a non-repressive society and can thus enable people to become emancipated from their oppression. Critical Theory, then, rejects the interests of the empirical–analytic sciences, but not necessarily all its methods, and it uses historical–hermeneutic methods and rational criticism in the interest of human emancipation. The clarification and systematization of Critical Theory by Fay (1975, 1987) stressed the need for the social sciences to expose the nature and origins of false consciousness, to describe the nature and development of social crises, to identify what needs to be done to resolve such crises, and to provide a plan of action as to how people can effect the transformation of society.

The versions of Realism which have come to dominate contemporary philosophy of science wish to replace both Positivism and Critical Rationalism with a view of science which it is claimed reflects what scientists do. The answer to the key question is 'Yes and No' but its ontology and epistemology distinguish it from all other approaches discussed. The view of reality advocated by Positivism, based on what can be perceived by the senses, becomes, for Bhaskar, but one domain of reality. Reality consists not only of events that are experienced but also of events that occur whether experienced or not, and of the structures and mechanisms that produce these events. The aim of science is to discover these structures and mechanisms, some of which may be reasonably accessible by the use of instruments that extend the senses. However, inaccessible mechanisms require the building of hypothetical models of them and a search for evidence of their existence. Structures and mechanisms, as the causal powers or the essential nature of things, are independent of the events they produce; they exist at a 'deeper' level of reality and may counteract each other to produce no observable event. Therefore, the constant conjunctions of Positivism are merely the observed regularities that need to be explained by establishing what links them.

Both Harré's and Bhaskar's versions of Realism accept the Interpretive view of social reality as socially constructed and, regardless of the differences in the subject matters of the natural and social sciences, the methods of both are considered to share the same principles, even if the actual techniques differ. This is a qualified anti-positivist naturalism. Bhaskar has rejected the Positivist principle of the separation of facts and values; social science both intervenes in social life and involves value judgements. While it is important to establish the meanings of actions from the point of view of the social actors, and the reasons they give for their actions, the social scientist is free to evaluate such reasons critically.

Modern Hermeneutics has further developed the two traditions of Classical Hermeneutics but with the majority of the attention being given to the one founded by Heidegger. Instead of looking for what the author of a text intended, or the 'real' meaning, Gadamer argued that the text must be engaged in dialogue in order to reconstruct the question to which it is the answer. Understanding involves the 'fusion of horizons' of the text and the interpreter, a process in which the interpreter's horizon is altered and the text is transformed; it is about mediation and the translation of languages. Different interpreters at different times are likely to produce different meanings. Unlike his predecessors in the hermeneutic tradition, Gadamer was not concerned with methodological questions. Rather, he saw the task of his philosophical hermeneutics as being ontological, of addressing the fundamental conditions which underlie all modes of understanding, be they scientific or everyday. He was not concerned with the methods of gaining knowledge, but with the openness required of interpreters of literary or historical texts. Gadamer's hermeneutics takes as 'reality' the ever-changing world in which people are participants. He was not concerned with their subjective meanings but with the meanings that are shared by the members. Neither was he interested in traditional views of 'objectivity' and 'truth'. For him, shared meanings are 'objective' and their 'truth' can be communicated. He was concerned 'to seek that experience of truth that transcends the sphere of the control of scientific method wherever it is found' (Gadamer 1989: xii).

Ricoeur distinguished between language and discourse, between the objective study of a text by structural linguistics and its interpretive study. He developed Gadamer's position by arguing that texts create a distance from spoken discourse. As texts have no social context, an unknown audience, and no dialogue is possible between the reader and the author, they can be read in many ways. Interpretation is achieved by the reader recovering what the text points to and, in the process, achieving self-interpretation. Social action can also be decontextualized and can also have a variety of interpretations, inferior interpretations being eliminated by argumentation.

As a background to his Structuration Theory, Giddens rejected Positivism as it was incorporated into sociology in the 'orthodox consensus' and he has embraced many features of Hermeneutics and Interpretivism. His concept of the *double hermeneutic* was sympathetic with Gadamer's notion of the 'fusion of horizons' and his argument that the language of social science is parasitic on lay language accepts key elements from both Schütz and Winch. However, he wished to differentiate between 'mutual knowledge' (what social actors believe) and 'common sense' (social actors' justifications for these beliefs); the social scientist must respect the authenticity of the former but is free to critique the latter.

Giddens not only rejected the positivistic view of the natural sciences, but he also argued that 'explanation' and 'understanding' are relevant to both the natural and social sciences. Nevertheless, he rejected the possibility of universal laws in the social sciences in favour of generalizations limited by time and space. The latter is a consequence of the preinterpreted nature of social reality and the fact that a basic element in all social contexts is the knowledge social actors have about their actions. As this knowledge can change, so too can generalizations produced by social scientists about their actions.

A primary concern of Structuration Theory has been to provide a conceptual scheme which identifies the ontological features of both 'agency' and 'structure', and their mutual dependence. The key concept, the *duality of structure*, recognizes that social actors are engaged in both producing and reproducing their social world. Therefore, in addition to arguing that social actors are knowledgeable and capable of acting differently, identifying their capacity reflexively to monitor their continuing actions and to rationalize their actions, and acknowledging the role of unconscious motives, Giddens has recognized, what Interpretivists have neglected, that these actions occur within a framework of unacknowledged conditions and unintended consequences.

For Giddens, social research needs to be conducted at various levels, including the elucidation of the frames of meaning in which a particular form of life occurs, the comparative investigation of the forms of everyday knowledge, the specification of the bounds of this knowledge, and the identification of the main institutional components of the social system in which social interaction occurs. Giddens has insisted that all social research is necessarily anthropological; it requires immersion in a form of life and a process in which the social scientist explicates and mediates divergent forms of life within the metalanguage of social science. These activities are ultimately critical in nature in that they can expose and undermine the capacity of dominant groups to maintain and impose their view of reality. In contrast to Critical Theory, Giddens' form of critique is incidental to rather than an integral part of his scheme.

In the context of a consideration of the nature of the natural and social sciences, Feminism has provided a collection of ideas about what is wrong with science, and what kind of science, particularly social science, will overcome these deficiencies. While these ideas cover a range of positions, some common elements are emerging. Lichtenstein (1988) has identified seven themes. The first, which deals with the problem of objectivity, refers to the solutions offered by Keller, Salleh and Fee. Keller (1985) has proposed the notion of 'dynamic objectivity' which connects emotional and cognitive experiences, Salleh (1984) has referred to the 'metabolism of subject and field' as if they were one organism (because there should be no gap between the self and the phenomenal world), and Fee (1986) has asserted that the knower should approach nature through 'conversation rather than command'.

The second theme deals with a 'new materialism' in which knowledge is to be grounded on personal experience, in a process in which personal and theoretical assumptions are made explicit (Flax 1983; Harding 1986; Rose 1986). The recognition of caring labour as a primary social activity must be linked with the labour of head and hand.

The third theme deals with the problem of the sociohistorical location of the researcher. Science will reflect the class, race, gender and cultural background of the scientist. Feminism aims to incorporate rather than negate the social and political influences on science by making the beliefs and assumptions of the scientist explicit. 'A scientific community is objective not when its work is totally free from politicization, but when it recognizes the possibility of such politicization and adopts for itself methods ... involving the exposure and criticism of background assumptions' (Longino 1981: 193).

The fourth theme deals with the reflexive nature of social enquiry. The process of research not only requires the researcher to reflect critically on the process, but to be open to being changed by it; the investigator, the participants, those who read and communicate the results, will all have their awareness changed. 'Such a science is maximally objective, continuously open to scrutiny, and continuously learning from itself, as each scientist consciously grows and changes in an understanding of the world' (Lichtenstein 1988: 145).

The fifth theme, an argument presented by Keller (1985) and Harding (1986), proposes that the social sciences, not physics, should provide the paradigm (exemplar) for all sciences. The sixth theme deals with the recognition that nature is active and complex (Salleh 1984; Bleier 1986; Fee 1986; Rose 1986). Rather than use reductive thought, linear logic and single causes, Feminism accepts the complexity and adopts what might be called an ecological or open systems approach. Finally, knowledge is to be used as a tool for liberation not domination (Fee 1986). Studies should be directed by moral and political emancipatory interests (Harding 1986); they should avoid elitist practices by making their knowledge available to anyone (Bleier 1986).

This review has begun to clarify the nature of the similarities and differences between these contemporary approaches to social science. They will be compared in chapter 7 around a number of basic issues. However, in the meantime, a more detailed critique of classic and contemporary approaches will be undertaken in chapter 4, and the research strategies associated with them will be explored in chapters 5 and 6.

Further Reading

Key References

Bhaskar, R. 1979. *The Possibility of Naturalism.*
Gadamer, H-G. 1989. *Truth and Method.*
Giddens, A. 1976. *New Rules of Sociological Method.*
—— 1979. *Central Problems in Social Theory.*
—— 1984. *The Constitution of Society.*
Habermas, J. 1970. 'Knowledge and Interest'.
—— 1972. *Knowlege and Human Interests.*
Harding, S. 1986. *The Science Question in Feminism.*
Harré, R. 1970. *The Principles of Scientific Thinking.*
—— 1972. *The Philosophy of Science.*
—— 1986. *Varieties of Realism.*
—— and Secord, R.F. 1972. *The Explanation of Social Behaviour.*
Outwaite, W. 1987. *New Philosophies of Social Science.*
Smith, D.E. 1974. 'Women's Perspective as a Radical Critique of Sociology'.
—— 1979. 'A Sociology for Women'.

General References

Bernstein, R.J. 1976. *Restructuring Social and Political Theory.*
Bryant, C.G.A. and Jary, D. 1991. *Giddens' Theory of Structuration.*
Cohen, I.J. 1989. *Structuration Theory.*
Fay, B. 1975. *Social Theory and Political Practice.*
—— 1987. *Critical Social Science.*
Guba, E.G. (ed.). 1990. *The Paradigm Dialogic.*
Harding, S. 1987. *Feminism and Methodology.*
—— and Hintikka, M.B. 1983. *Discovering Reality.*
Held, D. 1980. *Introduction to Critical Theory.*
—— and Thompson, J.B. (eds). 1989. *Habermas: Critical Debates.*
Keat, R. and Urry, J. 1975. *Social Theory as Science.*
—— 1982. *Social Theory as Science*, 2nd edn.
Lincoln, Y.S. and Guba, E.G. 1985. *Naturalistic Inquiry.*
McCarthy, T. 1973. 'A Theory of Communicative Competence'.
—— 1984. *The Critical Theory of Jürgen Habermas*, 2nd edn.
Outhwaite, W. 1983a. 'Towards a Realist Perspective'.
—— 1983b. *Concept Formation in Social Science.*
—— 1987. 'Laws and Explanations in Sociology'.
Palmer, R.E. 1969. *Hermeneutics: Interpretation Theory in Schleiermacher, Dilthey, Heidegger, and Gadamer.*
Sayer, A. 1984. *Method in Social Science.*
Stockman, N. 1983. *Antipositivist Theories of the Sciences.*
Thompson, J.B. 1981a. *Critical Hermeneutics.*
—— 1981b. *Paul Ricoeur: Hermeneutics and the Human Sciences.*

4

Review and Critique
of the Approaches

Introduction

Is there a correct or best answer to the question of whether the methods
of the natural sciences can be used in the social sciences? What methods
are appropriate for the social sciences? As the quotation at the beginning
of chapter 2 suggests, this has been a matter of vigorous debate for more
than a century. These issues were also part of the paradigmatic dispute in
the social sciences in the 1970s.[1] The protagonists usually had strong
commitments to their own position and presented their criticisms of other
positions on the assumption of the correctness of their own.

In this chapter, the approaches to social enquiry outlined in the previous
two chapters are reviewed and evaluated. For the most part, the critiques
are those offered by the adherents of competing approaches. As this
review must be selective, it will not be possible to pursue the dialogue
between critics and protagonists. The selection of critiques has been determined by what is considered to be helpful background for researchers
faced with a choice between approaches and research strategies. Some
aspects of the critiques have been encountered in the previous chapters
as later approaches responded to the alleged deficiencies in the earlier
approaches.

---

[1] See, for example, Winch (1958), Friedrichs (1970), Gouldner (1971), Douglas (1971), Filmer
et al. (1972), Giddens (1974, 1976a), Fay (1975), Keat and Urry (1975), Ritzer (1975),
Bernstein (1976, 1983), Benton (1977), Hindess (1977), Bhaskar (1979), Stockman (1983)
Johnson et al. (1984) and Habermas (1987).

Review of the Approaches: Ontology and Epistemology

Before undertaking the critique, the ontological and epistemological assumptions with which each approach works will be reviewed; the various answers to the key question are largely derived from these assumptions.[2] What follows are brief summaries of the major characteristics of seven of the approaches that have been outlined – Positivism, Critical Rationalism, Interpretivism, Critical Theory, Realism, Structuration Theory and Feminism. Hermeneutics has been excluded from this discussion as many of its elements can be found in other approaches. These seven represent the range of approaches to social enquiry with which social researchers are likely to have to deal.[3] The summaries contain some ideas which were not encountered in chapters 2 and 3 but which will be elaborated further in the following chapters.

Positivism

Positivism entails an *ontology* of an ordered universe made up of atomistic, discrete and observable events. This order can be represented by universal propositions or constant conjunctions. Only that which can be observed, i.e. experienced by the senses, can be regarded as real and therefore worthy of the attention of science. Human activity is understood as observable behaviour taking place in observable, material circumstances. *Social reality* is viewed as a complex of causal relations between events which are depicted as an emerging patchwork of relations between variables. The causes of human behaviour are regarded as being external to the individual.

In its *epistemology*, knowledge is seen to be derived from sensory experience by means of experimental or comparative analysis, and concepts and generalizations are shorthand summaries of particular observations. A correspondence is posited between sensory experiences and the objects of

---

[2] For an earlier review of Positivism, Interpretivism and Realism, see Blaikie (1991).

[3] There is another approach which has not been discussed because it does not lead to a research strategy that is likely to be of interest to social researchers. It has been described as Rationalism (Johnson et al. 1984). Rationalism entails an *ontology* of society as an objective and constraining structure of ideas. Society is real and general but not material; it is independent of individuals' consciousness and must not be reduced to the states of consciousness with which individuals enter social relations. Society should not be confused with the circumstances and conditions of human interaction; society determines both the consciousness of individuals and the particular relations of material objects. Society is, therefore, independent of the empirical world and is not immediately observable; it is a structure of ideas, separate from individual thoughts, which is shared by all human beings. This leads to an *epistemology* in which the direct examination of thought is the only path to knowledge of the real world. Rationalists set out to reveal the structures of mind itself in the belief that behind the world that can be observed lies a world of thought. What Positivists regard as unknowable is for Rationalists the reality that can and must be known. Validity is based on the criterion that what is real must conform to the canons of logic.

those experiences, and between observation statements and theoretical statements. Scientific laws are identical to empirical regularities.

> For the positivist, science is an attempt to gain predictive and explanatory knowledge of the external world. To do this, one must construct theories, which consist of highly general statements, expressing the regular relationships that are found to exist in that world. These general statements, or laws, enable us to predict and explain the phenomena that we discover by means of systematic observation and experiment. To explain something is to show that it is an instance of these regularities; and we can make predictions only on the same basis. Statements expressing these regularities, if true, are only contingently so; their truth is not a matter of logical necessity, and cannot be known by *a priori* means. Instead, such statements must be objectively tested by means of experiment and observation, which are the only source of sure and certain empirical knowledge. It is not the purpose of science to get 'behind' or 'beyond' the phenomena revealed to us by sensory experience, to give us knowledge of unobservable natures, essences or mechanisms that somehow necessitate these phenomena. For the positivist, there are no necessary connections in nature; there are only regularities, successions of phenomena which can be systematically represented in the universal laws of scientific theory. Any attempt to go beyond this representation plunges science into the unverifiable claims of metaphysics and religion, which are at best unscientific, and at worst meaningless. (Keat and Urry 1975: 4)

Critical Rationalism

Critical Rationalism shares some aspects of Positivism's *ontology* but rejects its *epistemology*. Nature and social life are regarded as consisting of essential uniformities – patterns of events. It is the aim of science to discover these uniformities, to find universal statements which are true because they correspond to the facts of nature – descriptions of observed states of affairs. However, sensory experience is rejected as a secure foundation for scientific theories.

Critical Rationalism makes no distinction between observational and theoretical statements; all observations are theory dependent and occur within a 'horizon of expectations'. Observation is used in the service of deductive reasoning and theories are invented to account for observations, not derived from them. Rather than scientists waiting for nature to reveal its regularities, they must impose regularities (deductive theories) on the world and, by a process of trial and error, use observation to try to reject false theories. Theories which survive this critical process are provisionally accepted but never proved to be true. All knowledge is tentative and subject to continuing critical evaluation.

> Without waiting, passively, for repetitions to impress or impose regularities upon us, we actively try to impose regularities upon the world. We try to discover similarities in it, and to interpret it in terms of laws invented by us.

Without waiting for premises we jump to conclusions. These may have to be discarded later, should observation show that they are wrong ... [S]cientific theories [are] ... conjectures boldly put forward for trial, to be eliminated if they clash with observations; with observations ... undertaken with the definite intention of testing a theory by obtaining, if possible, a decisive refutation ... [T]he belief that we can start with pure observation alone, without anything in the nature of a theory, is absurd ... Observation is always selective. It needs a chosen object, a definite task, an interest, a point of view, a problem. And its description presupposes a descriptive language, with property words; it presupposes similarity and classification, which in its turn presupposes interests, points of view, and problems ... It is quite true that any particular hypothesis we choose will have been preceded by observations – the observations, for example, which it is designed to explain. But these observations, in their turn, presuppose the adoption of a frame of reference: a frame of expectations: a frame of theories ... The critical attitude, the tradition of free discussion of theories with the aim of discovering their weak spots so that they may be improved upon, is the attitude of reasonableness, of rationality. It makes far-reaching use of both verbal argument and observation – of observation in the interest of argument, however ... [Therefore,] *there is no more rational procedure than the method of trial and error – of conjecture and refutation:* of boldly proposing theories; of trying our best to show that these are erroneous; and of accepting them tentatively if our critical efforts are unsuccessful. (Popper 1972: 46–51)

Interpretivism

Interpretivism entails an *ontology* in which social reality is regarded as the product of processes by which social actors together negotiate the meanings for actions and situations; it is a complex of socially constructed meanings. Human experience is characterized as a process of interpretation rather than sensory, material apprehension of the external physical world, and human behaviour depends on how individuals interpret the conditions in which they find themselves. Therefore, *social reality* is not some 'thing' that may be interpreted in different ways; it is those interpretations. Hence, in contrast to physical reality, social reality is preinterpreted.

In its *epistemology*, knowledge is seen to be derived from everyday concepts and meanings. The social researcher enters the everyday social world in order to grasp the socially constructed meanings, and then reconstructs these meanings in social scientific language. At one level, these latter accounts are regarded as redescriptions of everyday accounts; at another level they are developed into theories. The question of whether these accounts of social life are to be regarded as superior to everyday accounts is a matter of dispute.

The schools of 'interpretive sociology' ... have made some essential contributions to the clarification of the logic and method of the social sciences. In summary form, these are the following: the social world, unlike the world of nature, has to be grasped as a skilled accomplishment of active human beings; the constitution of this world as 'meaningful', 'accountable' or 'intelligible' depends upon language, regarded however not simply as a system of signs and symbols but as a medium of practical activity; the social scientist of necessity draws upon the same sorts of skills as those whose conduct he [sic] seeks to analyse in order to describe it; generating descriptions of social conduct depends upon the hermeneutic task of penetrating the frames of meaning which lay actors themselves draw upon in constituting and reconstructing the social world. (Giddens 1976a: 155)

Critical Theory

The *ontology* adopted by Habermas's Critical Theory shares much in common with Interpretivism. Both natural and social realities are seen to be socially constructed, although these realities are regarded as being fundamentally different. Cognitive interests – strategies for interpreting life experiences – determine the objects of reality. The world is not a universe of facts which exist independently of the observer; theoretical statements do not describe reality, they depend on assumptions embedded in theoretical constructs and common-sense thinking.

Objective observation is considered to be impossible in both the natural and social sciences due to the assumptions held by the observer. Therefore, cognitive interests also determine the procedures used to discover and justify knowledge; three types of interests lead to three types of knowledge. The *empirical–analytic* sciences are based on technical interests of prediction and control – exploitable knowledge; while the *historical–hermeneutic* sciences are based on practical interests of mutual understanding in everyday discourse – knowledge of human social existence. A third form of knowledge, derived from *critical theory*, is based on emancipatory interests – human autonomy freed from domination. In the *empirical–analytic* sciences the process is 'monologic' in which the researcher is a detached observer, while in the *historical–hermeneutic* sciences the process is 'dialogic' with the observer needing to become involved in the shared framework of cultural meanings.

Critical theory involves all three forms of knowledge, the one used being dependent on the interests of the researcher: causal explanation, interpretive understanding or human emancipation. The pursuit of the latter may require the use of one or both of the two other forms of knowledge. Causal laws are not regarded as universal truths but have a practical function as the basis for action. Truth is not based on the evidence but on consensus that could be expected in an ideal speech situation.

Habermas classifies processes of inquiry (*Forschungsprozesses*) into three categories: *empirical-analytic sciences*, including the natural sciences and the social sciences insofar as they aim at producing nominological knowledge; *historical-hermeneutic sciences*, including the humanities (*Geisteswissenschaften*) and the historical and social sciences insofar as they aim at interpretive understanding of meaningful configurations; and the *critically oriented sciences*, including psychoanalysis and the critique of ideology (critical social theory), as well as philosophy understood as a reflective and critical discipline. For each category of inquiry he posits a connection with a specific cognitive interest . . . These then are the basic elements of Habermas's theory of cognitive interests: a rejection of the "objectivist illusion" according to which the world is conceived as a universe of facts independent of the knower, whose task it is to describe them as they are in themselves; a thematization of the frames of reference in which different types of theoretical statements are located; a classification of processes of inquiry into three categories distinguished by their general cognitive strategies; and the connection of these strategies with specific cognitive interests that have their basis in the natural history of the human species. (McCarthy 1984: 58, 59)

Realism

In the Realist *ontology* the ultimate objects of scientific enquiry are considered to exist and act independently of scientists and their activity. A distinction is made between the domains of the empirical, the actual and the real. The empirical is made up of experiences of events through observation; the actual includes events whether observed or not; and the real consists of the processes that generate events. It is an ontology of intransitive structures and mechanisms which are distinguished from transitive concepts, theories and laws that are designed to describe them. These laws are descriptions of the real essences of things that exist in nature, such essences being their power or tendency to produce effects which can be observed.

Social reality is viewed as a socially constructed world in which either social episodes are the products of the cognitive resources social actors bring to them (Harré) or social arrangements are the products of material but unobservable structures of relations (Bhaskar). The aim of Realist science is to explain observable phenomena with reference to underlying structures and mechanisms.

Hence, Realist *epistemology* is based on the building of models of such mechanisms such that, if they were to exist and act in the postulated way, they would account for the phenomenon being examined. These models constitute hypothetical descriptions which, it is hoped, will reveal the underlying mechanisms of reality; these can only be known by constructing ideas about them. This is an epistemology of laws as expressing tendencies of things (as opposed to the conjunctions of events of Positivism).

The realist shares with the positivist a conception of science as an empirically-based, rational and objective enterprise, the purpose of which is to provide us with true explanatory and predictive knowledge of nature. But for the realist, unlike the positivist, there is an important difference between explanation and prediction. And it is explanation that must be pursued as the primary objective of science. To explain phenomena is not merely to show they are instances of well-established regularities. Instead, we must discover the necessary connections between phenomena, by acquiring knowledge of the underlying structures and mechanisms at work. Often, this will mean postulating the existence of types of unobservable entities and processes that are unfamiliar to us: but it is only by doing this that we get beyond the 'mere appearances' of things, to their natures and essences. Thus, for the realist, a scientific theory is a description of structures and mechanisms which causally generate the observable phenomena, a description which enables us to explain them. (Keat and Urry 1975: 5)

Structuration Theory

Structuration Theory is based on an *ontology* of recurrent social practices and their transformations; it is concerned with the nature of human action, the acting self, social institutions and the interrelations between action and institutions – with the relationship between agency and structure. It is an ontology of '*the constitutive potentials of social life: the generic human capacities and fundamental conditions through which the course and outcomes of social processes and events are generated and shaped in a manifold of empirically distinguishable ways*' (Cohen 1987: 279).

Social reality is produced and reproduced by the skilled activities of social actors but not necessarily under the conditions of their own choosing. Social structures are both constituted by human agency and are, at the same time, the medium of this constitution; as the conditions and the consequences of social interaction, they form the duality of structure.

While Structuration Theory does not conform to a predetermined set of *epistemological* principles, it nevertheless provides the grounds for gaining knowledge of the social world. Social scientists must use the same skills that social actors use to produce and reproduce their social world to penetrate the frames of meaning actors draw upon in these activities. In order to grasp this world it is necessary to get to know what social actors already know, and need to know in order to go about their daily activities, through a process of immersion in it. The resulting descriptions of this world have to be translated into technical concepts which can then be used to mediate the lay frames of meaning.

[T]he hallmark of the structurationist ontology is an abiding respect for the human potential to generate historically specific variations in the constitution of social life, and a corresponding renunciation of concepts which impose theoretical restrictions upon the substantive analysis of the constitution of social life in historically specific domains. (Cohen 1989: 252)

The social scientist studies a world, the social world, which is constituted as meaningful by those who produce and reproduce it in their activities – human subjects. To describe human behaviour in a valid way is in principle to be able to participate in the forms of life which constitute, and are constituted by, that behaviour. This is already a hermeneutic task. But social science is itself a 'form of life', with its own technical concepts. Hermeneutics hence enters into the social sciences on two, related levels; this double hermeneutic proves to be of basic importance to the post-positivist reformulation of social theory. (Giddens 1982: 7–8)

Feminism

The *ontological* claims of Feminism are that both the natural and social worlds are social constructions, and that these worlds are constructed differently by people who, in different social locations, have had different life experiences (e.g. men and women). Hence, multiple realities are possible. Feminism argues that it is necessary to counter the fact that the dominant forms of science have constructed these worlds from a male point of view, by focusing on women's constructions of the world. These may be different from male constructions: women tend to view nature as active rather than passive; they have different views of social relationships; they are more in touch with their feelings; and, they have different views of moral responsibility.

Feminist *epistemology* substitutes women's experiences for men's experiences as the basis for knowledge. It is argued that women have a privileged position in their ability to understand the social world because of the experience of caring labour. Conventional dualisms, such as objective/subjective, reason/emotion, fact/value, expert/non-expert, and the separation of the knower and the known, are rejected as part of androcentric epistemology. The researcher must be located in the same plane as the subject matter. Feminist researchers are encouraged to integrate thoughts and feelings, logical capacities and intuition, the rational and the emotional. There is a preference for researching natural settings rather than variables, using qualitative rather than quantitative methods. Traditional views of objectivity and rationality are rejected and replaced with notions of objectivity as drawing on the commonality of feelings and experiences, as a dialogical process located in a political context. Descriptions and explanations are seen to be not only theory-laden but also story-laden. However, while all knowledge is historically situated, some stories are better than others. Knowledge is based on shared visions, particularly visions of the future. Feminism is committed to change, to producing a better world for women and, hence, for men.

Feminist theory is that part of the new scholarship on women that implicitly or formally presents a generalized, wide-ranging system of ideas about the basic features of social life and of human experience as these can be understood from a woman-centered perspective. Feminist theory is women centred in three ways. First, its major 'object' for investigation, the starting point of all its investigation, is the situation (or the situations) and experiences of women in society. Second, it treats women as the central 'subjects' in the investigative process; that is, it seeks to see the world from the distinctive vantage point (or vantage points) of women in the social world. Third, feminist theory is critical and activist on behalf of women, seeking to produce a

better world for women – and thus, they argue, for mankind. (Lengermann
and Niebrugge-Brantley 1988: 400)

Critique of the Approaches

Positivism

As a philosophy of science, Positivism has been subjected to devastating
criticism. Some of the main points of dispute are: the claim that experience
can be a sound basis for scientific knowledge; that science should deal only
with observable phenomena and not with abstract or hypothetical entities;
that it is possible to distinguish between an a-theoretical observation language and a theoretical language; that theoretical concepts have a 1:1
correspondence with 'reality' as it is observed; that scientific laws are based
on constant conjunctions between events in the world; and, that 'facts' and
'values' can be separated. It is not possible to review these criticisms in
detail here.[4] Further comments related to claims about the appropriate
logic to be used in the development and testing of theories will be dealt
with in chapter 5.

Positivism has been attacked from the Interpretive, Critical Rationalist, Critical Theory, Realist and Feminist approaches, as well as from a
position labelled Conventionalist, derived largely from the work of
Kuhn (1970a). The Interpretive critique has focused on what is regarded
as Positivism's inadequate view of the nature of social reality – its inadequate ontology. Positivism simply takes for granted the socially constructed
world which Interpretivism regards as social reality. Positivism cannot
account for the way in which social reality is constructed and maintained,
or how people interpret their own actions and the actions of others.
Interpretivism requires that this everyday reality must be discovered and
described as the first and essential step in any social investigation.

> All forms of naturalism and logical empiricism simply take for granted this
> social reality, which is the proper object of the social sciences. Intersubjectivity,
> interaction, intercommunication, and language are simply presupposed as
> the unclarified foundation of these theories. They assume as it were, that the
> social scientist has already solved his fundamental problem, before a scientific
> enquiry starts. (Schütz, 1963a: 236)

Therefore, according to Schütz, Positivists and Critical Rationalists construct fictitious social worlds out of the meaning it has for *them*, and
neglect what it means to the social actors. Instead, he argued that the
'subjective' point of view of the social actors, as against the so-called
'objective' point of view of the social scientist, has to take precedence.

---

[4] For discussions with a social science orientation see, for example, Keat and Urry (1975),
Hindess (1977), Bhaskar (1979, 1986) and Stockman (1983).

'The safeguarding of the subjective point of view is the only but sufficient guarantee that the world of social reality will not be replaced by a fictional non-existing world constructed by the scientific observer' (Schütz 1970: 271).

The central feature of the Critical Rationalist critique of Positivism is its process for 'discovering' knowledge and the basis for justifying this knowledge. First, because it regards experience as an inadequate source of knowledge, and as all observation involves interpretation, Critical Rationalism has argued that it is not possible to distinguish between observational statements and theoretical statements; all statements about the world are theoretical at least to some degree.[5] Secondly, it is argued that experience is an inadequate basis for justifying knowledge, because it leads to a circular argument. On what basis can experience be established as a justification for knowledge except by reference to experience?

Positivism's claim that reality can be perceived directly by the use of the human senses has been thoroughly discredited. Even if it is assumed that a single, unique, physical world exists independently of observers – and this assumption is not universally accepted – the process of observing it involves both conscious and unconscious interpretation. Observations are 'theory-loaded'; 'there is more to seeing than meets the eyeball' (Hanson 1958).[6] The processes that human beings use to observe the world around them, be it in everyday life or for scientific purposes, are not analogous to taking photographs. In 'reading' what impinges on our senses, we have to engage in a complex process that entails both the use of concepts peculiar to the language of a particular culture, and expectations about what is 'there'. Furthermore, we do not observe as isolated individuals but as members of cultural or sub-cultural groups which provide us with ontological assumptions. Therefore, observers are active agents, not passive receptacles. And the particular baggage of experience, knowledge, expectations and language an observer brings to research will influence what is observed. It can be argued that we are only able to see those things for which we have concepts in our language. When two observers use very different languages, they are likely to see different things. Critical Rationalism claimed to have overcome these deficiencies of Positivism with its criteria of falsification rather than verification, and its tentative view of the truth of theories.

The Realist solution to the theory-laden nature of observation and description is to draw the distinction between the transitive and intransitive objects of science. While our descriptions of the *empirical* domain may be theory dependent, the structures and mechanisms of the *real* domain exist independently of our descriptions of them. Reality is not there to be observed as in Positivism, nor is it constructed as in Conventionalism, it is just there. Therefore, the relative success of competing theories to

---

[5] See Hesse (1974) for an alternative discussion of this issue.
[6] For a review of the 'theory dependence of observations' see Chalmers (1982).

represent this reality can be settled, according to the Realists, as a matter of rational judgement (Outhwaite 1983a: 323).

In their various publications between 1937 and 1969, the founders of Critical Theory worked with a rather broad and imprecise view of Positivism. Their criticism of it had three aspects: that it is an inadequate and misleading philosophy which is unable to attain an adequate understanding of social life; by focusing on what exists, it condones the present social order; and, that it is a major contributor to a new form of domination: technocratic–bureaucratic domination (Bottomore 1984: 28). Since this period, the critique of Positivism has continued in the work of Habermas.

Unlike the criticisms of Critical Rationalism, Critical Theory has operated both at the level of method and at the level of a theory of society. Its critique 'is motivated, not by a deep interest in the logic of the natural sciences, but by concern for the consequences of positivism's universalization of that logic for the human and social sciences' (Stockman 1983: 43). Habermas drew on Kant (1929) to replace the passive model of cognition of Positivism with an active model which attributed to observers the capacities both to perceive the world around them and to organize those perceptions. Kant argued that observers have to impose some structure on observations. According to Habermas (1972), Positivism suffers from an 'objectivist illusion' in believing that all knowledge is derived from 'objective facts' which are obtained free of the interests of the researcher. Positivism believes that it is obtaining knowledge of 'reality' and fails to recognize that it has an implicit standpoint in its interest in technical control. By denying the possibility of universal laws in the hermeneutic sciences, Habermas opened up the possibility of other realms of knowledge with different interests.

As well as accusing Positivism of having an inadequate ontology, Realism also attacked the Positivist method of explanation in terms of constant conjunctions between events. Even if two kinds of phenomena can be shown to occur regularly together, there is still the question of why this is the case. According to Realism, establishing regularities between observed events is only the starting point in the process of scientific discovery.

> Of course we must try to find correlations between types of occasions and types of social action ... But correlations are not science ... Correlations in non-positivistic science are the occasions for the investigation of the causal mechanisms responsible for these correlations, the discovery of which would be a contribution to science. Correlational studies remain at the level of natural history. (Harré 1977a: 333)

According to Bhaskar (1978), constant conjunctions of events occur only in closed systems, those produced by experimental conditions. In open systems characteristic of both nature and society, a large number of generative mechanisms will be exercising their powers to cause effects at the same time. What is observed as 'empirical' conjunctions may therefore not reflect the complexity of the mechanisms that are operating. The inter-action of mechanisms in open systems may cancel each other out and produce no observable outcomes. Bhaskar argued that Positivism and Critical Rationalism treat the world of nature as a closed system. Hence, because it conflates the domains of the empirical and the real, and the transitive and the intransitive, Positivism is not an adequate philosophy of science.

Conventionalism is a response to Positivism, Critical Rationalism and, to a certain extent, to Realism; its critique of Critical Rationalism will be discussed in the next section. In the meantime, three of its comments on Positivism will be reviewed briefly here (Keat and Urry 1975: 60–1). Conventionalism has argued, first, that scientific statements are the crea-tions of scientists rather than being true or false descriptions of some external, independently existing 'reality'. This claim leads to the view that the world which scientists study is created by theories and not described by them. Theories determine what is real, and when they change funda-mentally, or are replaced by other theories, we are faced with a different world, not a different view of the world. This makes decisions about whether a theory should be accepted or rejected a matter of judgement as it is not possible to establish universally valid criteria for this purpose. The second characteristic is that observations cannot provide an adequate basis for determining the truth or falsity of theories; it is not possible to establish any agreed facts that would assist in choosing between theories. Theories are 'under-determined' by empirical data because their claims usually go beyond what data can provide. The third claim of Conventionalism is that the processes of accepting or rejecting a theory are essentially related to the scientist's practical interests or aesthetic or moral values – there are no rational or universal criteria for evaluating scientific activity, thus making it a 'subjective' process. Conventionalism therefore undermines commonly held views on objectivity and rationality; science is viewed sociologically or psychologically rather than logically.

Critical Rationalism

Popper argued that falsification rather then justification should be regarded as embodying the appropriate methodological rules for both the natural and social sciences, and that this is most likely to facilitate the processes of gaining scientific knowledge. However, according to Stockman (1983), Popper lapsed into a positivistic justification for these rules, i.e. by regard-ing them as correct *descriptions* of the scientific method, rather than a matter of agreement.

> It would appear ... as if the methodological conventionalism of Popper's earlier work has now disappeared, and that there has been a relapse into precisely that which was earlier criticized as positivistic; for the doctrine

of the unity of method, rather than being proposed as a convention, is advanced as a correct description, either of the methods in fact in use, or perhaps of the 'essence' of both the natural and the social sciences. (Stockman 1983: 126)

The central requirement of Critical Rationalism is that hypotheses are compared with observation statements in order to eliminate those which do not conform with reality. But Hindess (1977: 182–7) has argued that the rejection of the idea of a theoretically neutral observation language removes any possible rational foundation for the idea of testing a theory against the facts of observation. The problem is how to establish a relationship between scientific language on the one hand, and real objects on the other. Popper's notion of truth depends on the possibility of establishing a correspondence between a theory and 'the facts'. Similarly, the Positivist principle of knowledge being derived from experience, or universal laws being built up from observations, faces the same problem. If the possibility of correspondence is problematic, then the certainty of both the laws of Positivism and the theories of Critical Rationalism cannot be established; they must rest on an act of faith. If there is no theory-neutral observation language, Critical Rationalism cannot work. 'To maintain, as Popper does, both the rationality of testing and the thesis that observation is an interpretation in the light of theory is to collapse into a manifest and absurd contradiction. Popper's theory of science is therefore strictly incoherent' (Hindess 1977: 186). The consequence is that theory testing cannot be a purely rational process as there is no way to observe reality directly.

The matter is further complicated by the fact that the process of testing theories which Popper advocated is not as simple as he has suggested. There are many elements in a theory: general statements which describe relationships between phenomena and are the core of the theory; other statements which specify conditions under which these general statements will hold; and logic of some form. If the test fails, the theory is supposed to be refuted. But a judgement has to be made as to which element must be rejected. Hindess (1977) has argued that refutation is always a matter of decision. Communities of scientists will develop their own rules for making these judgements and these rules will have no independent scientific basis (Habermas 1976: 204).

This epistemological difficulty of establishing the relationship between theories and reality is enough to undermine the claims that theory testing is a rational process. But the most influential challenge to this claim, and to the Critical Rationalist view of scientific progress, has come from the seminal work of Thomas Kuhn in *The Structure of Scientific Revolutions* (1970a), first published in 1962. From his background as a physicist, and later as a historian of science, Kuhn came to the conclusion that traditional accounts of science did not reflect the historical evidence. As an alternative to both the Positivist and Critical Rationalist views of scientific progress, either as the accumulation of observations, or as a process of trial and error, Kuhn argued for a psychological and sociological view rather than a logical one.

Kuhn's view of scientific progress is centred on the concepts of *paradigm*, *normal science*, *anomalies* and *scientific revolutions*, and on the communities of scientists who are practitioners of a scientific specialty. These scientists are considered to share a *paradigm* or 'discipline matrix' consisting of: the way in which a community of scientists views the nature of the reality which they study (their ontology) – the components that make it up and how they are related as reflected in concepts, laws and theories; the techniques which are appropriate for investigating this reality (their epistemology); and, accepted examples of past scientific achievements (exemplars), which provide both the foundation for further practice and models for students who wish to become members of the community.[7] He suggested that in a mature science a single paradigm will set the standards and provide the framework and direction for legitimate scientific activity.

Most of what scientists do is to engage in *normal science*, research which is firmly based on the assumptions and rules of the paradigm and which is dominated by 'puzzle-solving' activity. Normal science extends the knowledge which the paradigm provides by testing its predictions, and further articulating and filling out what is suggested by the paradigm. The aim is not for unexpected novelty of fact or theory but for articulation of problems within the expectations and prescriptions of the paradigm. The results of this research add to the scope and precision with which the paradigm can be applied. Practitioners will share criteria which will determine when a puzzle has been solved. As scientists are judged on their ability to solve puzzles, it is unlikely that puzzles will be chosen that do not have some chance of solution. In the course of normal science, the paradigm is not challenged or tested; failure to solve a puzzle will be seen as the failure of the scientist, not the paradigm – the practitioner is blamed, not the tools. Adherence to a paradigm by a community of scientists is analogous to an act of faith. However, the status of a paradigm will depend on its capacity to solve problems which its practitioners regard as important.

Occasions will arise when some puzzles cannot be solved, or gaps will appear between what the paradigm would have anticipated and what was observed. There is 'the recognition that nature has somehow violated the paradigm-induced expectations that govern normal science' (Kuhn 1970a: 52–3). These anomalies may initially be ignored as commitment to a paradigm makes for inherent resistance to their recognition. It is difficult for scientists to perceive phenomena for which the paradigm does not provide concepts; 'something like a paradigm is prerequisite to perception itself. What a man [sic] sees depends both upon what he looks at and also upon

[7] In an oft-quoted article, Masterman (1970) has pointed out that Kuhn has used the concept of *paradigm* in a variety of ways. However, for the present purposes, this broad definition, which includes the notion of a scientific worldview, accepted practices and exemplars, will be used.

what his previous visual-conceptual experience has taught him to see' (Kuhn 1970a: 113). But, in addition, to suggest that there is something wrong with the paradigm can also be interpreted as an act of heresy.

Anomalies require that the world be viewed differently. Eventually, this may lead to a crisis of confidence in the paradigm; the tools which it supplies are no longer able to deal with the puzzles it defines. There emerges a period of *extraordinary science*. 'The proliferation of competing articulations, the willingness to try anything, the expression of explicit discontent, the recourse to philosophy and to debate over fundamentals, all these are symptoms of a transition from normal to extraordinary research' (Kuhn 1970a: 91). The situation is ripe for the emergence of a new paradigm and novel theories.

The process of replacing the old paradigm with a new one is described as a *scientific revolution*. A new paradigm may be proposed to replace the existing one, a paradigm that can solve the new puzzles raised by the anomaly and, as well, handle the puzzles that the previous paradigm had solved. However, such revolutions occur only slowly; it may take a generation for the 'old guard' in the scientific community to be replaced by the 'young Turks', or it may take very much longer, as was the case with the Copernican revolution in astronomy. According to Kuhn, the process by which scientists move from working with the old paradigm to the new is analogous to a religious conversion; it involves not just adopting a fundamentally different way of viewing the world but also means living in a different world.

Once a new paradigm is established, a new phase of normal science will become established. In time, new anomalies will emerge and further revolutions will occur. This view of science can be represented as a cyclical process which proceeds through stages shown in Figure 1.

For Kuhn, scientific progress is not achieved either by the accumulation of generalizations derived from observation, or by the critical testing of new hypotheses, but by scientific revolutions which change the way a scientific community views the world and defines and goes about solving puzzles. It is a shift from criticism to commitment; from logic to community loyalty, from falsification to conversion. The critical tests which Popper saw as sifting out false hypotheses Kuhn regarded as 'extraordinary science', rare events that may be associated with the advent or the development of a scientific revolution. Hence, he has argued that Popper has overlooked the rather routine activities of *normal science*. Popper (1970) acknowledged this but regarded the uncritical features of normal science as bad science. 'The "normal" scientist, in my view, has been taught badly ... [H]e is a victim of indoctrination. He has learned a technique which can be applied without asking for the reasons why' (Popper 1970: 52–53).

Kuhn considered that on some occasions critical tests were not required to bring about a scientific revolution (Kuhn 1970b: 10). He regarded most scientific activity as *normal science* in which critical discourse is largely abandoned. Popper's distinction between science and pseudo-science, based

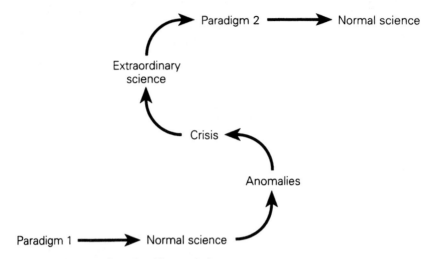

Figure 1 Stages of a scientific revolution.

on the criterion of the testability of theories, is replaced by the criterion of puzzle-solving; sciences have puzzles and non-sciences do not; astronomy has puzzles but astrology does not (Kuhn 1970b: 7–10).

Kuhn was critical of Popper's trial and error view of scientific progress, of learning from mistakes. He accepted that this process is inevitable in normal science, but only in the sense that an individual has failed to abide by pre-established rules of the community – mistakes in arithmetic, logic or measurement being the most common. For Popper, mistakes are wrong theories, but in extraordinary science this notion is problematic as paradigms are not wrong, just limited in their capacity to deal with particular puzzles. This difference between Kuhn and Popper hinges on whether or not science is regarded as the pursuit of absolute truths about the world. Popper claimed it was, although he recognized that we never know when we have arrived, while Kuhn can be interpreted as being agnostic on this point, being more concerned with the values which scientists use to make choices between competing theories and paradigms. Certainly, a paradigm is not true or false, only useful in solving puzzles which it defines, using criteria which it specifies. Truth becomes a matter of community consensus.

Kuhn has argued that as proponents of rival paradigms 'live in different worlds'; rival paradigms are incommensurable. This issue relates to his claim that as the concepts and propositions of theories produced by a community of scientists depend on the assumptions and beliefs in their paradigm for their particular meaning, and as paradigms embody different and incompatible worldviews, then it will be difficult for members of different scientific communities to communicate effectively, and it will be impossible to adjudicate between competing theories. There is no neutral language of observation, no common vocabulary and no neutral ground from which to settle claims.

Popper vigorously rejected the relativistic implications of Kuhn's thesis which he called 'the myth of the framework'. He accepted that

> at any moment we are prisoners caught in the framework of our theories; our expectations; our past experiences; our language. But ... if we try, we can break out of our framework at any time. Admittedly, we shall find ourselves again in a framework, but it will be a better and roomier one; and we can at any moment break out of it again. (Popper 1970: 56)

However, Popper was unwilling to acknowledge that a critical comparison of competing theories is impossible, and he rejected Kuhn's idea that sociology, psychology or history can be of assistance in understanding the nature of scientific activity. For Popper, the 'logic of discovery' has little to learn from the 'psychology or sociology of research'.

Kuhn's work has spawned a vast literature and has received detailed criticism by philosophers and historians of science.

> There is scarcely an aspect of Kuhn's work that has not been severely criticized – freqently from conflicting points of view. Critics have argued that the central notion of a paradigm is ambiguous and confused; that Kuhn has misinterpreted the history of science; that he has inaccurately described what he calls normal science; that the distinction between normal and revolutionary science is not nearly as sharp as he suggests; that his analysis of the paradigm shift makes science into an irrational, subjectivistic, and relativistic discipline, and fails to explain how sciences in fact do progress; that he not only confuses the history of science with the logic of science, but also surreptitiously passes off normative claims about what science ought to be, based on descriptions that do not warrant such norms. (Bernstein 1976: 88)

Nevertheless, Kuhn's view of science has had a great influence on the philosophy of the natural and social sciences, and has also provided a framework for some disciplines to understand their crises and revolutions. His ideas were taken up enthusiastically by many social scientists in the 1960s and 1970s (see, for example, Friedrichs 1970).

Another well-known, but more sympathetic, critique of Critical Rationalism has been made by Lakatos (1970). In order to overcome the piecemeal nature of the Critical Rationalist view of science, Lakatos argued that the growth of science is characterized by continuity which evolves from the existence of *research programmes*. 'The programme consists of methodological rules: some tell us what paths of research to avoid (*negative heuristic*), and others what paths to pursue (*positive heuristic*)' (1970: 132). The basic characteristic of a research programme is its *hard core* which cannot be rejected or modified. A *protective belt* of auxiliary hypotheses is invented and articulated to protect the hard core. 'It is the protective belt of auxiliary hypotheses which has to bear the brunt of tests and get adjusted and re-adjusted, or even completely replaced, to defend the thus-hardened core' (1970: 133). Such a research programme will be regarded as *progressive* if it predicts novel phenomena and *degenerating* if it fails to do so. Scientists will persist in developing the theory, even in spite of disconfirming evidence, as long as it continues to be progressive. However, a research programme may eventually be discarded if it degenerates, even if it has not been refuted; it is not overthrown by a crucial experiment, it is just neglected. It may even be revived at a later stage. He argued that as the history of science is characterized by research programmes, the advancement of scientific knowledge becomes an orderly and efficient process. Scientists are provided with both a relatively secure context in which to operate and some directions for their work.

Lakatos rejected Kuhn's idea of a single paradigm dominating a scientific community at any one time. What Kuhn called normal science, Lakatos regarded as a research programme that has achieved a monopoly. However, he regarded this situation as being rare, and then only for short periods, and, instead, favoured theoretical pluralism. '*The history of science has been and should be a history of competing research programmes (or, if you wish, "paradigms"), but it has not been and must not become a succession of periods of normal science: the sooner competition starts, the better for progress*' (Lakatos 1970: 155). Lakatos also objected to Kuhn's notion of a scientific revolution as being irrational as it suggested notions of contagious panic or mob psychology. Therefore, Lakatos charted a middle path between the extremes advocated by Popper and Kuhn; he accepted some aspects of both, while at the same time rejecting others. The outcome is a different view of the processes by which scientific progress occurs.

Interpretivism

The critics of Interpretivism come from within as well as from without the approach. Albert wanted to defend the doctrine of the unity of method. Giddens and Rex considered themselves within the tradition, drawing heavily on Gadamer's hermeneutics and Weber's interpretive sociology, respectively. Bhaskar, on the other hand, accepted some elements into his version of Realism, but was nevertheless critical of other elements. Similarly, Critical Theory has incorporated Interpretivism as an aspect of its overall scheme, but is aware of its limitations. As these critiques overlap at a number of points, they will be dealt with in an integrated way.

1   Albert's (1969) critique was based on a view that the Interpretivist concern to discover the meaningful nature of social life required the use of a method similar to that advocated by Positivism, i.e. as a process of gaining direct pre-theoretical access to the unique meanings used by people in particular situations. This, he argued, is analogous to the Positivist aim of achieving direct experience of the world.

2　Giddens has argued that the central concepts of Interpretivism, 'intention', 'reason' and 'motives', are all potentially misleading in that they imply that competent social actors engage in a countinuous monitoring of their conduct and are thus aware of both their intentions and the reasons for their actions. However, it is usually only when actors either carry out retrospective enquiries into their own conduct, or when their actions are queried by others, that this reflection occurs. It might be added that reflection is required when action breaks down and/or when social situations are disturbed, such that it is no longer possible for it to continue in a taken-for-granted manner. However, most of the time action proceeds without reflective monitoring. 'Routine . . . is the predominant form of day-to-day social activity. Most daily practices are not directly motivated' (Giddens 1984: 282).

3　Rex and others have argued that the social scientist should be able to give a different and competing account of social actors' actions from the actors' own accounts. His comments were made in the context of a position held by many Interpretivists that they should not meddle with, or seek to alter, the account which social actors give of their actions. (This will be elaborated in chapters 6 and 7.) Bhaskar has referred to the Interpretivist view, that social actors' concepts and meanings cannot be criticized by the social scientist, as the *linguistic fallacy*. This fallacy is based on a failure to recognize that there is more to reality than is expressed in the language of social actors. Social actors' constructions of reality are only one element in a Realist social science, rather than being its entire concern. Social actors' accounts are susceptible to critique, and 'social science (and, at a remove, philosophy) always and necessarily consists in a semantic, moral and political intervention in the life of the society under study' (Bhaskar 1979: 199).

4　Interpretivism fails to acknowledge the role of institutional structures, particularly divisions of interest and relations of power. Giddens has argued that the production and reproduction of the social world requires social actors to draw upon resources, and to depend on conditions, of which they are either completely or partly unaware. These structures are both the condition and the consequence of the production of interaction. Rex was also critical of Interpretive social scientists for dissociating themselves from any form of structural analysis, and argued that it was important for them to be interested 'in actual historical structures as they appear to the sociologist and not merely the structures which actors believe to exist, or believe that they make, in the process of thinking them to exist' (Rex 1974: 50).

5　From a Realist point of view, Bhaskar and Outhwaite have argued that Interpretivism also commits the *epistemic fallacy*. While 'interpretive processes are a significant part of what goes on in the social world, and . . . our access to the social world is necessarily via our understanding of these interpretive processes, it does not follow that this is all that exists, or can be known to exist' (Outhwaite 1987a: 76). Realists, of course, want to specify a domain of the 'real' which exists not only independently of the observer, but which includes intransitive structures and mechanisms about which social actors may be unaware, and which, unlike the structures referred to by Giddens and Rex, are unlikely to be obvious to the social scientist.

6   Fay (1975) considered that Interpretivism is not able to deal with the conditions which give rise to the meanings and interpretations, the actions, rules and beliefs.

> [I]t does not provide a means whereby one can study the relationships between the structural elements of a social order and the possible forms of behaviour and beliefs which such elements engender. A social scientist will want to investigate not only the meanings of particular types of actions, but those causal factors which give rise to and support the continuing existence of these meanings. (Fay 1975: 83–4).

In addition, focusing on people's intentions prevents Interpretivism from explaining the pattern of unintended consequences of actions (a point also made by Giddens).

7   Fay regarded Interpretivism as being implicitly conservative in that it ignores the possible structures of conflict in a society and, hence, the possible sources of social change. It is also unable to give an account of historical change – of why a specific institution or social order came to be what it is and why it changed in particular ways. However, Fay did not see these last two criticisms as undermining the basic foundations of Interpretivism. Rather, they indicate that there are some areas of interest to the social scientist with which Interpretivism cannot deal.

Critical Theory

It is neither possible nor necessary to undertake a comprehensive critique of Critical Theory here; the discussion will be confined to some specific methodological issues in Habermas's work.[8] Critical Theorists have exposed major flaws in traditional approaches to social enquiry but they have left unresolved a range of epistemological issues which they intended to solve (Held 1980: 399).

Some critics accuse Habermas of adopting a misleading differentiation between the natural and social sciences based on the distinction between causal explanation and interpretation. It was noted earlier that an interest in prediction and control is not specific to the natural sciences; it can be the concern of Positivist and Critical Rationalist social science. However, in adopting his view of the empirical–analytic sciences, which include some social sciences, Habermas has failed to address Positivism's many well-accepted deficiencies (Keat and Urry 1975: 227; Giddens 1976a: 68, 1977b: 148–151; Stockman 1983: 105).

---

[8] In the context of the positivist dispute in German sociology (Adorno et al. 1976), Albert (1976a,b) has offered a critique of Habermas's Critical Theory from the point of view of Critical Rationalism.

While Keat and Urry considered Habermas was correct in distinguishing between the forms of knowledge involved in the empirical–analytic and historical–hermeneutic sciences, between causal explanation and interpretive understanding, they considered that there is a danger that Critical Theory could be split between these two approaches, between research that does not involve an examination of the social actors' interpretations and research that concentrates on interpretive understanding. In the context of their support for Realism, they argued that both traditions of research must be combined (Keat and Urry 1975: 227).

In contrast, Giddens has argued that Habermas's classification of disciplines into the empirical–analytic and the historical–hermeneutic is unsatisfactory. First, hermeneutic problems are not confined to the human studies; an interest in meaningful understanding is more integral to science than Habermas allowed. As Kuhn (1970a) and Gadamer (1989) have pointed out in their own particular ways, with respect to 'paradigms' and 'traditions', 'all knowledge, whether in science, literature, or art, is achieved within and by means of frames of meaning rooted in natural-language communities' (Giddens 1977b: 150). Secondly, an interest in prediction and control, which Habermas associates with the empirical–analytic sciences, is not logically tied to concerns with causal explanation.

> On the contrary, they are of primary significance in interaction itself, and are manifestly crucial to the constitution of that form of knowledge . . . whereby the understanding of others is achieved. In this sense, the 'predictability' of interaction, and the control operated over its course, is a contingent accomplishment of parties to interaction. (Giddens 1977b: 151)

In a somewhat similar vein, Bernstein (1976) has suggested that Habermas's attempt to introduce categorical distinctions between forms of knowledge and enquiry has been unsuccessful. While it is difficult to deny that technical cognitive interests have played a major role in shaping the history and form of the empirical–analytic sciences, and that technical interests have come to dominate forms of knowledge, this does not mean that the empirical–analytic sciences are guided by technical interests that determine its form of knowledge.

> [T]he post-empiricist philosophy and history of science is deeply questioning the categorical distinctions that separate even the hard natural sciences from what Habermas calls the historical-hermeneutic disciplines. One of the lessons to be learned from such inquiries is that the very characteristics thought distinctive of disputes in the historical-hermeneutical disciplines have their analogies in research controversies in the natural sciences. Reference to technical interest is not sufficient to characterize the empirical-analytic sciences, for at their very foundation they require interpretive principles and a rational resolution of the conflict of interpretations. (Bernstein 1976: 221)

Bernstein also argued that there is a qualitative difference between the disciplines guided by a technical and a practical interest, and those guided by an emancipatory interest. In the case of the first two categories of science, Habermas specified the formal conditions which are required to produce the particular types of knowledge, the 'objects' that they study, the methods they employ, and the criteria used to evaluate competing interpretations. But the disciplines guided by an emancipatory interest appear to be different; it is not possible to specify formal procedures for such activity. In spite of Habermas's appeal to reason as a means of self-reflection, critique is a normative activity (Bernstein 1976: 209).

The problem faced by all members of the Critical Theory school was how to adopt an independent critical position while still being located in a particular cultural and historical context (Held 1980: 398–9). Is a solution to this problem possible? Habermas attempted to deal with it in terms of a consensus theory of truth. A major difficulty with this theory is that its own justification is based on the same process, thus leading to an infinite regress. However, depending on one's point of view, this can be viewed as either a reasonable method for dealing with the insoluble problem of the relativity of all knowledge, or an inadequate attempt to overcome the problem of relativism (see chapter 7).

Realism

In the early version of Realism proposed by Harré (1970), the aim of science was seen to be a search for the real essences of things which have powers to produce effects. The notion of 'real essence' goes back to Aristotle and has been the subject of much debate in philosophy. Positivism refused to deal with any notion that cannot be observed. However, while Popper also rejected such notions, it has been argued that his method of falsification *is* an attempt to discover essences, even if not mechanisms (Suppe 1977: 168). However, Hesse has argued that 'theories about essences are neither stable nor cumulative, and are therefore not part of the realistic aspects of science' (1974: 299).

A systematic critique of the early form of 'scientific realism' in the natural sciences has been presented by van Fraassen (1980) from a position which he has described as *constructive empiricism*.[9] He was also critical of Positivism, particularly Logical Positivism, and other philosophies of science known as Phenomenalism (Mach), Conventionalism (Poincaré), Fictionalism (Duhem) and Logical Empiricism (Reichenbach). He rejected two central features of Logical Positivism – the distinction between observational and theoretical languages, and the view of science as the search for truth – and, a central feature of scientific realism – the search for 'a true description of unobservable processes that explain observable ones' (van Fraassen 1980: 3). Instead, he argued for a view of science in which

[9] As van Fraassen directed his attack on the formulation of scientific realism presented by Smart (1963), and does not refer to the work of either Harré or Bhaskar, his critique must be viewed in the light of their precursors.

theories are regarded as giving an account of what is observable. To the extent that these theories postulate unobservable entities or processes, they do so to facilitate the description of what can be observed, and these unobservables need not themselves exist, or be true, 'except in what they say about what is actual and empirically testable' (1980: 3).

> To be an empiricist is to withhold belief in anything that goes beyond the actual, observable phenomena, and to recognize no objective modality in nature. To develop an empiricist account of science is to depict it as involving a search for truth only about the empirical world, about what is actual and observable ... [I]t must involve throughout a resolute rejection of the demand for an explanation of the regularities in the observable course of nature, by means of truths concerning a reality beyond what is actual and observable, as a demand which plays no role in the scientific enterprise. (van Fraassen 1980: 202–203)

Experimental activity in the natural sciences, according to van Fraassen, is concerned with testing for empirical adequacy, and filling in the blanks in developing theories. The former involves the use of hypotheses, but not the latter. The theory guides the kind of experiment that will show how blanks are to be filled if the theory is to be empirically adequate. This is a process of theory construction by experiment, not testing. Whereas Critical Rationalism is essentially about theory testing, and Realism is about constructing hypothetical models of mechanisms and then endeavouring to demonstrate their existence, constructive empiricism involves testing hypotheses and filling in the blanks.

Van Fraassen acknowledged that scientists work in communities which are likely to share a common worldview – a 'scientific world-picture' – and a commitment to a research programme (cf. Lakatos 1970), and that 'scientific activity is one of construction rather than discovery: construction of models that must be adequate to the phenomena, and not discovery of truth concerning the unobservable' (van Fraassen 1980: 5). His emphasis is on the empirical adequacy of a theory, its capacity to explain what is observed. A theory is empirically adequate 'exactly if what it says about the observable things and events in this world, is true' (1980: 12). However, as theories usually describe much more than what is observable, what matters, according to van Fraassen, is empirical adequacy and not the truth or falsity of how theories go beyond observable phenomena (1980: 64). It is possible for the scientist to accept a theory as empirically adequate without believing it to be true. Similarly, he acknowledged that it is not possible to make claims about the truth of these world-pictures, only about their empirical adequacy. After all, conceptual frameworks may change. In adopting this position, van Fraassen wished to reject conceptual relativism, but in doing so he appears to have adopted a realist assumption common to Positivism, Critical Rationalism and Realism, and he has failed to recognize the full implication of the theory-dependence of observations used in theory testing.

Van Fraassen's constructive empiricism has shaken the foundations of Realism. Such has been the power of his arguments that a group of eminent realist philosophers from around the world engaged him in debate (see Churchland and Hooker 1985). One described the effect of van Fraassen's work thus: 'At several points in the reading of van Fraassen's book, I feared I would no longer be a realist by the time I completed it. Fortunately, sheer doxastic inertia has allowed my convictions to survive its searching critique, at least temporarily' (Churchland 1985: 35). Musgrave acknowledged that while the work had given him sleepless nights, his belief in Realism had survived. He suggested that van Fraassen's anti-realism

> is more viable than earlier antirealist positions. But, in philosophy of science as well as in science, viability directly depends on weakness. Constructive empiricism is weaker then earlier antirealist views in all kinds of ways, and correspondingly closer to realism. This is why I conclude ... that realism emerges a little bloodied but unbowed from its encounter with constructive empiricism. (Musgrave 1985: 221)

There is clearly much that could be debated about the claims of constructive empiricism in the light of its criticisms of Positivism and Critical Rationalism, but it is not possible here to review the arguments and defences contained in Churchland and Hooker (1985), or to enter those debates. And some of those criticisms of Realism may not be relevant to many of the features of the versions proposed by Harré and Bhaskar. However, these latter versions of Realism have other critics.

While Critical Theorists have not yet presented a critique of Realism, Stockman has formulated the kind of critique that they could offer. He has suggested that Realism might be regarded as a new form of 'objectivism' and is therefore trapped in what Habermas has called the 'objectivist illusion'. 'This objectivism, in the shape of a doctrine of metaphysical realism, attempts to conceptualize an independent reality and develop a theory of its fundamental features without raising the question, central to a critical philosophy, of the constitution of that "reality" through synthetic activity' (Stockman 1983: 224). Realism claims for the domain of the real an objectivity which is not adequately justified, being at best based on the argument that this is how scientists regard reality.

Stockman went on to argue that because Realism has no theory for the way in which the objects of science are constituted, it can only differentiate the objects of the natural and social sciences in an *ad hoc* manner. He contrasted the ways in which Keat and Urry, and Harré and Secord, define the subject matter of the social sciences. The former are concerned with holistic social structures and the interrelationships of their elements, while the latter are concerned with the generation of social action by the conscious self-monitoring activity of social agents. By not recognizing the kind of distinction which Habermas made between sensory experience and communicative experience, the difference in accessibility of the mechanisms in the natural and social sciences is not, according to Stockman, fully appreciated. In the natural sciences, unobservable mechanisms are inaccessible to the senses, even although their effects may be detected by scientific instruments. However, in the social sciences the notion of unobservability is more complex.

> For structures of social relations are not 'unobservable' in the same sense as elementary particles or black holes; it is not that they are inaccessible to human sensory experience, requiring instead sociological equivalents of bubble chambers and radio telescopes in order to be perceived, but rather that they are only accessible to a form of experience which goes beyond sensory experience, namely communicative experience. (Stockman 1983: 207)

In other words, natural scientists can only observe their subject matter but social scientists can converse with theirs.

In his version of Realism, Bhaskar recognized that social structures are different from natural structures because the former are both produced by social activity and reproduce that activity (Bhaskar 1979: 48; cf. Giddens' notion of 'structuration'). However, like the objects of natural scientific enquiry, 'social structures' and 'society' are theoretical and unobservable, and can only be known by their effects. Nevertheless, social structures can neither be identified independently from their effects, nor do they *exist* independently of them. This places some limits on the possibility of a Realist naturalism, thus preventing the methods of the natural sciences being used in the social sciences without significant modification. Stockman has argued that, in spite of his recognition of this important difference, Bhaskar overlooks the dialogic nature of social research.

Keat and Urry have also argued that social structures are theoretical entities that cannot be perceived by direct observation. They claim, instead, that they are abstracted from such observations. This argument also ignores the claim of Critical Theory that access to structures of social relations has to be achieved by communicative experience. Therefore, in spite of the acceptance by some Realists that the social world is preinterpreted, there is a failure to recognize that this has a bearing on the manner in which the social world is studied (Stockman 1983: 209). This point could also be made by Interpretivists. However, the outstanding exception is the Realist social science of Harré.

Benton (1981) has argued that the objective of Realism, and Bhaskar's version in particular, is to transcend the polar opposition between Positivism and Interpretivism. However, he has suggested that Bhaskar has not achieved this because his position tends to support the differences between the natural and social sciences rather than present a qualified naturalism. By holding firm to Interpretive views about the nature of social reality, as existing only in and through the activities of human agents, problems are created for the transitive/intransitive distinction and for an understanding of the nature of power. At the same time, controlled experiment, prediction and decisive tests of theory are considered by Bhaskar to be impossible in the social sciences because of the open nature of social systems, and the lack of opportunity in the social sciences to create closed systems artificially. Benton has suggested that this latter argument indicates a residue of Positivistic conceptions of experiment/prediction/testing thinking. Some natural sciences (e.g. evolutionary biology) have to operate in open systems in which a plurality of mechanisms may be present. Hence, he has argued that a critique of the 'constant conjunction' conception of causal laws is insufficiently radical as it retains the view that experimental closure is possible in *all* the natural sciences. According to Benton, Bhaskar has made a series of concessions to Interpretivism which are quite unnecessary 'such that his position would be better described as a form of anti-naturalism, rather than as a naturalism, however qualified' (Benton 1981: 19). In other words, Bhaskar is not naturalistic enough.

> [M]y arguments against Roy Bhaskar's anti-naturalism are designed less to show that the social sciences are (or could be) more like the natural ones than he supposes, than to show that the natural sciences, or, at least, some of them, are more like the social than he supposes. More importantly, though, I remain committed, as he does, to the view that there are significant differences in the methods of the different sciences, which are grounded in real differences in the subject matters of those sciences and the relationships of those sciences to their subject matters. Where I differ from Roy Bhaskar and other anti-naturalists is that I think these differences to be always of a methodological rather than epistemological kind, and that I do not, whereas Roy Bhaskar does, align the whole range of methodological diversity along a single fault-plane, dividing the natural and the social. Methodologically, if not epistemologically, the sciences display a 'family resemblance' of cross-cutting and overlapping differences and similarities of method. (Benton 1981: 20–1)

Structuration Theory

It must be acknowledged that as the originator of Structuration Theory, Giddens has taken on a daunting task in attempting to rethink modern social theory. The magnitude of the task, the range of the territory traversed, and the ontological position adopted, create abundant scope for critics of various theoretical and philosophical persuasions to find something to debate.

It is neither possible nor necessary to attempt to review the extensive range of Giddens' work; there is already a thriving industry working on this. In addition to the numerous reviews of his many books, recent contributions include Cohen (1989), Held and Thompson (1989), Clark et al. (1990), Bryant and Jary (1991) and Craib (1992). Again, the discussion here shall be confined mainly to points that have a direct bearing on methodological issues.

In his most recent writings, Giddens has argued that Structuration Theory represents his concern to develop an ontology of social life. 'By "ontology" here, I mean a conceptual investigation of the nature of human action, social institutions and the interrelations between action and institutions' (Giddens 1991: 201). At the same time, he has eschewed any interest in epistemological issues, in spite of the fact that he has advocated 'new rules' of sociological method (1976a).

Many authors have argued that the central concepts in Giddens' scheme – *structure, structuration* and *duality of structure* – are ambivalent and inadequately developed (Dallmayr 1982): they are abstract and lack empirical examples (Layder 1981); the notion of rules and resources as the basis of structure generates confusion and obscures important issues (Thompson 1984, 1989); there is no allowance for negotiation of rules, which still imply an external force acting on people (Bauman 1989); the enabling character of structure has led to the underplay of the role of structural constraints (Thompson 1984, 1989); the relation between action and structure is one of tension rather than duality; and, the concepts of time and space are inadequate (Gregory 1989). Furthermore, the theory does not come to terms with the fact that structural constraints derive from prior, relatively enduring, inequalities of power of groups to which individuals belong and this determines their relative bargaining or negotiating strengths (Layder 1985); it underrates the role of domination as a prior structure (Clegg 1979).

In *The Constitution of Society*, Giddens has argued that '[s]tructuration theory will not be of much value if it does not help to illuminate problems of empirical research' (1984: xxix). However, he has suggested that neither the logic nor the substance of Structuration Theory precludes the use of any particular research technique; qualitative and quantitative methods may be used where appropriate. 'The points of connection of structuration theory with empirical research are to do with working out the logical implications of studying a "subject matter" of which the researcher is already a part and with elucidating the substantive connotations of the core notions of action and structure' (1984: xxx).

It is clear from his various writings that Giddens has a strong commitment to the importance of empirical research and that he has regarded theory as playing an important role in research. In particular, he has argued that Structuration Theory provides concepts which are relevant to social research: it provides the social researcher with an ontological framework; it provides orientations in the four levels of research (the hermeneutic elucidation of frames of meaning; the investigation of context and form of practical consciousness; the identification of bounds of knowledgeability; and the specification of institutional orders); and, it offers three guidelines for social research (that all social research involves an anthropological moment, that the skills of social actors and the time–space constitution of social life must be recognized).

In spite of the extent to which Giddens' work has been reviewed, few authors have specifically addressed the issue of the relation between Structuration Theory and social research (see, for example, Thrift 1985, Cohen 1989; Gregson 1989). Perhaps this is not surprising considering that Giddens has devoted comparatively little attention to it himself. In addition, those who have reviewed his work are primarily interested in theoretical and philosophical issues and there appears to be very little research that uses Structuration Theory as a framework. Some authors, however, have considered its practical implications. Bryant (1991) has discussed the broader issue of its relevance to applied or policy-oriented sociology and others have considered the extent to which it can be considered a critical theory (see, for example, Cohen 1989; Gregson 1989; Kilminster 1991).

Gregson (1989) has argued that the issue of the relevance of structuration theory to empirical research is important on two grounds: first, if it is unable to illuminate and explain social life it will have failed to fulfil the main objective of social science; and, secondly, given Giddens' commitment to a critical social science, in order for it to offer a process of social transformation it must be able to relate to what happens 'out there'. She has taken issue with Giddens's insistence that Structuration Theory has something to offer the social researcher other than an ontological framework and has argued that there in nothing about the three guidelines that would enable them to be used actively in empirical research.

> Thus, whilst few would disagree that social research has an ethnographic moment, that people demonstrate a vast number of skills in the course of daily life and that temporal and spatial structures are critical, for the purposes of empirical research the key questions concern *which* 'actors', *which* skills and *which* temporal and spatial structures we choose to investigate; and *how* we investigate them, *where* and *when*. (Gregson 1989: 240–1)

She went on to argue that structuration theory should be regarded as second-order theory (or meta-theory) as its concerns are with conceptualizing the general constitutents of human society rather than with theorizing the unique. Therefore, it would be unrealistic to expect Structuration Theory to have any direct relevance to social research. However, Giddens did not accept this distinction between first-order and second-order theory, but he did acknowledge a distinction between 'theory' as a generic category, and 'theories' as explanatory generalizations. In short, Giddens has accepted that structuration theory is a 'theoretical perspective' but he considered 'theory' to be as important as 'theories' in social science (Giddens 1989: 295).

In his review of *The Constitution of Society*, Sica (1986) proposed that Giddens' value as a general theorist will depend on the extent to which his approach is useful. He acknowledged that as a great deal of effort is required to comprehend Giddens' vocabulary and ideas, the reward needs to be large. Certainly, at the time Sica was writing, little social research had been conducted using the approach.

In spite of his insistence on the relevance of Structuration Theory for social research, Giddens has argued that there is no obligation on the social researcher to use the concepts of his theory in preference to those of ordinary language. He went even further in proposing that it is not necessary to 'bother with cumbersome notions like "structuration" and the rest if first-rate social research can be done without them' (1984: 326). Thrift (1985) has expressed his disappointment in this 'take it or leave it' argument. Kilminster saw Giddens' argument as deriving from the implicit worldview in Structuration Theory in which social actors are accorded the dignity of being extraordinarily skilled, rather than merely conforming to internalized values and beliefs. It embodies a 'liberalistic timidity about the possibility of representing and theorizing "social wholes", lest this procedure erases individuals' (Kilminster 1991: 78).

In his response to the criticism that he has failed to show how Structuration Theory generates specific research projects, Giddens has continued to maintain his position. However, he has argued that while Structuration Theory relates to the conduct of social research in a number of ways, it is not a research programme. Its concepts are to be regarded as sensitizing devices to be used in a selective way in thinking about research questions or interpreting findings.

> Structuration theory is not intended as a method of research, or even as a methodological approach. The concepts I have developed do not allow one to say: 'henceforth, the only viable type of research in the social sciences is qualitative field study'. I have an eclectic approach to method, which again rests upon the premise that research enquiries are contextually oriented. For some purposes, detailed ethnographic work is appropriate, while for others archival research, or the sophisticated statistical analysis of secondary materials, might be more suitable. But I do think the framework of structuration theory provides concepts relevant to empirical research and also warns against the pitfalls of some types of research procedure or interpretations of research results. (Giddens 1989: 296)

As a result of the criticisms of the usefulness of Structuration Theory for social research, Giddens has proposed what a structurationist programme of research might look like. First, 'it would concentrate on the orderings of institutions across time and space, rather than taking as its object the study of "human societies".' Secondly, it would analyse the regularities in social practices, i.e. social institutions, and the way they change through time. Thirdly, it 'would be continuously sensitive to the reflexive intrusions of knowledge into the conditions of social reproduction.' And, finally, it 'would be oriented to the impact of its own research upon the social practices and forms of social organization it analyses' (Giddens 1989: 300).

Another area of criticism concerns the extent to which Structuration Theory can be regarded in any sense as critical theory. Giddens has argued that social research is closely tied to social critique, and that 'structuration theory is intrinsically incomplete if not linked to a conception of social science as critical theory' (1984: 287).[10] However, Giddens' claims about the critical nature of Structuration Theory have been disputed by a number of authors.

Gregson has proposed that Structuration Theory does not constitute a critical social theory; 'in its current form it has no direct connection with practice and, consequently, no notion of possible alternatives' (1989: 248). While Bernstein is very supportive of Giddens' project, he is extremely sceptical of the extent to which Structuration Theory in its present form can be regarded as a critical theory. What is needed is a specification of the ends or purposes to which scientific knowledge should be put and standards or criteria for making critical judgements (Bernstein 1989: 31). Simply relying on the second half of the double hermeneutic as a means of transforming the social world is, for Bernstein, not good enough. While he has been critical of the use of the technological application of social knowledge in the same way as knowledge is used in the natural sciences,

> Giddens fails to realize how much of what he says is compatible with the 'technological' attitude that he opposes. For he leaves open the question *who* is to use social knowledge and to what ends. I do not think that Giddens gets any closer to answering these questions when he emphasizes the practical consciousness and knowledgeability of social agents and the double hermeneutic of social science. (Bernstein 1989: 33)

Giddens has made brief reference to the relation between social research and policy-making (1987: 44–8). During the period following the Second World War, there was a belief that social research could contribute to bringing about a better social order, whatever that might mean. However, for the most part, this work adopted an instrumental attitude in which research was designed to assist policy-makers to understand the social world better and, hence, to be able to influence it in a reliable way. Research assisted in providing efficient means of pursuing some objective but did not play a significant role in shaping these objectives. While this research may have been effective within this limited conception of its role, the presumptions that research findings are neutral, and that the context in which they are being applied is static, contributed to the disillusionment with the outcomes of such research programmes. The solution, according to Giddens, is to adopt a dialogical view of the role of social research in policy-making.

> A dialogical model introduces the notion that the most effective forms of connection between social research and policy-making are forged through an extended process of communication between researchers, policy-makers and those affected by whatever issues are under consideration. Such a model tends to reverse the traditional view that specific policy objectives should determine the character of research carried out. Primacy instead tends to be

---

[10] Some comments on this have already been made in chapter 3.

given to the process of research over the formulation of policy objectives, which this influences as much as the other way around. In a rapidly changing world, continuing processes of social research help indicate where the most urgent practical questions cluster, at the same time as they offer frameworks for seeking to cope with them. (Giddens 1987: 47)

Giddens has spelt out the relevance of Structuration Theory for the dialogical model. First, 'social research cannot just be "applied" to an independently-given subject matter, but has to be linked to the potentiality of persuading actors to expand or modify the forms of knowledge or belief they draw upon in organizing their contexts of action' (Giddens 1987: 47). Without this acknowledgement of the capability of social actors to grasp knowledge produced by social research, and of their ability to see its implications for their activities, policies are likely to be ineffective. Secondly, the recognition of the 'anthropological moment' of social research, through the mediation of forms of life, and the possibility of positing novel conceptual frameworks, opens up 'possible worlds' which programmes of reform might bring about. Thirdly, it is not the creation of sets of generalizations so much as the implications of the double hermeneutic that facilitates the contribution of social research to policy-making (1987: 47–8).

On a more general level, Giddens has accepted that knowledge generated by the social sciences is not cumulative because it gets absorbed into society itself. However, he has claimed that the social sciences have had more influence on society than the natural sciences have had on nature.

[T]he achievements of the social sciences tend to become submerged from view by their very success. On the other hand, exactly because of this we can in all seriousness make the claim that the social sciences have influenced 'their' world – the universe of human activity – much more strongly than the natural sciences have influenced 'theirs'. The social sciences have been reflexively involved in a most basic way with those very transformations of modernity which give them their main subject-matter . . . The practical impact of social sciences is both profound and inescapable. Modern societies, together with the organizations that compose and straddle them, are like learning machines, imbibing information in order to regularize their mastery of themselves. (Giddens 1987: 21)

In a sympathetic review of the relevance of Structuration Theory to policy research, Bryant (1991) has suggested that it is not in empirical research that Giddens has made a contribution – for he has not done any; rather it is his particular dialogical model of social science, which flows from elements of Structuration Theory, that is of value. It is a superior view of the relation of social research and policy to that presented by the most helpful of American writers (particularly, Weiss 1979, 1983; Weiss and Bucuvalas 1980). However, he acknowledged that the critical dimension of the dialogical model is incomplete. While Structuration Theory suggests that human agents can always act otherwise than they do, a critical social theory requires the support of a normative theory. In its present form, there is the danger that the dialogical model will

> reinforce the old conceit that sociologists have only to publish on topics of social concern for their work to apply. The danger of monologue puffed up as dialogue can be averted, however, as long as they remember that they have to make their sociology apply. Exactly how they should go about this they have to decide for themselves case by case. (Bryant 1991: 199)

Feminism

It is possible to critique *feminist empiricism* on the same grounds as the critiques of Positivism and Critical Rationalism, and, alternatively, to critique *standpoint feminism* on at least some of the same grounds as Interpretivism. However, this discussion will be confined to 'internal' critiques.

The experiences of women as subjugated members of their society are cross-cut by race, class and culture (or ethnicity) thus making it difficult to justify *a* feminist epistemological standpoint. The distinctive features of women's experiences in Western societies are probably also found in the experiences of other subjugated groups, for example, among the original inhabitants of colonized counties and third world nations. While it is not possible to have *a* women's epistemology, it is possible to have a number of other emancipatory epistemologies (Harding 1987d).

Harding has suggested two possible solutions to this dilemma. One solution is to regard feminist science and epistemology as being valuable in its own right alongside these other possible sciences and epistemologies, but not superior to them. Instead of seeking a new totalizing feminist theory and epistemology, a pluralistic situation would need to be accepted. Another solution would be to identify the goals which are shared by each of the standpoint epistemologies, be they feminist, third world, gay or working class.

The feminist postmodernists have raised serious questions about both of these attempts to establish a feminist science. They are sceptical about the possibility of establishing any kind of science which can avoid replicating undesirable forms of human existence. By drawing on such intellectual movements as semiotics, deconstructionism, psychoanalysis and structuralism, feminist postmodernists have challenged the assumptions common to both feminist epistemological strategies, namely, 'that through reason, observation, and progressive politics, the more authentic "self" produced by feminist struggles can tell "one true story" about "the world" ' (Harding 1987c: 188). It is argued that 'reality' may appear to be governed by one set of rules, or be made up of particular sets of social relations, only if it is dominated by one individual or group. Therefore, it is necessary to accept that there will always be many constructions of reality, which may be in conflict, and there may not be just one female reality.

> From this perspective, there can never be *a* feminist science, sociology, anthropology, or epistemology, but only many stories that different women tell about the different knowledge they have ... [F]eminism's opposition to domination stories locates feminism in an antagonistic position toward any attempts to do science – androcentric or not. (Harding 1987c: 188)

According to Harding, there are dangers in the feminist postmodern view if it supports an inappropriate relativist position. If reality is regarded as being viewed differently by people in different locations in the social structure, and if these views are regarded as being equally legitimate, then the political struggle of women is undermined. She has adopted the Marxist position that the views of the dominant group (i.e. men) are oppressive and false. 'For subjugated groups, a relativist stance expresses a false consciousness. It accepts the dominant group's insistence that their right to hold distorted views (and, of course, to make policy for all of us on the basis of those views) is intellectually legitimate' (Harding 1987d: 295).

Rather than be discouraged by these obstacles to the establishment of a unified feminist science, Harding has celebrated the opportunities which these dilemmas offer. In discussing both feminist theory and science, she has suggested that feminist analytical categories *should* be unstable. In an unstable and incoherent world, the establishment of consistent and coherent theories would be a hindrance to understanding and practice.

> In the field in which I have been working – feminist challenges to science and epistemology – this situation makes the present moment an exciting one in which to live and think, but a difficult one in which to conceptualize a definitive overview. That is, the arguments between those of us who are criticizing science and epistemology are unresolvable within frameworks in which we have been posing them. We need to begin seeing these disputes not as a process of naming issues to be resolved but instead as opportunities to come up with better problems than those with which we started. The destabilization of thought often has advanced understanding more effectively than restabilizations, and the feminist criticisms of science point to a particularly fruitful arena in which the categories of Western thought need destabilization. Though these criticisms began by raising what appeared to be politically contentious but theoretically innocuous questions about discrimination against women in the social structure of science, misuses of technology, and androcentric bias in the social sciences and biology, they have quickly escalated into ones that question the most fundamental assumptions of modern, Western thought. They therefore implicitly challenge the theoretical constructs within which the original questions were formulated and might be answered. (Harding 1987d: 287)

Review

In spite of the devastating criticisms Positivism has received from philosophers for over fifty years and, more recently, from social scientists, it and

Critical Rationalism, or some form of hypothesis testing, continue to hold sway, particularly in disciplines such as psychology and economics, and in mainstream American sociology. The various alternatives to Positivism differ, particularly, on the issue of whether they accept a Positivist view of the natural sciences. Critical Rationalism and Realism both reject Positivism and propose an alternative philosophy of the natural sciences. Additionally, in both cases, a naturalistic position is adopted, i.e. that this 'new' view of the natural sciences is also appropriate for the social sciences. However, some differences between the natural and social sciences are usually recognized. In the case of Critical Rationalism, the logic is the same but the methods may be different, while for Realism, there is an assumption that both natural and social realities have an independent existence, and the logic for investigating them (the building of hypothetical models) is the same, but the constitution of these realities is regarded as being different. Interpretivism, on the other hand, rejects Positivism in the social sciences but is largely uncritical of it or Critical Rationalism as being appropriate for the natural sciences. Its concern is to focus on the fundamental differences in natural and social realities and in the methods that are appropriate for investigating them.

These differences between Positivism and Interpretivism have led to them being presented as mutually exclusive positions. In the main, this was no doubt due to the desire of Interpretivists, especially in the 1960s and 1970s, to assert the legitimacy of their position in the face of the overwhelming dominance of Positivistic social science. This was particularly the case for those Interpretivists who were interested only in description, or in understanding rather than explanation. However, there are branches of Interpretivism which *are* concerned with explanation, some of which have adopted similar views to the Positivists, or Critical Rationalists, on the nature of theories. For example, Schütz, following Weber (1964), has adopted a middle ground (although it should be noted that his views precede much of what has been covered in this chapter). He did not accept the stark contrast between the two positions which he described in the quotation at the beginning of chapter 2.

[M]ost of these highly generalised statements are untenable under closer examination, and this for several reasons. Some proponents of the characterized arguments had a rather erroneous concept of the methods of the natural sciences. Others were inclined to identify the methodological situation in one particular social science with the method of social science in general. Because history has to deal with unique and non-recurrent events, it was contended that all social sciences are restricted to singular assertory propositions. Because experiments are hardly possible in cultural anthropology, the fact was ignored that social psychologists can successfully use laboratory experiments at least to a certain extent. Finally, and this is the most important point, these arguments disregard the fact that a set of rules for scientific procedure is equally valid for all empirical sciences whether they deal with objects of nature or with human affairs. Here and there, the principles of controlled inference and verification by fellow scientists and the theoretical ideals of unity, simplicity, universality and precision prevail. (Schütz 1963a: 232)

Schütz went on to argue that this confusion was due to the fact that the modern social sciences developed during the period when the natural sciences had established a monopolistic imperialism on what was regarded as the only scientific method. In the face of a realization that the methods of the natural sciences were inadequate, at least without modification, social scientists lacked the same philosophical basis for the methods which they were trying to develop.

It is in his views on the foundations of the scientific method that Schütz agreed with the Positivists, particularly Nagel and Hempel. He argued that 'all empirical knowledge involves discovery through processes of controlled inference, and that it [knowledge] must be stateable in propositional form and capable of being verified by anyone who is prepared to make the effort to do so through observation.' However, this observation need not be sensory in the way in which Positivists have argued. He agreed that ' "theory" means in all empirical sciences the explicit formulation of determinate relations between a set of variables in terms of which a fairly extensive class of empirically ascertainable regularities can be explained' (Schütz, 1963a: 235). Furthermore, he claimed that the fact that these regularities in the social sciences are restricted in the extent to which they can be generalized, and that they permit prediction to only a limited extent, does not constitute a basic difference between the natural and social sciences. While these views of Schütz have much in common with those of Popper, he departed from the Positivists on the issues of ontology and epistemology.

It is clear that none of these approaches has escaped criticism, although it must be recognized that the majority of the criticism comes from exponents of other approaches. It has been argued that there are incommensurable differences between these approaches (see, for example, Feyerabend 1978); there is no neutral ground from which it is possible to make 'objective' evaluations. When a social researcher makes choices about which approach to adopt, a judgment will have to be made about the status of these criticisms.

The next chapter explores the research strategies which are associated with the major approaches to social enquiry.

Further Reading

Key References

Bernstein, R.J. 1976. *Restructuring Social and Political Theory.*
Bhaskar, R. 1979. *The Possibility of Naturalism.*
Bryant, C.G.A. and Jary, D.Y. 1991. *Gidden's Theory of Structuration.*

Chalmers, A.F. 1982. *What is this Thing Called Science?*
Fay, B. 1975. *Social Theory and Political Practice.*
Giddens, A. 1977. 'Positivism and its Critics'.
—— 1984. *The Constitution of Society.*
Habermas, J. 1970. 'Knowledge and Interest'.
—— 1972. *Knowledge and Human Interests.*
Harding, S. 1987. 'Introduction: Is There a Feminist Method?'.
Keat, R. and Urry, J. 1975. *Social Theory as Science.*
—— 1982. *Social Theory as Science,* 2nd edn.
Kuhn, T.S. 1970a. *The Structure of Scientific Revolutions.*
—— 1970b. 'Logic of Discovery or Psychology of Research'.
Lakatos, I. 1970. 'Falsification and the Methodology of Scientific Research Programs'.
Popper, K.R. 1961. *The Poverty of Historicism.*
—— 1970. 'Normal Science and its Dangers'.
Riggs, P.L. 1992. *Whys and Ways of Science.*
Stockman, N. 1983. *Antipositivist Theories of the Sciences.*

General References

Adorno, T.W. et al. 1976. *The Positivist Dispute in German Sociology.*
Bryant, C.G.A. 1985. *Positivism in Social Theory and Research.*
Fay, B. 1987. *Critical Social Science.*
Giddens, A. 1974. *Positivism and Sociology.*
—— 1976. *New Rules of Sociological Method.*
—— 1979. *Central Problems in Social Theory.*
—— 1987. *Social Theory and Modern Sociology.*
—— 1989. *'A Reply to my Critics'.*
—— 1991. 'Structuration Theory: Past, Present and Future'.
Halfpenny, P. 1982. *Positivism and Sociology: Explaining Social Life.*
Harré, R. and Secord, P.F. 1972. *The Explanation of Social Behaviour.*
Held, D. 1980. *Introduction to Critical Theory.*
Hindess, B. 1977. *Philosophy and Methodology in the Social Sciences.*
Lakatos, I. and Musgrave, A. (eds). 1970. *Criticism and the Growth of Knowledge.*
McCarthy, T. 1973. 'A Theory of Communicative competence'.
—— 1984. *The Critical Theory of Jürgen Habermas,* 2nd edn.
Outhwaite, W. 1983a. 'Towards a Realist Perspective'.
—— 1983b. *Concept Formation in Social Science.*
—— 1987. *New Philosophies of Social Science.*
Popper, K.R. 1972. *Conjectures and Refutations.*
—— 1976. 'The Logic of the Social Sciences'.
—— 1979. *Objective Knowledge: An Evolutionary Approach.*
Thomas, D. 1979. *Naturalism and Social Science.*
Thompson, J.B. 1981a. *Critical Hermeneutics.*
—— 1981b. *Paul Ricoeur: Hermeneutics and the Human Sciences.*
Tudor, A. 1982. *Beyond Empiricism: Philosophy of Science in Sociology.*

Part II
Research Strategies

5

Inductive and Deductive Strategies

[S]cientists and philosophers use a logic – they have a cognitive style which is more or less logical – and some of them also formulate it explicitly. I call the former the *logic-in-use*, and the latter the *reconstructed logic* . . . [T]here are many logics-in-use [and] there are many reconstructed logics.

A. Kaplan, *The Conduct of Inquiry*

Introduction

Scientific research is about answering questions by means of controlled enquiry. These questions may be divided into three kinds, 'what', 'why' and 'how' questions. 'What' questions are directed towards discovering and describing the features of some phenomenon. What does it looks like? What does it consist of? What does it do? 'Why' questions are directed towards understanding and explanation. Why did it come to be as it is? Why does it behave as it does? Why does it change, or remain stable? Why does it have particular consequences? 'How' questions are about intervention. How could it be made different? How could it be made to change in a particular direction? How could it be made to stop changing, or to slow down or speed up its rate of change?

The crucial issue for the researcher is how to discover, describe, explain and intervene in the phenomenon under investigation. In other words, how can 'what', 'why' and 'how' questions be answered. And this leads to another question – where does the research process begin? Does it start with observations or gathering data which are then used to develop explanations, or does it begin with a theory, a hypothesis or a model which is then tested by making observations or gathering data? The major approaches to social enquiry which were outlined and discussed in the previous chapters each imply a particular position on this issue.

In the next two chapters the four research strategies associated with these approaches will be explored in more detail. These strategies are labelled *Inductive*, *Deductive*, *Retroductive* and *Abductive*. They are used to answer 'what', 'why' and 'how' questions, but particularly 'why' questions, and they differ in terms of their views on where the researcher begins and on the 'logic' adopted. As a background to the *Inductive* and

Deductive strategies, it is necessary to examine the two forms of logical reasoning on which they are based.

Inductive and Deductive Reasoning

The Inductive and Deductive strategies are based on alternative cognitive styles of reasoning – induction and deduction. Both styles consist of two main kinds of statements: *singular statements*, which refer to a particular event or state of affairs at a particular time and place; and, *general statements*, which refer to all events of a particular kind at all places and times.

This long-term unemployed factory worker from Melbourne has lost his self-respect

is an example of a singular statement which might result from undertaking an investigation of a specific problem in a particular context.

Long-term unemployed people lose their self-respect

is a general statement related to the same phenomenon.

An *inductive argument* begins with singular or particular statements and concludes with a general or universal statement(s). The premises of the argument are statements about specific instances of some event or state of affairs, and the conclusion is a generalization drawn from these premises. The premises might consist of statements about many unemployed factory workers who have lost their self-respect. If all these statements were consistent, and no instances were observed of unemployed workers who have not lost their self-respect to some degree, then it might be concluded that *long-term unemployed people lose their self-respect*. This general statement makes no restrictions about the type of former employment, where people live, or when they were unemployed. However, if some of the singular statements about unemployed people did not refer to loss of self-respect, the argument might conclude with another form of general statement.

Long-term unemployed people are at risk of losing their self-respect.

This statement is general but not universal because it leaves open the possibility that some long-term unemployed people, under certain conditions, may not lose their self-respect. In either case, in an inductive argument, the conclusion makes claims that exceed what is contained in the premises; it promises to extend knowledge by going beyond actual experience.

A deductive argument is the reverse of this. The argument moves from premises, at least one of which is a general or universal statement, to a conclusion that is a singular statement. The conclusion contains less than the premises. Using the same example, the deductive form of argument might set out to explain why a particular individual, or category of individuals, suffers from loss of self-respect. Put simply, the argument might read as follows.

1 *Long-term unemployed people lose their self-respect.*
2 *Mary Smith has been unemployed for two years.*
3 *Therefore, Mary Smith suffers from loss of self-respect.*

The premises (statements 1 and 2) include a general statement and a singular statement, and the conclusion (statement 3) is a singular statement. Nothing has been added to the premises to get to the conclusion; the truth of the premises guarantees the truth of the conclusion.

These two forms of argument have been used as strategies for constructing scientific theories.

The Inductive Research Strategy

Induction in the Natural Sciences

The Inductive strategy corresponds to a popular conception of the activities of scientists, i.e. of persons who make careful observations, conduct experiments, rigorously analyse the data obtained, and hence produce new discoveries or new theories. Personal opinions are excluded from this process in order to arrive at what is believed to be objective knowledge.

The earliest form of induction used to develop knowledge about the world has been attributed to Aristotle and his disciples. Known as 'enumerative induction', it will be referred to here as *naive induction.* Knowledge is produced about a restricted class of things or events from a limited number of observations. However, a more challenging use of induction is to produce general conclusions about open or unrestricted classes of things and events (Quinton 1980).

This is the Positivistic view of science, advocated by Bacon and Mill; it is sometimes referred to as *empiricism* because of the stress on observation being the foundation of scientific knowledge. These philosophers were arguing against relying on Greek philosophy and the Bible as sources of knowledge about the world. If you want to understand nature, then you must consult nature and not the writings of Aristotle. Science was seen to be built on facts gained by observation, not on some preconceived notions about how the world works.

A problem for this view of science is how to make contact with that reality. The solution is to eliminate the bias that might arise from personal beliefs and opinions, and let nature write its experiential message on the passively receptive mind.

Thus if you want to be a good scientist it follows from crude empiricism that you must begin by ridding yourself of all preconceptions about what you are going to study. Indeed, this is one of the main things a good scientific education is thought to achieve. You will then be in a position to collect particular observations which you hope will reflect the regularities of nature or society relevant to the problem you wish to solve. When you have collected what you consider to be enough evidence, you may develop an explanation of the problem by generalizing from it. If your explanation is firmly grounded in such evidence, it can be assumed to be certain. The less firmly grounded, the less probable the explanation. (Doyal and Harris 1986: 2)

It is important to note here that 'observation' or 'experience' is not restricted to what can be perceived directly by the human senses. It includes the use of machines and other instruments which extend the senses, the readings from which can be inspected and interpreted. The discussion in chapter 4, and what will follow later in this chapter, makes it clear that both direct and indirect observation are theory-dependent, through the concepts and theories which explicitly or implicitly make it possible for a scientist to observe at all, and through the theories that are used to construct the instruments. However, in the meantime, it is necessary to examine the origins and characteristics of Induction.

Bacon, the first major philosopher of science of the modern period, set out in his *Novum Organum* (1620) an elaborate account of the method of induction[1] which is still regarded by many as *the* scientific method.[2] He held firmly to the view that this method must be based on presuppositionless observation, and he identified four types of 'idols' which can distort the mind and inhibit the acquisition of true knowledge. The 'idols of the tribe' are tendencies to see things from our own point of view rather than letting nature reveal itself; we are inclined to impose our own order on nature rather than learning to obey nature. The 'idols of the cave' refer to the differences in personality and experience which lead individuals to approach 'the facts' in different ways and not see them as they really are. Then there are the 'idols of the market' which are the result of imposing on nature concepts which do not stand for anything, which do not relate to objects in the real world. And, finally, there are the 'idols of the theatre' in which philosophical systems influence our minds and hence predetermine what we see in nature. Bacon argued that Aristotle's work was influenced by these idols, and he set out to deal with them. He wished to develop a method based on the 'cleansing of the mind of all its presuppositions and prejudices, and reading the book of nature with fresh eyes' (O'Hear 1989: 16).

Rather than simply accumulating knowledge by generalizing from observations, Bacon argued that it is necessary to focus on negative in-

---

[1] There is some dispute amongst philosophers as to whether Bacon's method is strictly inductive. See, for example, Harré (1972: 38) and O'Hear (1989: 12).

[2] The following discussion of Bacon's ideas is drawn mainly from Quinton (1980) and O'Hear (1989).

stances. His became an *eliminative* method of induction. The first stage is to prepare 'a complete and accurate natural and experimental history' of all the things relevant to the phenomenon being investigated. This material is then arranged in tables of three kinds: the table of presence; the table of absence; and the table of degrees. In the table of presence, cases in which a characteristic associated with the phenomenon is present are listed and described and a general account of these characteristics is produced. In the table of absence, cases are listed which have a similar characteristic but in which the phenomenon is absent. In the table of degrees, cases are included which have more or less of this characteristic associated with more or less of other characteristics.

Bacon illustrated his method with reference to the nature of heat. He collected and described known instances of heat of various kinds, 'ranging from the rays of the sun, through bodies rubbed violently, boiling liquid, compost and horse dung, to the effects on us of fortified spirits of wine and aromatic herbs' (O'Hear 1989: 14). He then collected other cases that were similar in some way to these first cases but which lacked heat, such as the rays of the moon and non-boiling liquid. He then prepared a list of cases in which different levels of heat are associated with different levels of these characteristics. The aim was to find the characteristics that are present in all the positive cases, which are absent in all the negative cases, and which vary in appropriate degrees.

By stressing negative instances rather than just positive instances, Bacon argued that this method had a better chance of producing true theories than was possible by other methods. He claimed that it controls the tendency to jump to conclusions from a few cases; it forces the scientist to examine a wide range of different cases; and it involves a search for possible causes, one of which is associated with every natural phenomenon we can observe. However, in spite of the systematic nature of his method, it could not escape the problem of the theory-dependence of observations discussed in chapter 4. For example, in collecting his cases of various kinds of heat, he had to rely on an everyday use of the concept. In doing so, he made a judgement about which cases are similar and which ones different. But this judgement may not correspond to the actual physical constitution of the phenomena. It is possible to group cases together according to some common-sense criterion for which there is no physical equivalent (O'Hear 1989: 19). If observation without presuppositions is not possible, then Bacon's method will not work.

For more than two centuries Bacon's view of science was dominant. It was elaborated by Mill in *A System of Logic*, originally published in 1843. Mill believed that the purpose of science was to discover causes and hence produce general laws. He set out a number of methods, or Canons of Induction, the most important of which are the Canon of Agreement and the Canon of Difference.

1   The Canon of Agreement: 'If two or more instances of the phenomenon under investigation have only one circumstance in common,

the circumstance in which alone all the instances agree, is the cause (or effect) of the given phenomenon.'

2 The Canon of Difference: 'If an instance in which the phenomenon under investigation occurs, and an instance in which it does not occur, have every circumstance in common save one, that one occurring only in the former; the circumstance in which alone the two instances differ, is the effect, or the cause, or an indispensable part of the cause, of the phenomenon.' (Mill 1879: Bk iii, ch. 8)

To put this in simpler language, in the method of agreement, two instances of a phenomenon need to be different in all but one characteristic, while in the method of difference, two situations are required to be similar in all characteristics but one, the phenomenon being present with this characteristic. In the both cases, the different characteristic can be considered as either the cause or the effect of the phenomenon.

While Mill advocated the use of the methods of the natural sciences in the social sciences, he held the view that experimentation associated with his Canons was not possible in the social sciences. This was based on an assumption that the social sciences are concerned with entire societies, and that it is not possible to find two societies that conform to the requirements of his Canons; no two societies are ever completely similar or completely dissimilar. However, Nagel has suggested that Mill's methods underestimate or ignore the fact that no two situations are ever completely alike or completely unalike in all but one respect. They require a set of assumptions about what features of a situation are to be considered as relevant. Further, it is impossible in any experimental situation to control all but one factor or characteristic (Nagel 1961: 454–5).

Therefore, as with Bacon's method, Mill's Canons also require the scientist to have some ideas about possible causes for the phenomenon in order to know to which 'circumstance' to pay attention. As Harré has suggested, if we wished to explain why plants grow more vigorously in warm weather than in cold, the choice between heat and light as possible causes could not be made using Mill's Canons. It would be possible to set up a controlled experiment to test the independent effects of heat and light, and we might come to the conclusion that light seems to be the predominant cause, but that some heat is also necessary. However, would this process lead us to photosynthesis as the mechanism of growth?

> Our reasons for thinking that one kind of phenomenon is the cause of an-other kind are not just a matter of seeing if the two kinds of phenomena appear together or in a sequence, and the second never without the first, but are based much more upon our knowledge or speculations about the mechanisms by which the two are related, and by which the first kind of phenomenon produces the second. (Harré 1972: 41)

Mill's Canons may be useful guides for the preliminary stages of an investigation but, according to Harré, they are inadequate as a method for discovering or testing theories.

In spite of these difficulties, which were recognized in the early forms of the Inductive Strategy, it has been a very seductive view of science. In its more recent forms, the Inductive Strategy has been described as consisting of three principles.

> *The Principle of Accumulation*: that scientific knowledge is a conjunction of well-attested facts, and that such knowledge grows by the addition of further well-attested facts, so that the addition of a new fact to the conjunction leaves all previous facts unaltered ...
>
> *The Principle of Induction*: that there is a form of inference of laws from the accumulated simple facts, so that from true statements describing observations and the results of experiments, true laws may be inferred ...
>
> *The Principle of Instance Confirmation*: that our belief in the degree of plausibility of (or our degree of belief in) a law is proportioned to the number of instances that have been observed of the phenomenon described in the law. (Harré 1972: 42)

The Inductive strategy has been characterized as consisting of four main stages.

1 All facts are observed and recorded without selection or guesses as to their relative importance.
2 These facts are analyzed, compared and classified, without using hypotheses.
3 From this analysis, generalizations are inductively drawn as to the relations between them.
4 These generalizations are subjected to further testing (Wolfe 1924: 450; Hempel 1966: 11).

Medewar (1969a: 40) expressed the Inductive strategy this way.

> Let us first assemble the data; let us by observation and by making experiments compile the true record of the state of Nature, taking care that our vision is not corrupted by preconceived ideas; then inductive reasoning can go to work and reveal laws and principles and necessary connections.

Apart from the necessary observational equipment and skills, and the ability to set aside preconceptions, all that the scientist needs is to be able to think logically. The generalizations will follow logically from the data. If these generalizations are challenged, the defence of the inductive scientist will be that they are based on the facts and only objective and logical procedures have been used.

The Inductive strategy embodies the realist ontology which assumes that there is a reality 'out there' with regularities that can be described and explained, and it adopts the epistemological principle that the task of observing this reality is essentially unproblematic as long as the researcher adopts objective procedures. It claims that there is a correspondence between sensory experiences and the objects of those experiences; that reality impinges directly on the senses; that what we 'see' is what exists. As shall be seen, the other research strategies have different ontological and epistemological assumptions.

Induction in the Social Sciences: an Example

The Inductive strategy was advocated in sociology by Emile Durkheim (1858–1917). He was not the first sociologist to argue for a science of society, having continued a tradition already established by Comte in France and Spencer in England. However, he largely rejected their ideas on what a science of society should look like. It is his conception of the nature of this new science that sets him apart from these earlier contributors and it is this conception that determined the dominant style of empirical research as sociology developed. His method is still held up as a model to students of social science.

Durkheim differed from the earlier Positivistic sociologists in that he focused his attention on very limited problems rather than searching for grand theories of society. He set out his approach in *The Rules of Sociological Method* (1964) and he illustrated it in his research on suicide (Durkheim 1952). He wished to move away from the modes of explanation of social life that were dominant in his day, based on the analysis and combination of *ideas*, to a process of observing, describing and comparing *things*. In other words, he wanted sociologists to base their explanations on some kind of empirical evidence rather than just philosophical or metaphysical theories. More particularly, he wished to avoid the form of explanation in which an argument is supported by examples, even if based on observation, in favour of the form of explanation in which generalizations (or theories) are *produced* from observations. In short, he argued for the method of induction.

Durkheim's argument is based on the view that every discipline has its own subject matter which, for sociology, he called 'social facts'. Social facts are ways of acting, thinking and feeling, external to the individual. They exist in their own right and have the ability to exercise control over people. Durkheim was particularly concerned with laws and codes of morality, the more obvious forms of social constraint, but he was also interested in crowd behaviour which, he argued, is controlled by rather more transitory social facts. He argued that explanations of social phenomena must be in terms of independently existing forces that act on individuals from without and that these forces, while perhaps lacking the more tangible form of forces that act in nature, nevertheless have the same objective thing-like quality. If nothing else, their presence can be established by the effects that they produce, somewhat analogous, for example, to gravity. 'I consider extremely useful this idea that social life should be explained, not by notions of those who participate in it, but by more profound causes which are unperceived by consciousness, and I think also that these causes are to be sought mainly in the manner according to which the associated individuals are grouped' (Durkheim, cited in Winch 1958: 23).

In order to observe these social facts, Durkheim set out three rules.

1 'All preconceptions must be eradicated' (Durkheim 1964: 31).
2 'The subject matter of every sociological study should comprise a group of phenomena defined in advance by certain common external characteristics, and all phenomena so defined should be included within this group' (1964: 35).
3 'When, then, the sociologist undertakes the investigation of some order of social facts, he [sic] must endeavour to consider them from an aspect that is independent of their individual manifestations' (1964: 45).

According to Durkheim, as social phenomena have an independent existence, they can and should be treated as if they are things, and observed in a manner similar to natural phenomena. However, there is the danger that the observer may allow common-sense ideas or preconceptions to distort the process of observation. If these preconceptions are set aside, and the phenomenon under investigation is defined in advance, it will be possible to recognize the relevant facts that must be accumulated in order to produce a scientific explanation. The aim is to produce objective data and thus true generalizations about an independent reality.

According to Durkheim, the object of sociology is to construct theories about human conduct inductively on the basis of prior observations about that conduct: these observations, which are made about externally 'visible' characteristics of conduct, are necessarily 'pre-theoretical', since it is out of them that theories are born. Such observations, it is held, have no particular connection with the ideas actors have about their own actions and those of others; it is incumbent upon the observer to make every possible effort to separate himself [sic] from common-sense notions held by actors themselves, because these frequently have no basis in fact. In Durkheim's presentation of this kind of standpoint, the social scientist is instructed to formulate his concepts for himself, at the outset of his research, and to break away from those current in everyday life. The concepts of everyday activity, Durkheim says, 'merely express the confused impression of the mob'; 'if we follow common use', he continues, 'we risk distinguishing what should be combined, or combining what should be distinguished, thus mistaking the real affinities of things, and accordingly misapprehending their nature'. The investigations which the social scientist makes have to deal with 'comparable facts' whose 'natural affinities' cannot be distinguished by the 'superficial examination that gives rise to ordinary terminology'. The assumption that there are discriminable 'natural affinities' of objects (physical and social), which pre-exist and determine what the observer does in describing and classifying those objects, appears throughout Durkheim's writings. (Giddens 1976a: 132)

Therefore, according to Durkheim, in order to study society 'as it really is' the sociologist must first set aside his or her own assumptions and prejudices and then make observations in terms of the external (presumably obvious) characteristics of the phenomenon which are stated in its definition. By adhering to such a definition the sociologist will not only be 'firmly grounded in reality', but will also be observing phenomena of the same kind.

Problems of Induction

In spite of convincing critiques dating back to the 1930s, the Inductive method persisted in some scientific and philosophical circles until the 1960s. However, it is now rejected by most natural and social scientists and, as we have seen, is regarded by philosophers of science as flawed.

The first difficulty which Inductivism raises is how the principle of induction can be justified. An Inductivist might appeal to logic. But can inductive inferences be logically justified? Some earlier philosophers argued that as the principle of induction is widely accepted in both science and everyday life, its truth is based on experience. Popper has responded by arguing that to claim that the principle of induction is a universal statement derived from experience is to use the principle in order to justify it; it involves an infinite regress (1959a: 29). It therefore follows that there is no purely logical or mechanical induction process for establishing the validity of universal statements from a set of singular statements (Hempel 1966: 15).

This deficiency alone is enough to demolish the claims of the Inductive strategy. However, there are a number of other important criticisms that need to be examined. In an inductive argument, if the premises are true, it does not follow that the conclusion will be true. It may be the case that all observed cases of long-term unemployment exhibit loss of self-esteem, but a further observation may reveal a case that is different. Hence on the basis of the original observations, the conclusion that *long-term unemployed people lose their self-respect,* cannot be regarded as true. The response of an Inductivist might be that while we cannot be one hundred per cent sure of the conclusion to an inductive argument, it might be regarded as probably true. The greater the number of observations, and the greater the variety of conditions under which the observations are made, the greater the probability that the conclusion will be true. However, a major difficulty with this modification is that it is not possible to establish just how probable a conclusion might be. It is not possible to be certain about the proportion of observation statements that are not consistent with the universal statement because all observations cannot be made.

Another deficiency concerns the number of observations that need to be made before a generalization is possible. In order to produce a valid logical argument, it is necessary to make all the necessary observations, in the present, in the past, and in the future. Even if all past occurrences are ignored, all future observations would have to wait to the end of the world (assuming that there will be an end). And even if the period of observation is restricted to some contemporary time period, there is still the problem of when to stop observing.

> Though some earlier positivists believed that it is possible, by means of observation, to conclusively verify scientific theories, there is an important feature of scientific laws which, as all modern positivists have emphasised, rules this out. No finite amount of observational evidence (and this is all we ever have) can finally establish the truth of a law which is held to apply to all times and places, and whose instances are therefore potentially infinite in number. (Keat and Urry 1975: 15)

An Inductivist might argue that it is simply necessary to make all 'relevant' observations. But relevant to what? All research is directed towards answering questions or solving some problem. The example of long-term unemployment and loss of self-esteem is incomplete because the research questions were not specified. If one of the questions is, *What factors lead to loss of self-esteem?*, long-term unemployment is only one possible area on which to focus attention; other factors can contribute to loss of self-esteem. But how do we know where to look for them, and why did we think unemployment might be relevant? If everything has to be observed in order to discover patterns of association – such as unemployment and loss of self-esteem – the task gets even more difficult. Whether we are aware of it or not, we make choices in what we observe.

The Inductive strategy implies that all that is required in research is numerous observations of the phenomenon under investigation. If we study enough cases of loss of self-esteem, we will discover those factors with which it is associated, and hence provide an explanation of it, e.g. that it is a consequence of long-term unemployment. However, at best, what this strategy produces is descriptions of patterns of association. But no matter how confident we are about an association – such as between long-term unemployment and loss of self-esteem – we cannot conclude that loss of self-esteem is a *consequence* of long-term unemployment. It could be that it is produced by something else, and that this has led to unsatisfactory performance at work, which has led to unemployment. Therefore, an explanation of loss of self esteem requires more than a description of it. Even a well-established association still requires an explanation. There is always a need to go beyond the mere reporting of events in order to explain them. The critical question is where to look for the explanation? The Inductive strategy provides no answer. In fact, it deliberately prohibits the researcher from even pursuing any hunches – only objective observation is permissible. 'The facts must speak for themselves.'

As has already been mentioned in this and the previous chapters, there is another more serious objection to the Inductive strategy which has to do with the activity of observing. The Inductivist operates with two important assumptions about observation: that all science starts with observation; and that observation provides a secure basis from which knowledge can be derived (Chalmers 1982: 22). However, Popper has argued that all observation is interpretation. In fact, 'in the social sciences it is even more obvious than in the natural sciences that we cannot see and observe our objects before we have thought about them. For most of the objects of the social sciences, if not all of them, are abstract objects; they are *theoretical* constructions' (Popper 1961: 135).

Two of the early critics of the Inductive strategy, Popper and Hempel, summarized their views as follows.

> I do not believe that we ever make inductive generalizations in the sense that we start with observations and try to derive our theories from them. I believe that the prejudice that we proceed in this way is a kind of optical illusion, and that at no stage of scientific development do we begin without something in the nature of a theory, such as a hypothesis, or a prejudice, or a problem – often a technological one – which in some way *guides* our observations, and helps us to select from the innumerable objects of observation those which may be of interest. (Popper 1961: 134)

> There are, then, no generally applicable 'rules of induction', by which hypotheses or theories can be mechanically derived or inferred from empirical data. The transition from data to theory requires creative imagination. Scientific hypotheses and theories are not *derived* from observed facts, but *invented* in order to account for them. They constitute guesses at the connections that might obtain between the phenomena under study, at uniformities and patterns that might underlie their occurrence ... [T]he ways in which fruitful scientific guesses are arrived at are very different from any process of systematic inference. (Hempel 1966: 15)

The application of the Inductive strategy has been illustrated in a somewhat exaggerated form in the context of medical practice by the eminent biologist and Nobel lauriate, Peter Medewar.

> A patient comes to his physician feeling wretched, and the physician sets out to discover what is wrong. In the inductive view the physician empties his mind of all prejudices and preconceptions and *observes* his patient intently. He records the patient's colour, measures his pulse rate, tests his reflexes and inspects his tongue (an organ that seldom stands up to public scrutiny). He then proceeds to other, more sophisticated actions: the patient's urine will be tested; blood counts and blood cultures will be made; biopsies of liver and marrow are sent to the pathology department; tubing is inserted into all apertures and electrodes applied to all exposed surfaces. The factual evidence thus assembled can now be classified and 'processed' according to the canons of induction. A diagnosis (e.g. 'It was something he ate') will thereupon be arrived at by reasoning which, being logical, could in principle be entrusted to a computer, and the diagnosis will be the right one unless the raw factual information was either erroneous or incomplete. (Medewar 1969a: 42–3).

Medewar then illustrated an alternative strategy.

The second clinician always observes his patient with a purpose, with an idea in mind. From the moment the patient enters he sets himself questions, prompted by foreknowledge or by sensory cues; and these questions direct his thought, guiding him towards new observations which will tell him whether the provisional views he is constantly forming are acceptable or unsound. Is he ill at all? Was it indeed something he ate? An upper respiratory virus is going around: perhaps this is relevant to the case? Has he at last done his liver an irreparable disservice? Here there is a rapid reciprocation between an imaginative and a critical process, between imaginative conjecture and critical evaluation. As it proceeds, a hypothesis will take shape which affords a reasonable basis for treatment or for further examination, though the clinician will not often take it to be conclusive. (Medewar 1969a: 44)

Popper and Hempel have argued for this Deductive strategy which will be examined shortly.

It is a commonly held belief that one of the strengths of *the* scientific method is that it is objective; that it eliminates or at least controls the biases of the scientist. Just what is meant by 'objective' and 'biased' is a complex issue on which some discussion has already occurred in previous chapters, and which will be discussed further in chapter 7. However, for the moment, there is the troublesome implication that if researchers are influenced by their past experiences, knowledge and expectations, and they inevitably work from within some language, and that all observations entail theoretical assumptions, how is objectivity possible? Different researchers, from different cultural backgrounds and biographical trajectories, working with different theoretical assumptions, will, at best, have different views of reality. If the critics of the Inductive strategy are correct, we are left with the question of whether objectivity is possible at all. And if objectivity is not possible, then the discovery of truth is also impossible.

The Deductive Research Strategy

Deduction in the Natural Sciences: Naive and Sophisticated Falsification

Deductivism can be traced back to antiquity. More than two thousand years ago Euclid developed a system of geometry in which a large number of propositions (theorems) are demonstrated, or proved, if they can be deduced from a few assumptions (axioms or postulates). Euclidian geometry was later followed by Aristotelian logic – the simple syllogisms which were used as the basis of developing knowledge by logical argument. So powerful were these axiomatic and syllogistic systems that they led to the view that scientific theories should also be constructed in this deductive form.

The Deductive Strategy is sometimes referred to as the *hypothetico-deductive* or the *falsificationist* approach, or the method of conjecture and refutation; it is the strategy associated with Critical Rationalism. Its modern pioneer and most outspoken advocate is Karl Popper. Whereas Inductivists look for evidence to confirm their generalizations, sometimes referred to as *justificationism*, Deductivists try to refute their hypotheses, to falsify them. The Deductive strategy begins with a question or a problem that needs to be understood or explained. Instead of starting with observations, the first stage is to produce a possible answer to the question, or an explanation for the problem.

> Science starts with problems, problems associated with the explanation of the behaviour of some aspect of the world or universe. Falsifiable hypotheses are proposed by scientists as solutions to the problem. The conjectured hypotheses are then criticized and tested. Some will be quickly eliminated. Others might prove more successful. These must be subject to even more stringent criticism and testing. When an hypothesis that has successfully withstood a wide range of rigorous tests is eventually falsified, a new problem, hopefully far removed from the original solved problem, has emerged. This new problem calls for the invention of new hypotheses, followed by new criticism and testing. And so the process continues indefinitely. It can never be said of a theory that it is true, however well it has withstood rigorous tests, but it can hopefully be said that a current theory is superior to its predecessors in the sense that it is able to withstand tests that falsified those predecessors. (Chalmers 1982: 45)

Braithwaite has expressed the Deductive strategy as one in which the scientist has great freedom to propose a theory but has to hand over to Nature the task of deciding whether any of the conclusions drawn from it are false. 'Man [sic] proposes a system of hypotheses: Nature disposes of its truth or falsity. Man invents a scientific system, and then discovers whether or not it accords with observed fact' (Braithwaite 1953: 368). The 'aim is not to save the lives of untenable systems, but, on the contrary, to select the one which is by comparison the fittest, by exposing them all to the fiercest struggle for survival' (Popper 1959a: 42).

> The falsificationist freely admits that observation is guided by and presupposes theory. He [sic] is also happy to abandon any claim implying that theories are established as true or probably true in the light of observational evidence. Theories are construed as speculative and tentative conjectures or guesses freely created by the human intellect in an attempt to overcome problems encountered by previous theories and to give an adequate account of the behaviour of some aspects of the world or universe ... Science progresses by trial and error, by conjectures and refutations. Only the fittest theories survive. While it can never be legitimately said of a theory that it is true, it can hopefully be said that it is the best available, that it is better than anything that has come before. (Chalmers 1982: 38)

Popper's strategy can be summarized as follows.

1   Begin by putting forward a tentative idea, a conjecture, a hypothesis or a set of hypotheses that form a theory.
2   With the help, perhaps, of other previously accepted hypotheses, or by specifying conditions under which the hypotheses are expected to hold, deduce a conclusion, or a number of conclusions.
3   Examine the conclusions and the logic of the argument that produced them. Compare this argument with existing theories to see if it would constitute an advance in our understanding. If you are satisfied with this examination –
4   Test the conclusion by gathering appropriate data; make the necessary observations or conduct the necessary experiments.
5   If the test fails, i.e. if the data are not consistent with the conclusion, the 'theory' must be false. The original conjecture does not match up with reality and must therefore be rejected.
6   If, however, the conclusion passes the test, i.e. the data are consistent with it, the 'theory' is temporarily supported; it is *corroborated*, not proved to be true. (Popper 1959a: 32–3)

Popper also set out a number of requirements for this strategy. First, for any theory to be regarded as scientific, it must be possible, at least in principle, to falsify it – to use evidence to challenge it. A theory that is not capable of being tested, cannot be called scientific (Popper 1959a: 40, 48). A good theory is falsifiable because it makes definite claims about the world. And the more precisely a theory is stated, the more falsifiable it becomes. This requirement is known as the 'demarcation criterion'. Secondly, tests should be as demanding as possible, for a theory which can survive such a test must be more acceptable than one that has been subjected to weaker tests. 'In order to make the method of selection by elimination work, and to ensure that only the fittest theories survive, their struggles for life must be made severe for them' (Popper 1961: 134). The more falsifiable a theory is the better. 'The more a theory claims, the more potential opportunities there will be for showing that the world does not in fact behave in the way laid down by the theory' (Chalmers 1982: 42).

This view of the process of generating theories is somewhat paradoxical. Why do we not try to find support for a fledgling theory rather than try to destroy it? Popper argued that

> if we are uncritical we shall always find what we want: we shall look for, and find, confirmations, and we shall look away from, and not see, whatever might be dangerous to our pet theories. In this way it is only too easy to obtain what appears to be overwhelming evidence in favour of a theory which, if approached critically, would have been refuted. (Popper 1961: 134)

Popper has suggested that there is no great logical difference between explanation, prediction and testing. Rather, it is one of emphasis and depends on what we regard as given. If the task is explanation, then the conclusion to the argument is what we want to explain, and the general propositions that form the basis of the argument constitute the explanation; we take the propositions as given on the basis, presumably, that they had previously survived some tests. If the task is prediction, then, again, the propositions are taken as given, the conditions are specified, and the conclusion to the argument becomes the prediction. Finally, if the task is theory testing, then the propositions are regarded as being tentative and the conclusion is what has to be tested against some data.

Nagel (1961) has argued that the most comprehensive and impressive forms of explanation are deductive in form, and those forms of explanation that do not meet its requirements assume it as the ideal. An influential elaboration of the deductive form of theories can be found in Braithwaite's *Scientific Explanation* in which he viewed deductive theories as forming a system of propositions in which observable consequences logically follow from a set of general, or initial, propositions.

> Every deductive system consists of a set of propositions (to be called the *initial propositions*) from which all other propositions (to be called the *deduced propositions*) follow according to logical principles. Some of these propositions follow immediately from a set of initial propositions, others follow immediately from propositions which follow immediately from the initial propositions, others follow from these propositions, and so on. Every proposition of the system follows immediately or mediately from the set of initial propositions. Every deduced proposition in a deductive system occurs at the end of a chain of deductive steps which starts with the set of initial propositions. The chain which leads to any particular proposition may be short or long, but it is always a finite length, so that the proposition is reached after a limited number of steps of immediate deduction. (Braithwaite 1953: 22)

While Popper's view of science began to gain acceptance in the 1960s, there were features of it with which some commentators were dissatisfied. In his early work, he regarded a single refutation as being sufficient for the demise of a theory. Later, he allowed for theories to be modified in order for them to survive. This did not mean introducing *ad hoc* modifications that had no testable consequences, such as an extra condition which arbitrarily restricted the scope of the theory, but it did allow for testable conditions to be introduced. For example, if we take the universal statement that 'water boils at 100 degrees Centigrade', and put it to the test (assuming we can recognize when water boils), we may find that the temperature reading is not as predicted. It would not be legitimate to rescue this theory by introducing a condition that excludes the day on which the test was applied, but it would be legitimate to introduce conditions about the purity of the water and air pressure. The former condition does not advance our knowledge, while the latter conditions do. Popper accepted this modification in his later work.

Popper's view of the logic of science has come to be known as *naive falsificationism.* Lakatos (1970) set out to improve on Popper's method by developing what he called *sophisticated falsificationism.* He moved the emphasis away from establishing the level of falsifiability of a single theory to the comparison of the degree of falsifiability of competing theories. For a new theory to be acceptable it needs to be more falsifiable than its rival and preferably be able to predict new kinds of phenomena. Hence, as science progresses, theories should become increasingly more falsifiable by making greater claims than their predecessors.

> Sophisticated falsificationism differs from naive falsificationism both in its rules of *acceptance* (or 'demarcation criterion') and its rules of *falsification* or elimination. For the naive falsificationist any theory which can be interpreted as experimentally falsifiable, is 'acceptable' or 'scientific'. For the sophisticated falsificationist a theory is 'acceptable' or 'scientific' only if it has corroborated excess empirical content over its predecessor (or rival), that is, only if it leads to the discovery of novel facts. (Lakatos 1970: 116)

In order for a theory to be replaced, the new theory must provide additional information, i.e. it must be able to predict facts that the existing theory would regard as improbable or not allowed; it must be able to explain what the existing theory can explain, and there must be *some* corroboration for this additional information. *'There is no falsification before the emergence of a better theory'* (Lakatos 1970: 119).

Sophisticated falsificationism allows for confirmation as well as falsification of theories; it distinguishes between bold and cautious conjectures. A conjecture is bold if its claims are unlikely, and it makes novel predictions in terms of the state of knowledge at the time. Little is to be gained from falsifying bold conjectures or corroborating cautious conjectures. 'Significant advances will be marked by the *confirmation* of *bold* conjectures or the *falsification* of *cautious* conjectures' (Chalmers 1982: 54). Cautious or apparently self-evident statements need to be discarded if they are in fact false, while failing to falsify a bold conjecture constitutes a leap forward.

Sophisticated falsificationism replaces the concept of 'theory' with the notion of a series of theories. *'It is a succession of theories and not one given theory which is appraised as scientific or pseudo-scientific.* But the members of such a series of theories are usually connected by a remarkable *continuity* which welds them into *research programmes'* (Lakatos 1970: 132).

Some philosophers of science (e.g. Braithwaite) have argued that explanations in all sciences form a pyramid-like network of propositions such that theories in all disciplines are interrelated and are derived from a limited number of very general scientific 'laws'. Hawking (1988) and others have argued that it may be possible to demonstrate that all theories in all disciplines can be derived from a single 'law'. Others have argued that the theories of the social sciences (e.g. sociology) are derived from the theories of the behavioural sciences (e.g. psychology) which, in turn, are derived from the theories of biology, chemistry and physics. This view, known as *reductionism*, might be better expressed as the principle of the 'unity of the sciences'. However, a rejection of the 'unity of method' in the natural and social sciences entails a rejection of this principle.

Deduction in the Social Sciences:
an Example

In his seminal work on *The Structure of Science*, Nagel (1961) discussed the natural, biological and social sciences, as well as historical enquiry. While he considered the deductive form of explanation as the ideal, he acknowledged three other types: probabilistic explanations, functional or teleological explanations, and genetic explanations. Probabilistic explanations, which occur in most disciplines, are characterized by the fact that the premises are logically insufficient to establish the truth of the conclusion. One of the high-level propositions may be in the form of a statistical relationship which indicates a less than perfect association between two phenomena. It is sometimes suggested that probability explanations are halfway theories which may become deductive theories in due course; all that is needed is to replace the statistical statements with a general statement. However, in some disciplines, particularly the social sciences, statistical regularities are all that can be expected. Hence, Nagel concluded that probabilistic explanations cannot be ignored.

Functional or teleological explanations are particularly common in the biological and social sciences. They take the form either of the specification of the functions a part of a system performs for the system as a whole, or of stating that a particular action is designed to achieve a particular goal; that it is a means to some end. It is not necessary to assume that functional explanations require a conscious social actor. For example, the existence of parts of the human body, or of social systems, has been explained in terms of the functions they must perform if the organism or system is to survive. However, in the means–ends case, it is usually the actions of conscious social actors that are being explained.

Genetic explanations are characteristic of historical enquires. The task of such explanations is to propose a sequence of events which have led to an earlier form of society being transformed into a later one. They include many singular statements about past events, although these events will have been selected on the (usually) tacit assumption of there being a causal connection between them. If general or law-like propositions are entertained they would deal with developmental stages.

Criticisms of both the probabilistic and genetic forms have already been encountered. However, later in this chapter the latter will be revisited. The former might be a more correct description for the following example of Deductivism in the social sciences, based on a reconstruction of Durkheim's theory of egoistic suicide.

Durkheim, as has already been discussed, was a staunch advocate of the Inductive strategy. He chose to study suicide to demonstrate the superiority of an inductive sociological explanation over all existing explanations. However, his application of the Inductive strategy, and the validity of the theory, have been severely criticized (see, for example, Douglas 1967; Atkinson 1978). The Deductive reconstruction is not designed to deal with these problems; the theory just lends itself to this.

A Deductive theory, as outlined above, consists of a set of hypotheses or propositions which are arranged in such a way that from some of the propositions as premises all the other propositions follow. Such a theory has the form of a logical argument which leads to certain conclusions. The following reconstruction from Homans (1964) consists of five propositions using three main concepts: 'suicide rate' (the number of suicides per thousand of a population); 'individualism' (the tendency for people to think for themselves and act independently rather than conform to the beliefs and norms of some group);[3] and 'Protestantism' (a collection of Christian groups formed after the Reformation).

1   In any social grouping, the suicide rate varies directly with the degree of individualism (egoism).
2   The degree of individualism varies directly with the incidence of Protestantism.
3   Therefore, the suicide rate varies with the incidence of Protestantism.
4   The incidence of Protestantism in Spain is low.
5   Therefore, the suicide rate in Spain is low. (Homans 1964: 951)

The theory contains two universal propositions (1 and 2) which state the form of relationships between pair of concepts. The meaning of each proposition could be elaborated and reasons given for including it. The third proposition follows logically from the first two and links the suicide rate with 'Protestantism', a less abstract concept than 'individualism'. On its own each proposition explains nothing, but all three propositions together constitute an explanation for differences in suicide rates. What Durkheim wanted to explain was why Protestants have a higher suicide rate than Catholics; he claimed that these propositions provide such an explanation. The addition of proposition 4, a descriptive statement, allows for a prediction (proposition 5) that can be tested (assuming that relative suicide rates can be satisfactorily established). Similarly, predictions could be made about other countries (e.g. Republic of Ireland) to provide further tests of the theory. Alternatively, if proposition 5 needs to be explained, then the preceding propositions provide the explanation. In this particular theory it would be possible to test propositions 1 to 3 directly by gathering data on these pairs of concepts in various populations. Hence, when theories are

[3] An alternative concept is 'social integration' which refers to the acceptance and practice of a group's beliefs and norms by its members. Durkheim discussed what he called a spirit of free enquiry which some religious groups may encourage, and which can lead to schisms within the group, in contrast to the strict adherence to beliefs and practices which some groups require, and which therefore socially integrates its members.

structured in this deductive way, the differences between explanation, prediction and testing, as Popper has argued, is just a matter of emphasis.

Another reconstruction of Durkheim's theory of suicide, using different concepts, has similar characteristics.

1   Social cohesion provides psychic support to group members subjected to acute stress and anxieties.
2   Suicide rates are functions of *unrelieved* anxieties and stresses to which persons are subjected.
3   Catholics have greater social cohesion than Protestants.
4   Therefore, lower suicide rates should be anticipated among Catholics than among Protestants. (Merton 1957: 97)

This form of the theory includes two very general propositions, a descriptive statement, and a conclusion which is the proposition to be explained.

Problems of Deduction

It has been argued that Deductivism involves the use of induction. In spite of his strong support for Deductivism, Hempel has claimed that in the case where a theory has not been falsified, its acceptance relies on data that lend 'inductive support' (1966: 18). Salmon (1988) has raised the issue of whether Deductivism provides any rational basis for choosing between all the unrefuted alternative theories in order to make some practical prediction. Popper had argued that such a choice would be based on the degree to which these theories have stood up to severe criticism and testing. Salmon has replied that basing claims about the capacity of a theory to make practical predictions by appraising its past performances provides no basis for choice. Like Hempel, he claimed that corroboration involves some elements of induction with the result that it is not possible to make a rational choice. He believed Popper's arguments to be unsatisfactory.

> I must confess to the feeling that we have been given the runaround. We begin by asking how science can possibly do without induction. We are told that the aim of science is to arrive at the best explanatory theories we can find. When we ask how to tell whether one theory is better than another, we are told that it depends upon their comparative ability to stand up to severe testing and critical discussion. When we ask whether this mode of evaluation does not contain some inductive aspect, we are assured that the evaluation is made wholly in terms of their comparative success up to now; but since this evaluation is made entirely in terms of past performance, it escapes inductive contamination because it lacks predictive import. When we then ask how to select theories for purposes of rational prediction, we are told that we should prefer the theory that is 'best tested' and that 'in the light of our *critical discussion*, appears to be the best so far,' even though we have been explicitly assured that testing and critical discussion have no predictive import. Popper tells us, 'I do not know of anything more "rational" than a

well-conducted critical discussion.' I fail to see how it could be rational to judge theories *for purposes of prediction* in terms of a criterion that is emphatically claimed to be lacking in predictive import. (Salmon 1988: 55–6)

In spite of describing himself as a neo-Popperian, Watkins (1968, 1984) has also contributed to this debate on the basis for choosing between competing theories. In his recent work he wished to correct what he regarded as 'some lingering traces of inductivism' in Popper's position. However, with Popper, he argued that corroboration implies nothing about the future performance of a theory and, against Salmon, he argued that prediction is certainly possible. On the question of theory choice, Watkins (1984) has gone to great lengths to develop a logical argument to support the case that such choice can be made without the use of induction.

More recently, O'Hear (1989) has discussed Popper's claim that the best theory at any time is the one that has survived the severest tests. He has suggested that it is difficult to talk of severe tests without using some notion of inductive reasoning. The degree of corroboration of a theory is always based on its past performance and the judgement of the severity of a test is based on past evidence. But how is it possible to move from past experience to the calculation of present or future probability? 'The crucial point is that it is only against a background of expectations built up from past experience that we can speak of some outcomes being improbable, and hence of severe tests in the Popperian sense. Without some sort of inductive argument, all tests are liable to look equally severe' (O'Hear 1989: 40). Knowledge concerning the past success of a theory to pass tests is not an adequate basis for future actions based on the theory, except on the basis of inductive assumptions. Therefore, the Popperian method of falsification does not provide a basis for believing in theories that have survived severe tests.

O'Hear has proposed that as the testing of theories occurs against a background of existing knowledge about the world, this knowledge should be used to judge which theories are worth testing. Theories should not be generalized from background knowledge, nor should the results of the tests be able to be predicted from this knowledge. However, some prior evidence that a theory is worth testing is necessary to ensure some probability that it will survive the testing process; severe testing is not all that is needed. This probability is increased both with the severity of the test and the initial probability of the theory surviving the test.

This concern to find a strictly logical strategy for science has been attacked by Feyerabend (1978) who claimed that a strict adherence to rational procedures inhibits scientific progress. The principles of Critical Rationalism, he argued,

give an inadequate account of science because science is much more 'sloppy' and 'irrational' than its methodological image. And they are liable to hinder it, because the attempt to make science more 'rational' and more precise is bound to wipe it out ... For what appears as 'sloppiness', 'chaos' or 'opportunism' . . . has a most important function in the development of those very theories which we today regard as essential parts of our knowledge of nature . . . Thus anarchism is not only *possible*, it is *necessary* for the internal progress of science and for the development of our culture as a whole. (Feyerabend 1978: 179–80)

Other criticisms of the Deductive strategy fall into four main categories: those concerned with the source of the propositions that make up deductive theories; those concerned with practical aspects of making observations; those related to the theory-dependence of observations; and, those associated with the fact that scientists are members of scientific communities.

An important issue for the practising researcher is where the propositions that form the basis of a deductive theory come from. Popper had no interest in this question. He distinguished between what he called the *logic of knowledge* – the method by which theories are justified – and the *psychology of knowledge* – the process by which a new idea is conceived.

The initial stage, the act of conceiving or inventing a theory, seems to me neither to call for logical analysis nor to be susceptible to it. The question of how it happens that a new idea occurs to a man [sic] – whether it is a musical theme, a dramatic conflict, or a scientific theory – may be of great interest to empirical psychology; but it is irrelevant to the logical analysis of scientific knowledge . . . [T]here is no such thing as a logical method of having new ideas, or a logical reconstruction of this process. (Popper 1959a: 31, 32)

According to Popper, every discovery contains an 'irrational element' or a 'creative intuition'; the issue of how theories are tested is the only scientifically relevant one. Similar arguments have been presented by Reichenbach and Braithwaite. Reichenbach argued that philosophers of science cannot be concerned with reasons for suggesting hypotheses, only with reasons for accepting them (1948: 382), and Braithwaite proposed that it is a matter of 'the individual psychology of thinking and the sociology of thought' (1953: 20–1), neither of which is of concern to the philosopher. Unfortunately, these arguments are not particularly helpful to the practising researcher. Are the propositions derived by imaginative conjecture, as Popper maintained, or by some form of inductive reasoning, which Popper wished to avoid (Hesse 1974: 2).

Medewar was critical of this aspect of the Deductivist strategy.

The major defect of the hypothetico-deductive scheme, considered as a formulary of scientific behaviour, is its disavowal of any competence to speak about the generative act in scientific inquiry, 'having an idea', for this represents the imaginative or logically unscripted episode in scientific thinking, the part that lies outside logic. The objection is all the more grave because an imaginative and inspirational process enters into all scientific reasoning at every level: it is not confined to 'great' discoveries, as the more simple-minded inductivists have supposed. (Medewar 1969a: 55)

Because of the reluctance of Deductivists to deal with the process by which hypotheses come into being, Medewar argued that they do not offer a complete account of the scientific process. He regarded this process as involving a great deal of intuition and creativity, as well as logic; it is about both discovery and justification.

> The scientific method is not deductive in character: it is a well-known fallacy to regard it as such: but it is rigorous nevertheless, and logically conclusive. Scientific laws are *in*ductive in origin. An episode of scientific discovery begins with the plain and unembroidered evidence of the senses – with innocent, unprejudiced observation, the exercise of which is one of the scientist's most precious and distinctive faculties – and slowly builds upon it a great mansion of natural law. Imagination kept within bounds may ornament a scientist's thought and intuition may bring it faster to its conclusions, but in a strictly formal sense neither is indispensable. (Medewar 1969b: 147)

This view seems to have almost brought us full circle, back to some kind of induction. Medewar, however, wished to stress the central role of imagination in the scientific process of discovery.

A somewhat similar position was adopted by Mary Hesse.

> I have maintained that scientific theories are not constructed solely out of sense-data or out of operational definitions, but are 'hypothetico-deductive' in form; that is, they consist of hypotheses which may not in themselves have any reference to immediate observations, but from which deductions can be drawn which correspond to the results of experiments when suitably translated into experimental language. The main point that emerges from such a description of theories is that there can be no set of rules given for the procedure of scientific discovery – a hypothesis is not produced by a deductive machine by feeding experimental observations into it: it is a product of creative imagination, of a mind which absorbs the experimental data until it sees them fall into a pattern, giving the scientific theorist the sense that he [sic] is penetrating beneath the flux of phenomena to the real structure of nature. (Hesse 1953: 198)

Stated like this, the process of scientific discovery may seem to be relatively straightforward. However, seeing data 'fall into a pattern' is a complex and difficult process (see chapter 6).

The second area of criticism of the Deductive strategy is concerned with the problem of using data to test a theory. From a practical point of view, the process of testing a theory is dependent not only on making accurate observations, but also on the stage of development of both the theories behind the observations and the instruments which are used. Popper recognized this problem but gave it only limited attention; he was unable to provide a satisfactory solution. 'In point of fact, no conclusive disproof of a theory can ever be produced; for it is always possible to say that the experimental results are not reliable or that the discrepancies which are asserted to exist between the experimental results and the theory are only apparent and that they will disappear with the advance of our understanding' (Popper 1959a: 50).

Medewar and Chalmers echoed the same concern but they saw it as being serious.

> We could be mistaken in thinking that our observations falsified a hypothesis: the observations may themselves have been faulty, or may have been made against a background of misconceptions; or our experiments may have been ill-designed. (Medewar 1969a: 53–4)

> [I]t is precisely the fact that observation statements are fallible, and their acceptance only tentative and open to revision, that undermines the falsificationist position. Theories cannot be conclusively falsified because the observation statements that form the basis for the falsification may themselves prove to be false in the light of later developments ... Conclusive falsifications are ruled out by the lack of a perfectly secure observation base on which they depend. (Chalmers 1982: 63–4)

The third area of criticism, reviewed briefly in chapter 4, derives from the problem of the theory dependence of observation; it is the problem of the relationship between theories and 'reality'. One of the central features of the Inductivist strategy is the distinction made between observation languages and theoretical languages. The Deductivists deny the existence of an observational language because of the theory-dependence of observations. To some degree, all statements must be in a theoretical language. Therefore, if there is no observation language, and all observations are interpretations, there is no way of comparing theoretical statements with 'reality'; they can only be compared with theory-impregnated observations. There is no way of knowing whether theoretical statements match 'reality' because it cannot be directly observed.

Hesse (1974) has called this the circularity objection, and has offered a solution to it in terms of *a network model* of theories. While she accepted that all observation may be 'theory-laden', the status of any 'observation report' depends on its relationship to a network of theoretical statements with a high level of coherence. In contrast to the Deductive strategy in which propositions form a hierarchy, from theoretical to observational, or from abstract to concrete, the network model regards all statements to be reciprocally related at some level of probability. If some of these theoretical statements form a 'hard core' which, for the present, has received a high level of confirmation, 'observation reports', which show some level of consistency with it, can be accepted, inductively, in the meantime.

Pawson (1989) has addressed this question in the context of developing his theory of social measurement. In order to avoid the circularity problem, he has adopted a *transformation model of measurement* based on the notion of information transfer. He provided an example of how the heat produced by an internal combustion engine might be measured. 'The basic strategy in the measurement of a physical property is to harness an output of energy from a physical system, transforming that output into some kind of "signal" and transmitting that information to some kind of recording device' (Pawson 1989: 110). The consequence of viewing measurement this way is that rather than the theory which is being tested providing the guidance for observation, a whole family of theories is called upon to produce data. '[C]ircularity is avoided since theories or expectations which lead us to inquire about the measured are not the theories and principles used in the measurement' (1989: 115).

The fourth category of criticism has to do with the intellectual and social contexts within which science is practised. The history of science provides many examples of theories for which there was disconfirming evidence but which were nevertheless not rejected. A classic example is the theory of planetary motion developed by Copernicus in the sixteenth century as an alternative to that developed by the early Greek astronomers. More recent examples can be found in Newton's gravitational theory, Bohr's theory of the atom, and the kinetic theory of gases (Chalmers 1982). Why did this happen? Answers to this question by Lakatos and Kuhn were reviewed in the previous chapter (see pp. 105–110).

A recognition of the role of scientific communities is also related to the issue of the source of hypotheses. These ideas can be drawn from what Cohen (1968) has called 'meta-theories', Inkeles (1964) has called 'models', Willer (1967) has called 'general models', Cuff and Payne (1979) and others have called 'perspectives', and Kuhn (1970a) has called 'paradigms'. Although there are differences in the meaning of these various concepts, they all recognize that social theorists and researchers operate in the context of a set of abstract ontological and epistemological assumptions about what society looks like, what are its fundamental units and how they are related, how society works, what constitutes appropriate methods for studying it, where one should look for explanations (i.e. what explains what), and what will be acceptable as an adequate explanation. These ideas are frequently taken for granted, they may not be explicitly formulated, they are not subjected to critical scrutiny or testing, and they may be modified but cannot be refuted. They provide the backdrop to the work of social scientists and thus make 'observation' and 'understanding' of the social world possible, and set limits to what is 'seen' and 'known'. If intuition or creativity is at work, it is occurring within the possibilities and limits of this body of ideas.

In spite of its shortcomings, Kuhn's work, together with that of Polanyi (1958), Lakatos (1970), Hesse (1974), Laudan (1977) and Feyerabend (1978), has helped to discard the limited views of science proposed by both Inductivists and Deductivists. 'These investigations have taught us how vital and central the role of theory is for any scientific discipline. And they have also shown that even the . . . concept of scientific theory as consisting of hypothetical-deductive systems is far too narrow and misleading to account for the varied functions of theory in science' (Bernstein 1976: 105).

Combining Inductive and Deductive Strategies

The relationship between induction and deduction has been debated for about one hundred and fifty years. For example, Jevons (1874) has suggested that all inductive reasoning is the inverse application of deductive reasoning, and Whewell (1847) has argued that induction and deduction went upstairs and downstairs on the same staircase. Is it possible to combine these two strategies and thereby capitalize on their strengths and minimize their weaknesses?

Wallace (1971) has proposed such a scheme and, in the process, has endeavoured to overcome the deficiencies of both naive induction and naive falsification. He defined science as 'a way of generating and testing the truth of statements about events in the world of human experience' (Wallace 1971: 11). He included both the generation *and* testing processes as part of science.

In Wallace's scheme (see figure 2),[4] two sets of overlapping processes are involved: theorizing and doing research; and induction and deduction. These processes are related in a series of cyclical stages which, for example, could occur in the following order: from observation to empirical generalization to theory to hypotheses to tests through further observations. Wallace was at pains to point out that this reconstruction of the scientific process is not intended to imply inflexibility. For example, the process of moving from one stage to another may involve a series of preliminary trials, including mental experiments, pre-tests and pilot studies, i.e. feedback loops may be built in. It is also possible to begin the process at any stage in the cycle, with observations, with empirical generalizations, with a theory or with hypotheses. He discussed the process beginning with observations.

Wallace does not hold a naive inductivist view of observations. He argued that while observations are almost the prime arbiters of the scientific process, 'the primacy of observations in science should not be taken to mean that observations are "immediately given" or wholly detached in their origins from empirical generalisations, theories, and hypotheses to which they then give rise' (Wallace 1971: 33). Thus, observations provide information for, as well as being the output of, the scientific process. In social research, data gathered from samples of some population can, by means of techniques of statistical inference, produce statistical (i.e. empirical) generalizations. Following Merton (1957), he regarded these empirical generalizations as nothing more than summaries of observed uniformities, not the universal laws as claimed by the naive inductivists.

---

[4] What follows is based mainly on Wallace's earlier work (1971). However, a more elaborate scheme, which distinguishes between the processes involved in both 'pure' and 'applied' science, can be found in his later work (Wallace 1983).

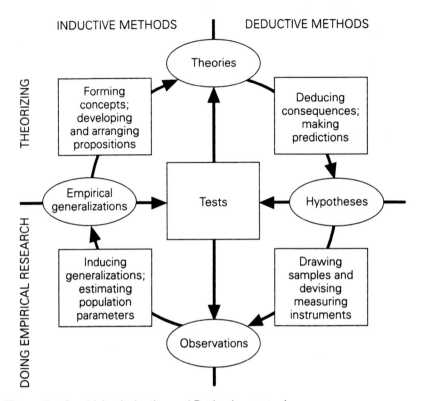

INDUCTIVE METHODS   DEDUCTIVE METHODS

Figure 2   Combining Inductive and Deductive strategies.

Source: Wallace, Walter L. *The Logic of Science in Sociology.* (New York: Aldine de
Gruyter) Copyright © 1971 Walter L. Wallace, and Wallace, Walter L. *Principles of Scientific
Sociology.* (New York: Aldine) Copyright © 1983 Walter L. Wallace.

For Wallace, this process is the *inductive research stage* of the cycle. It can
be illustrated by means of the reconstruction of Durkheim's theory of
egoistic suicide. What is required is to translate the observation that
'Protestants commit suicide more than Catholics' into a measurable relationship between the variables 'religious affiliation' (or 'degree of Protestantism') and 'suicide rate'.

The next stage in the process is to construct theories from empirical
generalizations by forming concepts and developing and arranging propositions – the *inductive theorizing stage*. According to Wallace, these
processes involve making the terms in the empirical generalizations and
their relationships more abstract. It is necessary to climb the ladder
of abstraction (Phillips 1966: 28–9). A creative jump has to be made to
identify 'degree of individualism' as a theoretical concept related to the

descriptive variable 'religious affiliation'. Thus, the most abstract proposition in the theory, that 'the suicide rate varies directly with the degree of individualism', is arrived at, and it can now be arranged with propositions of similar abstractness to form a theory. Unfortunately, Wallace appears to have underestimated the complexity of this process, which can hardly be called inductive. This issue is one of the central concerns of the next chapter.

Assuming for the moment that it is possible to construct a theory from empirical generalizations, in *deductive theorizing,* the first step in the next stage, the theory is examined for internal consistency and compared with other theories to see whether it is superior in terms of having greater breadth of scope, a higher level of abstraction, and whether it is more parsimonious. It is then possible to deduce hypotheses or predictions from the theory in the manner already discussed.

The *deductive research stage* requires the translation of the concepts in the hypotheses into measurement procedures involving instruments, scales and sampling techniques. It is then possible to test the theory by making new observations. The latter can be compared with the predictions and a decision made as to whether the theory has been corroborated or confirmed, whether it has been refuted, or whether it can be modified for further testing. By measuring the theoretical concepts in various ways and in different contexts, several tests of an initially corroborated theory are possible. Results which do not fully corroborate a theory may provide a stimulus for the modification of the theory or the development of a new theory. Merton has described this as the 'serendipity' component of research, 'the fairly common experience of observing an *unanticipated, anomalous and strategic* datum which becomes the occasion for developing a new theory or for extending a different theory' (1957: 104).

In view of the conflicts between Positivism and Critical Rationalism, the purist may have some difficulties with the way in which Wallace has combined elements of these two positions. For example, their different positions on the nature of 'observation' would seem to be a problem. Wallace dealt with this by both accepting that observations are dependent 'on other elements in the scientific process', and arguing that 'they are also partly independent of them' (1971: 35). On this issue and others, Wallace has essentially accommodated aspects of the Inductive strategy within the Deductive strategy, although in a way to which Popper would have objected. Given that the two research strategies differ mainly in their logic of theory construction, and that they share a common ontology, viewing them as complementary has some merits.

It is important to recognize, however, that Wallace's scheme remains within the confines of a Positivist and Critical Rationalist ontology and therefore adopts an outside or monologic relationship to social reality; it makes no provision for its socially constructed character. Any attempt to graft on an input from social actors' constructions could only lead to ontological and epistemological confusion.

More recently, Rubinstein *et al.* (1984) have argued that science is a process that progressively explores the world by means of a systematic alternation between induction and deduction, an iterative process for refining and testing ideas. However, this process offers no assistance in the difficult activity of finding ideas that make sense of collected data.

Review

These two strategies of social research have dominated philosophical views on the processes by which theories are constructed in both the natural and social sciences. The Inductive strategy can be traced back to the establishment of modern natural science and it was vigorously advocated as being appropriate for the social sciences as their foundations were being laid. In time, however, it came under attack, particularly because of its naive view of the role of observation and the unsatisfactory nature of inductive logic on which it was based. Nevertheless, it still represents a popular view of *the* scientific method.

While elements of a Deductive view of theory testing were adopted by some Positivists, as a process which followed the inductive generation of theory, it was the Critical Rationalists, and Popper in particular, who adopted it as an exclusive strategy. The shift was intended to solve the problems of the truth status of scientific theories and to provide a criterion for demarcating science from non-science. Scientific research was about refuting false conjectures rather than inductively confirming derived generalizations; falsification rather than verification became the catch cry.

The Deductive strategy was intended to overcome the deficiencies of the Inductive strategy. However, various attempts were made to refine and elaborate the former and, in some cases, to transform it. Naive falsification was replaced with sophisticated falsification; the testing of isolated hypotheses was replaced with the notion of theories as structured wholes, as networks or paradigms; the worldviews of scientific communities were elevated to the status of mutually exclusive and incommensurate ontological and epistemological arbiters. These shifts in approach involved some fundamental changes; a move from the Inductivist position that the truth of theories could be conclusively established, through the Deductivist position which claimed that while the pursuit of truth is the goal of science all scientific theories are tentative, to the Conventionalist position that all scientific theories are the relativistic products of scientific communities. The outcome of this development, and the controversies which it engendered, was a proposal for scientific anarchism.

> The idea of a method that contains firm, unchanging, and absolutely binding principles for conducting the business of science meets considerable difficulty when confronted with the results of historical research. We find then, that there is not a single rule, however plausible, and however firmly grounded

in epistemology, that is not violated at some time or other. It becomes evident that such violations are not accidental events, they are not the results of insufficient knowledge or of inattention which might have been avoided. On the contrary, we see that they are necessary for progress . . . There is only *one* principle that can be defended under *all* circumstances and in *all* stages of human development. It is the principle: *anything goes.* (Feyerabend 1978: 23, 28).

This principle has received an enthusiastic reception, particularly among social science students who find the intricacies of philosophical debate difficult and tedious, and the prescription of research procedures inhibiting. However, it can become an excuse for sloppy research. But this is not the end of the story. There are two further research strategies which are based on different approaches to social enquiry, the Retroductive and the Abductive.

Further Reading

Key References

Chalmers, A.F. 1982. *What is this Thing Called Science?*
Hempel, C.E. 1966. *Philosophy of Natural Science.*
Lakatos, I. and Musgrave, A. (eds). 1970. *Criticism and the Growth of Knowledge.*
O'Hear, A. 1989. *An Introduction to the Philosophy of Science.*
Popper, K.R. 1959. *The Logic of Scientific Discovery.*
—— 1961. *The Poverty of Historicism.*
—— 1972. *Conjectures and Refutations.*
Wallace, W.L. 1971. *The Logic of Science in Sociology.*

General References

Bernstein, R.J. 1976. *Restructuring Social and Political Theory.*
—— 1983. *Beyond Objectivism and Relativism.*
Braithwaite, R.B. 1953. *Scientific Explanation.*
Doyal, L. and Harris, R. 1986. *Empiricism, Explanation and Rationality.*
Durkheim, E. 1952. *Suicide.*
—— 1964. *The Rules of Sociological Method.*
Grünbaum, A. and Salmon, W.C. (eds). 1988. *The Limits of Deductivism.*
Harré, R. 1972. *The Philosophy of Science.*
Hindess, B. 1977. *Philosophy and Methodology in the Social Sciences.*
Hughes, J. 1980. *The Philosophy of Social Research.*
Kaplan, A. 1964. *The Conduct of Inquiry.*
Kuhn, T.S. 1970. *The Structure of Scientific Revolutions,* 2nd edn.
Laudan, L. 1977. *Progress and its Problems.*
Medewar, P.B. 1969a. *Induction and Intuition in Scientific Thought.*
—— 1969b. *The Art of the Soluble.*
Phillips, D.C. 1987. *Philosophy, Science and Social Inquiry.*

Richards, S. 1983. *Philosophy and Sociology of Science.*
Riggs, P.L. 1992. *Whys and Ways of Science.*
Wallace, W.L. 1983. *Principles of Scientific Sociology.*
Watkins, J.W.N. 1984. *Science and Scepticism.*

6

Retroductive and Abductive Strategies

Every inquiry whatsoever takes its rise in the observation ... of some surprising phenomena, some experience which either disappoints an expectation, or breaks in upon some habit of expectation ... The inquiry begins with pondering these phenomena in all their aspects, in search of some point of view whence the wonder shall be resolved.
C.S. Peirce, 'A Neglected Argument for the Reality of God'

Introduction

The Inductive and Deductive research strategies are based on two contrasting forms of reasoning for generating new scientific knowledge. Alleged deficiencies in the Inductive and Deductive research strategies has lead to the development (or perhaps reclaiming) of two alternative strategies, Retroduction and Abduction, which are based on cyclic or spiral processes rather than linear logic. Retroduction has been advocated for use in both the natural and social sciences. Abduction, a relatively unknown strategy, was proposed as a method for generating hypotheses in the natural sciences, but is now advocated as the appropriate method of theory construction in Interpretive social science.

The Retroductive strategy, adopted by the Realist approach to social enquiry, has been discussed by philosophers for many years and, it is claimed, has been practised by scientists from various disciplines. However, its incorporation into an articulated philosophy of science is a recent development. Research based on the Realist approach begins in the domain of the actual, with observed connections between phenomena – perhaps correlations between variables. The task is to explain why such connections or relationships occur. The second step is to postulate the existence of 'real' structures and mechanisms which, if they existed, would explain the relationship. And the third step is to attempt to demonstrate the existence and operation of these structures and mechanisms, either by experimental activity designed to isolate and perhaps observe them, or by eliminating alternative explanations. The central problem for Realism is how to establish the plausibility of hypothesized structures and mechanisms given that they are not immediately available to experience (Harré 1979: 160).

In those branches of Interpretivism that are concerned to go beyond description to explanation and prediction, it is argued that Abduction is the appropriate research strategy. Such a strategy involves constructing theory which is derived from social actors' language, meanings and theories, or is grounded in everyday activities. Such research begins by describing these activities and meanings and then deriving from them categories and concepts that can form the basis of an understanding or an explanation of the problem at hand.

A critical issue for Realism is how to arrive at the postulated structures and mechanisms, and for these branches of Interpretivism, how to derive theories from everyday activities and meanings. Is there an appropriate mode of reasoning that will assist the researcher to find these ideas? Is there a *logic of discovery?*

This issue has been a matter of some dispute. It has already been noted that Popper had a distaste for induction and considered that there is only a logic for testing theories. However, a number of writers with a Critical Rationalist persuasion have suggested that it involves imagination, intuition or guesswork. For Popper, it is a matter of '*free* creations of our own minds, the result of an almost poetic intuition' (1972: 192). Hempel (1966) has described the logic of discovery as requiring creative imagination in which theories are not derived from observations but are invented, or guessed at, to explain them. For Medewar (1969b), it is an inductive process involving imagination and intuition, and for Feynman (1967) it is a matter of guesswork.

Before discussing the strategies used by Realism and Interpretivism, it is necessary to examine some attempts that have been made to understand this creative process.

Retroductive and Abductive Reasoning

There is a much neglected logic of science which was one of Aristotle's three types of logical reasoning; induction, deduction and *reduction*. Writing mainly in the second half of last century and early this century, Peirce translated this third form of reasoning as 'abduction' or 'retroduction', or sometimes as 'hypothesis'.

Peirce used the full range of concepts – Induction, Deduction and Abduction/Retroduction – to present his ideas on forms of reasoning involved in the scientific process. He illustrated the three forms of reasoning by a series of syllogisms.

Suppose I enter a room and there find a number of bags, containing different kinds of beans. On the table there is a handful of white beans; and, after some searching, I find one of the bags contains white beans only. I at once infer as a probability, or as a fair guess, that this handful was taken out of that bag ... We have then –

DEDUCTION

Rule – All the beans from this bag are white.
Case – These beans are from this bag.
Result – These beans are white.

INDUCTION

Case – These beans are from this bag.
Result – These beans are white.
Rule – All the beans from this bag are white.

HYPOTHESIS

Rule – All the beans from this bag are white.
Result – These beans are white.
Case – These beans are from this bag. (Peirce 1931b: 374)

His view of Deductive reasoning is the same as that outlined in chapter 5. It begins with a general statement, a *rule*, and with a statement of some conditions, the application of the rule to a specific *case*, a conclusion or a *result* is drawn. Such arguments are analytic because the truth of the conclusion is contained in the premises; it is the reasoning of mathematics (Peirce 1931b: 373). He characterized Induction as like 'rowing up the current of deductive sequence, and ... concluding a rule from the observation of a result in a certain case' (1931b: 373–4). It is what is involved in the experimental testing of a theory. 'Induction consists in starting from a theory, deducing from it predictions of phenomena, and observing those phenomena in order to see how nearly they agree with the theory' (1934a: 105).[1]

Unlike Deductive reasoning, Inductive and Retroductive reasoning, are synthetic or ampliative, because they make claims that do not follow logically from the premises. In addition, neither Induction nor Deduction can produce any new ideas (1934a: 90). On the other hand, Retroductive/ Abductive reasoning involves 'making an hypothesis' which appears to explain what has been observed; it is observing some phenomenon and then claiming what it was that gave rise to it. 'All the ideas of science come to it by way of Abduction ... Its only justification is that if we are ever to understand things at all, it must be in that way' (1934a: 90).

Given that enquiry is stimulated by 'the observation of some surprising phenomena', Peirce regarded the process of Retroduction, or hypothesis formulation, as being the first stage of an enquiry. It is a process akin to finding the right key for the lock, although the key may never have been observed before. The hypothesis must than be tested and, according to Peirce, this involves both Deduction and Induction; in the second stage of an enquiry consequences are deduced from the hypothesis and, in the

---

[1] This use of 'induction' is clearly different from those discussed in the previous chapter. It is more akin to 'deduction', but included the inductive elements identified by Hempel (1966). Peirce also distinguished between what he called 'Crude Induction', which involves simple enumeration of instances, and 'Gradual Induction' in which each new observed instance provides a changing estimate of the truth of the hypothesis.

third stage, these consequences are tested by means of Induction. Therefore, Peirce regarded scientific enquiry as involving all three forms of reasoning used in sequence. Deduction performs a very mechanical role, and while Induction links ideas to the natural or social worlds, Retroduction/Abduction is the most critical step. In scientific enquiry,

> we are building a cantilever bridge of induction, held together by scientific struts and ties. Yet every plank of its advance is first laid by Retroduction alone, that is to say, by the spontaneous conjectures of instinctive reason; and neither Deduction nor Induction contributes a single new concept to the structure. (Peirce 1934b: 324)

The main difference which Peirce saw between Induction and Retroduction (or hypothesis) is that 'induction infers from one set of facts another set of facts, whereas hypothesis infers from facts of one kind to facts of another' (1931b: 386). Retroduction proposes something that may not have been observed or could not be observed directly. He also argued that 'Abductive and Inductive reasoning are utterly irreducible, either to the other or to Deduction, or Deduction to either of them' (1934a: 91).

Peirce regarded Kepler's discovery that the planets move in elliptical orbits as the greatest piece of Retroductive reasoning ever performed. Kepler did not merely describe or generalize from what had been observed. Through a long process of investigation and the most careful and judicious reflection, he was able to modify his theory until it was in a form that fitted the observations. This was not a random process of casting around for ideas but a methodical and thoughtful process. Retroduction, therefore, is no easy task which, while involving a process of reasoning, does not lead to certainty; it culminates in finding *a* solution to the research problem.

According to Peirce, all established scientific theories are due to the operation of Retroduction/Abduction, but he continued to be puzzled about how the process occurred. That it is possible for human beings to have a new idea at all Peirce found remarkable; that correct theories can be imagined seems to be like a natural instinct.

> However man [sic] may have acquired his faculty of divining the ways of Nature, it has certainly not been by a self-controlled and critical logic. Even now he cannot give any exact reason for his guesses. It appears to me that the clearest statement we can make of the logical situation ... is to say that man has a certain Insight, not strong enough to be oftener right than wrong, but strong enough not to be overwhelmingly more often wrong than right ... An Insight, I call it, because it is to be referred to the same general class of operations to which Perceptive Judgments belong ... If you ask an investigator why he does not try this or that wild theory, he will say, 'It does not seem *reasonable*.' (Peirce 1934a: 107)

For Peirce, therefore, a hypothesis must eliminate the puzzlement which arises from some surprising observations, it must be able to answer the research question(s), and it must be possible to test it. Eliminating the puzzlement is a necessary first step, for without it the scientist would not consider testing to be worthwhile. Popper did not make this requirement; he encouraged scientists to think of unusual or even outrageous hypotheses but did not consider whether the scientist, or research funding bodies, would take such hypotheses seriously. Kuhn, on the other hand, in regarding 'normal science' as puzzle-solving, was aware of this critical element in the process of theory construction. Science, according to Peirce, is much more a struggle for intelligibility than it is a matter of strictly following logical procedures. He expressed the form of inference in Retroduction as follows:

> The surprising fact, C, is observed;
> But if A were true, C would be a matter of course,
> Hence, there is reason to suspect that A is true. (Peirce 1934a: 117)

In Positivistic Induction, A is supposed to emerge from repeated observations of C and, in Critical Rationalist Deduction, C is derived from some unaccounted for creation of A as a higher-level hypothesis (Hanson 1965: 86).

The process of arriving at a hypothesis, according to Peirce, begins by drawing together isolated observations and, in the end, involves being overwhelmed by an idea that cannot be resisted.

> It begins always with colligation, of course, of a variety of separately observed facts about the subject of the hypothesis ... Something corresponding to iteration may or may not take place. And then comes an Observation ... The act of observation is the deliberate yielding of ourselves to that *force majeure* – an early surrender at discretion, due to our foreseeing that we must, whatever we do, be borne down by that power, at last. Now the surrender which we make in Retroduction, is a surrender to the Insistence of an Idea ... It is irresistible; it is imperative. We must throw open our gates and admit it at any rate for the time being. (Peirce 1934a: 404–5)

Following Whewell, he defined *colligation* as the binding together of facts by means of a general description or hypothesis which applies to them all; it involves classifying and ordering observed patterns into categories or sequences. Kepler, for example, became interested in the proportions of interplanetary space occupied by Mercury, Venus, Earth, Mars, Jupiter and Saturn. He established the ratios of the radii of the orbits of adjoining planets such as Earth and Mars. An examination of the relative magnitudes of these ratios and their geometrical properties was an important step on the road to the elliptical hypothesis.

The emergence of a new idea is neither a quantum leap to an unrelated state of affairs, nor is it a continuous transition from one state to another. While both processes are involved in discovery, Peirce gave more weight to continuity than to abruptness (Tursman 1987: 22).

In addition to these three forms of reasoning, Peirce used another which he called Analogy. This is the inference 'that a not very large collection of objects which agree in various respects may very likely agree in another respect. For instance, the Earth and Mars agree in so many respects that it seems not unlikely that they agree in being inhabited' (Peirce 1931a: 29). Analogy, which is also an ampliative form of inference, combines characteristics of Induction and Retroduction. Peirce seemed to be suggesting that drawing analogies from other disciplines is a useful aid to Retroduction. However, he did not develop Analogical reasoning nor did he see analogies playing an integral role in the research process.

It is clear that Peirce's use of Induction is very different from that proposed by the Positivists and criticized by the Critical Rationalists. His view of the relationship between Induction and Deduction is also different from that proposed by Wallace (1971). It might be argued that his ideas on the nature of observation, both as a preliminary to scientific enquiry and as it is involved in the process of hypothesis testing through Induction, is naive in that it ignores the theory-dependence of observation. However, the time at which he was writing must provide him with some excuse on this issue.

Peirce used the concepts of Retroduction, Abduction and Hypothesis interchangeably in his work. However, while it will be necessary to follow the general sense in which he has used Retroduction and Abduction, for the present purposes they will be applied to different research strategies.

As well as being the originator of the idea of observations being theory-laden, Hanson is an exponent of Peirce's views on the logic of discovery and a critic of the hypothetico-deductive method. Hanson concurred with Peirce's views and elaborated them with reference to physics.

> Physical theories provide patterns within which data appear intelligible. They constitute a 'conceptual Gestalt'. A theory is not pieced together from observed phenomena; it is rather what makes it possible to observe phenomena as being of a certain sort, and as related to other phenomena. Theories put phenomena into systems. They are built up 'in reverse' – retroductively. A theory is a cluster of conclusions in search of a premise. From the observed properties of phenomena the physicist reasons his way towards a keystone idea from which the properties are explicable as a matter of course. The physicist seeks not a set of possible objects, but a set of possible explanations. (Hanson 1965: 90)

Like Peirce, Hanson was impressed with the process which Kepler used to arrive at his theory of elliptical orbits. He also illustrated the process with reference to Galileo's theory of falling bodies.

> Galileo's thirty-four year march towards his final explanation is punctuated with misconceptions and erroneous arguments. [H]e always tries to explain the original data by fashioning general hypotheses and theories 'in their image'. His hypotheses are never inductive summaries of data; nor does he

actively doubt them until he can deduce new observation statements which experiments confirm. Galileo knew he had succeeded when the constant acceleration hypothesis patterned the diverse phenomena he had encountered for thirty years. His reasoned advance from insight to insight culminated in an ultimate physical *explicans*. Further deductions were merely confirmatory; he could have left them to any of his students. (Hanson 1965: 89)

Achinstein (1971) has raised some difficulties with the Peirce and Hanson view of Retroduction. First, in claiming that scientists start by considering observed phenomena neglects the background of theory that the scientist has available. While Hanson is to be commended for recognizing the theory-dependence of observations, he seems to have overlooked the theory-dependence of Retroduction. Secondly, it may be possible to think of more than one reasonable hypothesis to account for the puzzling observations. Other evidence is needed in order to select from among such hypotheses the one that seems to provide the best explanation. Harman (1965, 1968) has made a similar proposal for improving the Peirce and Hanson view of Retroduction. For a hypothesis to be acceptable it must be 'the best of *competing* explanations and not the best of *alternative* explanations' (Harman 1968: 530). It must not only fit with existing knowledge, it must also fit best with that knowledge.

Reference to background assumptions raises the issue of the role of paradigms or research programmes in the setting of criteria for evaluating competing hypotheses. Retroduction/Abduction occurs in the context of ontological, conceptual and theoretical assumptions; the researcher does not start with a blank slate in the manner implied by Inductivists.

It is surprising that Peirce's views have received almost no attention outside the United States. The exception is Habermas (1972) who accepted Peirce's approach as being appropriate for the *empirical–analytic* sciences but not for the *historical–hermeneutic* sciences. Habermas's critique of Peirce's ontology and epistemology need not detain us here. However, the Abductive research strategy, to be developed later in this chapter, is intended to overcome these deficiencies and provide a logic which is consistent with the Interpretive approach to social enquiry.

The Retroductive Research Strategy

Following Bhaskar's suggestion (1979: 15), the term Retroduction will be restricted to the process of building models of structures and mechanisms which characterizes the Realist approach. The term Abduction will be used to refer to the process by which theories are constructed within the Interpretive approach.

The Retroductive research strategy involves the construction of hypothetical models as a way of uncovering the real structures and mechanisms which are assumed to produce empirical phenomena. It requires a disciplined scientific imagination.

When a non-random pattern is identified, the first step is to undertake a series of experiments to determine the range of conditions under which it appears. Then the processes which generate the pattern are to be looked for in the natures of the things and materials involved. It is the fact that these are usually not known that brings into action the model building process. The creative task is to invent a plausible analogue of the mechanism which is really producing the phenomenon. (Harré 1976: 21)

A frequently quoted example of how this process works is the case of the discovery of viruses. Certain diseases could not be explained by the presence of bacterial agents. Viruses were postulated to explain their occurrence and in time their existence and mode of operation was demonstrated. The same process led to the 'discovery' of the structure of the atom. Initially, atoms were hypothetical entities; only after some time were they actually observed. Similarly, the genetic explanation for inherited characteristics started as an idea which took hundreds of years to establish.

Some mechanisms may be reasonably accessible by the use of instruments which provide a modest extension of the senses, such as in biology by the dissection of organisms. Quasi-accessible mechanisms can be discovered from empirical studies, particularly of an exploratory kind, with an input from an associated field of knowledge in which some process is used as an analogy for the one under investigation. For example, the behaviour of electricity might be understood as being analogous to a hydraulic system of water in pipes. 'Accessible mechanisms are discovered wholly by exploration, quasi-accessible mechanisms by a joint method of exploration and imagination' (Harré and Secord 1972: 73). The discovery of inaccessible mechanisms requires a combination of reason and imagination and the use of iconic models in which the inaccessible mechanism is represented by a real or imagined thing or process.

Typically, then, the construction of an explanation for ... some identified phenomenon will involve the building of a model, utilizing such cognitive materials and operating under the control of something like a logic of analogy and metaphor, of a mechanism, which *if* it were to exist and act in the postulated way would account for the phenomenon in question (a movement of thought which may be styled 'retroduction'). The reality of the postulated explanation must then, of course, be subjected to empirical scrutiny ... Once this has been done, the explanation must then in principle itself be explained. (Bhaskar 1979: 15)

For Bhaskar, science conceived in this way involves three closely inter-related steps. First, a phenomenon, or range of phenomena, is identified, explanations based on the postulated existence of a generative mechanism are constructed and empirically tested, and this mechanism then becomes the phenomenon to be explained, and so on. Hence, Realist science involves a process of description, explanation and redescription, in which layers of reality are continually exposed.

This process is analogous to pealing the layers off the proverbial onion. As one set of structures and mechanisms is postulated, tested and 're- vealed', others at a 'lower' level go through the same process. Distinctions between the domains of the *actual* and the *real* therefore keep changing as the strata of reality are unfolded; reality has *ontological depth*. 'In this continuing process, as deeper levels or strata of reality are successively unfolded, science must construct and test its explanations with the cogni- tive resources and physical tools at its disposal, which in this process are themselves progressively transformed, modified and refined' (Bhaskar 1979: 15).

The Retroductive research strategy can be summarized as follows.

1   In order to explain observable phenomena, and the regularities that obtain between them, scientists must attempt to discover appropriate structures and mechanisms.
2   Since these structures and mechanisms will typically be unavailable to observation, we first construct a model of them, often drawing upon already familiar sources.
3   The model is such that, were it to represent correctly these structures and mechanisms, the phenomena would than be causally explained.
4   We then proceed to test the model as a hypothetical description of actually existing entities and their relations. To do so, we work out further consequences of the model (that is, additional to the phenomena we are trying to explain), that can be stated in a manner open to empirical testing.
5   If these tests are successful, this gives good reason to believe in the existence of these structures and mechanisms.
6   It may be possible to obtain more direct confirmation of these existen- tial claims, by the development and use of suitable instruments.
7   The whole process of model-building may then be repeated, in order to explain the structures and mechanisms already discovered (Harré 1961; Keat and Urry 1975: 35).

The Use of Models in the Natural Sciences

The use of models and analogies has a long history in the natural sciences. However, more recent discussions have been directed to overcoming the deficiencies of Positivism and Critical Rationalism, and avoiding the ex- tremes of Kuhn's paradigmatic relativism (Hesse 1976: 2).

Harré (1970) has identified some common uses for the term 'model'. For example: the parliaments of many countries have been *modelled on* the British Parliament; the dress was *modelled by* Mary; the image was *modelled in* clay; she made a living *modelling for* the art class; he was a *model* or ideal husband; she bought the latest *model* car.

Various attempts have been made to classify models (see, for example, Black 1962; Achinstein 1968; Harré 1970). Five main types of model have been used in the natural sciences; representational, analogue, mathematical, theoretical and imaginary.

1   In *representational* models the characteristics of importance to the scientist are reproduced to scale, either larger of smaller, although different scales may be used for various characteristics, e.g. for length and width.
2   In *analogue* models other objects or systems are used to represent the object or phenomenon under investigation; they share, more abstractly, the same structure or pattern of relationships as the original, e.g. when the structure of the atom is modelled on the movement of planets around the sun.
3   *Mathematical models* involve a translation into a set of abstract terms and functions of a different 'language'; the model is conceived of as being simpler and more abstract than the original.
4   *Theoretical models* consist of extending a familiar theory into a new domain of application; they draw from some more basic theory or theories a set of assumptions about an object or system, including its inner structure, composition or mechanism. Theoretical models differ from theories in that they use approximations, omit complicating factors, and introduce idealised relationships.
5   *Imaginary models* are similar to theoretical models in some respects and to analogue models in other respects. An object or system is described in terms of a certain set of assumptions to show how it would behave under certain conditions. Whether the model is plausible or even an approximation of what actually occurs is an open question.

An important distinction needs to be made between *models of* and *models for*. Some models *represent* the characteristics of a known object or phenomenon (a model of), while other models *speculate* on the characteristics of an unknown object or phenomenon (a model for). Harré distinguished between the source and the subject of a model. The *subject* of a model is what it is intended to represent; it is a model of. The *source* is whatever the model is based on; what has been used to construct it. He identified two broad categories of models (1970): *homeomorphs*, where the subject is also the source of the model as, for example, in a model aeroplane; and, *paramorphs*, where the subject and the source differ as, for example, when models of unknown mechanisms are constructed. Homeomorphs are models *of* a subject, and are modelled *on* the same subject as a source. Paramorphs are models *for* an unknown subject, the processes and things which are responsible for the phenomena being studied, and are modelled *on* things and process we know or imagine (adapted from Harré 1972: 174–5). Thus, scale models are homeomorphs, and analogue, mathematical, theoretical and imaginary models are various forms of paramorph.

A model of an unknown mechanism can be both a paramorph and a homeomorph. It is a paramorph of that unknown mechanism, constructed in the hope that the behaviour of the mechanism hypothesized in the model may be parallel to the behaviour of the actual mechanism. But it is also a homeomorph with respect to each of the sources on which it is modelled. For example, Darwin's hypothetical mechanism of 'the process of natural selection' is a paramorph of the real but unknown processes by which biological change occurs. But is also a homeomorph of the domestic breeding of species without the deliberate acts of the breeder and of Malthus's theory of the effect of population pressure on the division of resources (Harré 1970: 57–8).

To have scientific value, a paramorph must be existentially plausible. It is possible to construct models which can introduce existential novelty, that propose the existence of a mechanism which is in conflict with what is currently known to exist. In some cases such models will be discarded even though later changes in the way the world is viewed would have made them acceptable. However, there are some models, such as the Bohr–Rutherford atom, that seemed to contain unacceptable notions but which turned out to be extremely plausible and useful. Unfortunately, there are no logical or routine procedures for establishing plausibility. 'Plausibility for a model is determined partly by the slowly changing general assumptions of the scientific community as to what the world is really like, partly by the way the model fits in to the particular circumstances for which it was created' (Harré 1970: 50).

The Retroductive research strategy, therefore, involves the building of models in order to explain some observed regularity. The models used are likely to be of the theoretical or imaginary type (Achinstein) or paramorphs (Harré).

> [T]heory construction is primarily model building, in particular imagining paramorphs. Imagined paramorphs involve imaginary processes among real and imagined entities. The crucial point for the understanding of science is that in either case they may invite existential questions, since like homeo-morphs, they introduce additional entities other than the given, provided it seems plausible to treat them as causal mechanisms. It is through imagined paramorphs and their connection with their sources, multiple, single, semi or fragmentary, that theoretical terms gain part, and a vital part, of their meaning ... A scientific explanation of a process or pattern among pheno-mena is provided by a theory constructed in this way. (Harré 1970: 46–7)

The Use of Models in the Social Sciences

One common view of the concept 'model' in the social sciences is to equate it with a formalized theory, i.e. with an integrated set of propositions which state relationships between various concepts and which have been successfully subjected to empirical testing. This is sometimes referred to as a *theoretical* model. When the propositions are translated into symbolic terms, it might be referred to as a *mathematical* model. Alternatively, the concept 'theory' is sometimes regarded as being synonymous with a particular perspective (or paradigm), e.g. conflict theory or consensus theory, leading to expressions such as 'theoretical perspective' or 'general model'. Such perspectives might be more usefully regarded as 'meta-theories' which contain the principles and assumptions upon which the propositions of a theory are based.

A more restricted use of 'model' has been proposed by Willer (1967) in his distinction between 'theoretical models' and 'general models'. Theoretical models contain a rationale which explains the nature of the phenomena under study and provides the definitions of the concepts and the structure of their relationships. It is 'a conceptualization of a group of phenomena, constructed by means of a rationale, where the ultimate purpose is to furnish the terms and relations, the proposition, of a formal system which, if validated, becomes a theory' (Willer 1967: 15). A formal system (a set of propositions which have still to be tested) is derived from the model and, if successfully tested, will become a theory. The model provides the propositions for the theory. A rationale in a theoretical model of society, for example, would be the view of how the parts of society either come together to form a stable whole (the consensus model), or come into conflict with each other (the conflict model). The model might also contain a mechanism which describes the way a society moves from one stage of development to another.

What Harré (1972, 1976) had in mind for theories and models in both the natural and social sciences was different from these uses. Theories provide answers to the question: 'Why is it that the patterns of phenomena are the way they are?' The theory supplies an account of the constitution and behaviour of those things which, in their interactions with each other, produce the manifested pattern. His scheme has four main components: observed patterns, the generative mechanism, the iconic model and the source of ideas for the model. The relations between the iconic model and the generative mechanism are analogous since the observed pattern is produced by the iconic model hypothetically and by the generative mechanism actually, while the relations between the iconic model and the model source is metaphorical since the laws of behaviour of the iconic model are like the laws of behaviour of aspects of the model source. Harré used the example of the relationships between stage actors, social role-players and the patterned behaviour of people. The behaviour of people is analogous to imaginary social role players (hence the common use of the concept 'social actor') and these role players are, at least in some respects, like stage actors. The stage provides the source for the iconic model which, in turn, provides a hypothetical mechanism for the explanation of patterned behaviour (Harré 1979).

Harré (1976) has elaborated how models are used in what he has called the ethogenic point of view, an approach which draws on many aspects of Interpretivism. Human beings are regarded not as passive responders to the contingencies of their social world, but as agents who use theories about people and their situations, and a related social technology. In line with his interest in psychology, he regarded human powers as being ontologically basic and the social order as one of their epiphenomena.

A person's social capacities are viewed as being related to the cognitive equipment s/he possesses. As this cognitive equipment is not readily available for inspection by the social actor, by other social actors or by social scientists, it is necessary to construct models from the relevant fragments of the cognitive structure of the person. Social actors do this in their interaction with each other and social scientists need to do it in order to explain patterns in social life. Social actors construct models of people who they know well and with whom they interact on a regular basis, as well as of people who are more remote. Like Schütz and Giddens, Harré considered everyday methods of understanding as being of the same form as social scientific methods. 'Theories of social action, whether they are those held by an ordinary social actor in terms of which he [sic] develops his own action and construes the actions of others, or whether they are those special versions of that kind of theory developed by social scientists, have a similar structure' (Harré 1976: 25).

Ethogenists see the social world primarily in episodes of individual encounter. People bring their cognitive resources to these microsocial situations which are constrained by rules and social sanctions. In order to grasp these episodes, it is necessary to construct *homeomorphs* of them. Then *paramorphs* of the largely unknown natures of people, their cognitive resources, or psychological 'mechanisms', need to be constructed. And, finally, the macrostructures of the social world need to be identified, which, according to Harré, exist only as iconic models within people's minds as part of their cognitive resources for interaction management.

Social episodes range from formal social acts which can be identified as rituals, to informal or enigmatic interactions which lack any explicit rules, the ceremonial nature of which actors may not be aware. The enigmatic episodes are understood by using formal episodes as a model.

> Thus, the structure of an enigmatic episode is conceived of on the model of a formal episode comparable as to social act achieved, while the mechanism by which the episode is produced is conceived of on the model of the mechanism by which the formal episode is produced, namely explicit rule-following. In this way we generate both a homeomorph of the episode, and a paramorph of the processes of its production. (Harré 1976: 30–1)

Harré set his approach within the context of Goffman's dramaturgical perspective. He identified two types of homeomorphic model for identifying episodes: the ritual or *liturgical model*, and the game or *agonistic model*. They are of equal importance as a source of paramorphic models, and can both be used to provide concepts for analysing the content of elements, moves, actions and sayings of social interaction. He also proposed four kinds of *models of people*: the *ethogenic*, the *cybernetic*, the *system theoretic* and the *physiological*. These models are links in a chain: at one end is the interaction of a social episode; it can be modelled in terms of rule-following (ethogenic model); this can then be modelled mathematically as a series of operations (cybernetic model); this, in turn, can be modelled on an abstract structure which could perform in a way described in the cybernetic model (system-theoretic model); and, finally, it can take concrete form in an iconic model of the nervous system (Harré 1976).

In addition to these four kinds of person models, Harré suggested that social actors use models of the social order, such as 'the class system'. He regarded the social order as nothing more than the models people have of an imaginary structure, and these models are part of the cognitive resources used in the management of social interaction. 'Each person has a mode of representing to himself the structure of the social world, and he [sic] manages his social action, when rules and habits run out, by reference to that representation' (Harré 1976: 37). These images of society are models in a double sense: they are models *for* a reality which has to be constructed for people to inhabit; and they are modelled *on* some real or imagined view of the world. These models of the social order may be realistic in that they relate to real differences in the world, such as people being viewed as either male or female, or they may be fictitious in that they picture the social world as a structure which is 'brought to the world' rather than being 'derived from it'.

An important difference between the natural and social sciences with regard to model building is that the natural scientist creates models of an existing world whereas social actors create the world based on some model.

In an analysis of the theories about people and their social actions that we deploy in the management of ourselves and our interaction with others, images of society have the place that metaphysical visions of the world have in natural science. The image of society gives us our ideas of what roles there can be, and then we discover empirically if they are filled, how and by whom – the only difference from natural science being the crucial fact that we can and do construct worlds to fulfil images. (Harré 1976: 36)

These constructions of the social world need to be used as elements in explanations.

At the end of the day, the social scientist has to establish the plausibility of the iconic models that have been created as a surrogate for a generative mechanism. How can this be done? Harré has argued that the Deductivist strategy, of making predictions as a way of testing an explanation, is unsatisfactory because 'the source of a model of the unknown inner structure of some entity is usually sufficiently rich to allow ameliorating additions to be made to the original model should it fail hypothetico-deductively, additions whose pedigree ensures they escape the stricture of being merely *ad hoc*' (Harré 1976: 38). There are also limits to the observations that can be made to test existential models, these being the extent to which the senses can be extended by the use of instruments.

To a large extent, models will be regarded as being plausible if they conform to the scientific worldview dominant in the particular discipline or scientific community at the time. Models that lie outside the ontological assumptions of the worldview will have great difficulty in being accepted; the worldview determines what will be considered as real.

These models go beyond what participants can report about a social episode, and involve elements and structures of which they are unaware and, perhaps, could never become aware. However, according to Harré, their authenticity can be checked by endeavouring to replicate the social processes based on the assumptions contained in the model. If this is successful, the model can be assumed to be analogous to those cognitive structures which produced the patterns of behaviour. He considered the best check on the model would be to locate the physiological mechanisms that produced the social behaviour, although he recognized that this is impossible at present and will be unlikely for some time to come.

The Abductive Research Strategy

The Abductive research strategy is based on the Hermeneutic tradition, and is used by Interpretivism and approaches which include Interpretive ontological and epistemological elements, such as Critical Theory, Realism, Structuration Theory and Feminism. Abduction is the process used to produce social scientific accounts of social life by drawing on the concepts and meanings used by social actors, and the activities in which they engage.

Interpretivism takes what Positivism and Critical Rationalism ignore – that is, the meanings and interpretations, the motives and intentions, which people use in their everyday lives, and which direct their behaviour – and elevates them to the central place in social theory and research. For Interpretivism, the social world *is* the world perceived and experienced by its members, from the 'inside'. Hence, the task of the social scientist is to discover and describe this 'insider' view, not to impose an 'outsider' view on it. Therefore, the major task of Interpretive social science is to discover why people do what they do by uncovering the largely tacit, mutual knowledge, the symbolic meanings, intentions and rules, which provide the orientations for their actions. It is the everyday beliefs and practices, the mundane and taken for granted, which have to be grasped and articulated in order to provide an understanding of these actions. Mutual knowledge is background knowledge that is largely unarticulated, it is constantly being used and modified by social actors as they interact with each other – it is produced and reproduced by them in the course of their lives together.

The Abductive strategy has many layers to it. The basic access to any social world is the accounts that people can give of their own actions and

the actions of others. These accounts contain the concepts that the participants use to structure their world, and the 'theories' that they use to account for what goes on. However, much of the activity of social life is
routine, and is conducted in a taken-for-granted, unreflective attitude. It is
when enquiries are made about their behaviour by others (such as social
scientists) or when social life is disrupted, and/or ceases to be predictable,
that social actors are forced consciously to search for or construct meanings and interpretations. Therefore, the social scientist may have to resort
to procedures which encourage this reflection in order to discover the
meanings and theories. Ultimately, it is necessary to piece together the
fragments of meaning that are available from their externalized products.

For some Interpretivists, reporting social actors' accounts is all that
is possible and necessary in order to understand social life. Others are
prepared to turn these accounts into descriptions of the way of life of a
particular social group (community or society) but they would insist on
keeping such descriptions tied closely to the language that the social actors
use. However, once these descriptions are produced, the Interpretivist may
then wish to understand them in terms of some existing social theory or
perspective. A different group of Interpretivists will generate abstract
descriptions, or even theories, from the descriptions produced from social
actors' accounts.

These layers can be summarized as follows:

Everyday concepts and meanings

provide the basis for

Social action/interaction

about which

Social actors can give accounts

from which

Social scientific descriptions can be made

from which   OR   and understood in terms of

Social theories can be generated   *Social theories or perspectives*

In whatever way it is described, the relationship between everyday or
lay concepts and meanings and social scientific or technical concepts and
theories is, according to Bhaskar (1979: 198), the central question of method
in the social sciences. However, it still remains a largely neglected area of
concern among social theorists and social researchers. *It is to the process
of moving from lay descriptions of social life, to technical descriptions of
that social life, that the notion of Abduction is applied.*

The following review of Abductive strategies is selective; it includes
only those Interpretivists who are concerned with achieving explanation
and excludes those concerned primarily with description. For example,

because ethnomethodology does not attempt to construct theory from members' methods, it has been excluded from consideration. The review begins with Weber's use of ideal types as a means for developing explanations. However, Schütz and Winch can be regarded as providing the foundation for the Abductive research strategy. There follows a review of more recent developments in the US, in Douglas's social phenomenology or existential sociology, and adaptations of the Abductive strategy in Britain by Rex and Giddens. And, finally, the rather different use of Abduction in the Grounded Theory of Glaser and Strauss will be discussed, the difference being the relative lack of concern with social actors' meanings and a primary focus on the generation of theory from data.

Weber's Ideal Types

In the process of trying to establish a science of subjective meanings, Weber did not specifically address the problem of the relationship between languages. His ideal types, which incorporated the social actors' intended meanings, required the investigator to construct them. Weber wanted sociology to be a generalizing science in which abstract concepts are used to represent actual historical events and concrete courses of action. For him, sociology is concerned with generalizations and causal explanations of historically and culturally important phenomena, and with the analysis of individual actions, structures and processes possessing cultural significance. '[S]ociological analysis both abstracts from reality and at the same time helps us to understand it, in that it shows with what degree of approximation a concrete historical phenomenon can be subsumed under one or more of these concepts' (Weber 1964: 109–10).

Weber dealt with the relationship between such abstract concepts of meaningful action and concrete historical meaningful action by means of ideal types. They are abstractions, constructed by the social scientist to approximate an actual state of affairs, and they must have 'the highest possible degree of logical integration by virtue of their complete adequacy on the level of meaning' (1964: 110). The notion of 'adequacy on the level of meaning' was central to his concern with both generating adequate explanations and ensuring that these explanations are related to the actual meaning actors use. The action under consideration must constitute a regular pattern, but no matter how regular (statistically probable) it is, it is not explained without providing the meanings which are typically associated with such action. Further, the meanings which ideal types contain must fit with *normal* expectations about the motives people acting in that particular situation would have. However, the question of whose view of normal is critical here.

Weber recognized that the process of constructing ideal types of subjective meaning associated with particular action entails some practical difficulties for the social scientist because people are not always aware of the meanings they are using.

The theoretical concepts of sociology are ideal types not only from the objective point of view, but also in their application to subjective processes. In the majority of cases actual action goes on in a state of inarticulate half-consciousness or actual unconsciousness of its subjective meaning. The actor is more likely to 'be aware' of it in a vague sense than he [sic] is to 'know' what he is doing or be explicitly self-conscious about it. In most cases his action is governed by impulse or habit. Only occasionally and, in the uniform action of large numbers often only in the case of a few individuals, is the subjective meaning of the action, whether rational or irrational, brought clearly into consciousness. The ideal type of meaningful action where the meaning is fully conscious and explicit is a marginal case. Every sociological or historical investigation, in applying its analysis to the empirical facts, must take this fact into account. But the difficulty need not prevent the sociologist from systematizing his concepts by the classification of possible types of subjective meaning. That is, he may reason as if action actually proceeded on the basis of clearly self-conscious meaning. (Weber 1964: 111–12)

For Weber, then, it is up to the social scientist to construct a hypothetical ideal type of meaning that might account for the action under consideration, and then proceed to test this hypothesis. Rex has summarized the procedure as follows.

What we mean by the verification of an ideal type of meaningful action is this. We posit that, in controlled and fully ascertainable circumstances, a particular explanation is applicable. This particular explanation may include other such notions as goals, means, norms, conditions and other elements. We then argue that, if our claim as to the applicability of this ideal type is valid, certain empirical events will occur. If they do occur we may then say that our ideal type is verified (or, more modestly, following Popper, that it has not been falsified). (Rex 1974: 41)

Clearly, Weber's strategy for developing ideal types is able to circumvent a direct exploration of the actual meanings used by social actors. He ends up with what looks very like a very Popperian method but which also has some similarity to Realism; the postulated typical meaning could be regarded as a model of mechanism. However, it must be acknowledged that in his own historical work he had little option but to proceed this way.

Schütz's First-order and Second-order Constructs

Schütz, like Weber, was also concerned with the problem of how to generate concepts and theories of subjective meaning structures. He accepted Weber's view that this can be achieved by the use of ideal types but he adopted a different conception of their nature and origin. Whereas Weber was prepared to allow the sociologist to attribute typical meaning to an ideal type, Schütz insisted that social scientists' types (second-order

constructs) must be derived from everyday typifications (first-order constructs) which constitute social actors' social reality.

> The thought objects constructed by the social scientist, in order to grasp this
> social reality, have to be founded upon the thought objects constructed by
> the common-sense thinking of men [sic], living their daily life within their
> social world. Thus, the constructs of the social sciences are, so to speak,
> constructs of the second degree, that is, constructs of the constructs made by
> the actors on the social scene, whose behaviour the social scientist has to
> observe and to explain. (Schütz, 1963a: 242)

The critical difference between first- and second-order constructs is that
they are constructed with different purposes in mind and within different
contexts. First-order constructs take a particular social stock of everyday
knowledge for granted and are designed to deal with a social problem – to
make social interaction possible and understandable to the participants.
Second-order constructs are designed to deal with a social scientific problem – to explain social phenomena – and have to relate to a sometimes
taken-for-granted social scientific stock of knowledge (Schütz, 1963b:
337–9).

The move from first-order to second-order constructs requires the social
scientist to select from the activities and meanings of everyday life those
considered to be relevant to the purpose at hand and to construct models
of the social world – typical social actors with typical motives and typical
courses of action in typical situations.

> Yet these models of actors are not human beings living within their bio-
> graphical situation in the social world of everyday life. Strictly speaking, they
> do not have any biography or any history, and the situation into which they
> are placed is not a situation defined by them but defined by their creator, the
> social scientist. He [sic] has created these puppets or homunculi to manipu-
> late them for his purpose. A merely specious consciousness is imputed to
> them by the scientist, which is constructed in such a way that its presupposed
> stock of knowledge at hand (including the ascribed set of invariant motives)
> would make actions originating from it subjectively understandable, pro-
> vided that these actions were performed by real actors within the social
> world. (Schütz 1963b: 339–40)

Therefore, Schütz claimed that all scientific knowledge of the social world
is indirect. The social sciences cannot understand people as living individuals, each with a unique consciousness. Rather, they can only be understood as personal ideal types existing in an impersonal and anonymous
time which no one has actually experienced or can experience.

> In the process of ideal-typical construction, subjective meaning-contexts that
> can be directly experienced are successively replaced by a series of objective
> meaning-contexts. These are constructed gradually, each one upon its suc-
> cessor, and they interpenetrate one another in Chinese-box fashion, so that

it is difficult to say where one leaves off and the other begins. However, it is precisely this process of construction which makes it possible for the social scientist, or indeed for any observer, to understand what the actor means. (Schütz 1976: 241–2).

According to Schütz, ideal types are constructed by the social scientist on the assumption that the social action is rational, that if a person were to perform the typified action with full knowledge of all the elements which the social scientist has included as being relevant, and only those elements, then using the most appropriate means available s/he would achieve the goals as defined by the ideal type (Schütz 1963b: 334). Thus ideal types are models of rational (means–end) action and, as such, can be compared with actual social action as a way of developing understanding. In addition, elements of a model can be varied in order to produce several models, the outcomes of which can be compared. Like Weber, Schütz wished to develop explanations from ideal types which he regarded as theoretical systems embodying testable hypotheses (1963a: 246).

The ultimate constraint on the researcher in constructing ideal types is contained in Schütz's *postulate of adequacy*. He argued that the concepts of social science have to remain consistent with common-sense, first-order concepts.

Each term in a scientific model of human action must be constructed in such a way that a human act performed within the life-world by an individual actor in the way indicated by the typical construct would be understandable for the actor himself as well as for his fellow-men [sic] in terms of common-sense interpretation of everyday life. (Schütz 1963b: 343)

In short, if social actors cannot identify with the types which have been constructed to represent their actions or situations, then the researcher has either got it wrong or has strayed too far from the concepts of everyday life.

Winch's Lay Language and Technical Language

Whereas Weber and Schütz were concerned with meanings and motives, Winch (1958) argued that social behaviour is to be understood as rule-following behaviour and not as causally regular behaviour; rules provide the reasons and the motives, the meaning for behaviour. Like Schütz, Winch was concerned with the relationship between the language of the social actors and the language used by investigators. He discussed this in the context of observing regularities and how judgements are made that the same action has been performed. He recognized that as the only language available in the natural sciences is that of the investigator, rules for making such decisions will be those derived from this language. However, in the social sciences, two languages and hence two sets of rules are available; those of the social scientist and those of the participants. It is the rules associated with human activity, 'rather than those which govern the sociologist's investigations, which specify what is to count as "doing the same kind of thing" in relation to that kind of activity' (1958: 87). The judgement needs to be made from the context of the investigation, not from the context of the investigator.

Winch was also concerned with the problem of understanding other forms of life, particularly those with a very different language and culture from that of the investigator. This issue concerns what is involved in understanding, interpreting and explaining alien societies, their beliefs, rituals, institutions and practices, without distorting them (Bernstein 1983: 28). Or it is 'how to make intelligible in our terms institutions belonging to a primitive [sic] culture, whose standards of rationality and intelligibility are apparently quite at odds with our own' (Winch 1964: 315). This, of course, is the central problem addressed by the Hermeneutic approach.

Winch took the position 'that the concepts used by primitive peoples can only be interpreted in the context of the way of life of those peoples' (1964: 315). He objected to the ethnocentric attitude in which the rationality of alien cultures is judged in terms of the criteria of rationality used in the culture of the investigator. He therefore introduced the distinction between 'our standards' and 'their standards' of rationality, and argued that beliefs and practices in alien cultures must be understood in terms of 'their standards', not ours.

> Winch seems to be suggesting that forms of life may be so radically different from each other that in order to understand and interpret alien or primitive societies we not only have to bracket our prejudices and biases but have to suspend our Western standards and criteria of rationality. We may be confronted with standards of rationality about beliefs and actions that are incompatible with or incommensurable with our standards. (Bernstein 1983: 27)

The outcome of this argument is to raise the spectre of relativism which most philosophers appear to be unable to handle. It also raises questions about Weber's use of *verstehen* in terms of the observer's attribution of meaning.

Winch offered very little help on how to grasp 'their standards' except to say that by learning the language of the alien culture it may be possible to discover the rules which people follow, and hence to understand their activities as they understand them.

For Winch, the relationship between lay language and technical language involves building the latter on the former, but he was not dogmatic about restricting technical concepts to those derived from lay concepts. He considered that while the social scientist may find it necessary to use concepts which are not derived from the form of life being investigated, but are drawn from the technical concepts of the discipline, these latter concepts will, nevertheless, imply an understanding of social actors' concepts. He used the example of the concept of 'liquidity preference' in economics, a concept which is not generally used by people in business to conduct their everyday activities but which is used by economists to explain certain kinds of business behaviour.

> Winch does not forbid us to go on from there; we can analyse religion, politics, art or whatever else, in a way that the participants do not. The claim is not one which dictates where our inquires shall end, but one which says where they can logically be said to start; and the claim is that whatever we may go on to say, we must root our story in that which is told by the agents themselves. (Ryan 1970: 143)

Douglas's Theoretic Stance

Douglas's existential sociology is based on a rejection of absolutist approaches to social science.[2] He relied heavily on Schütz and Garfinkel but went beyond both of them. The critical questions for Douglas were what stance to adopt towards everyday life and what methods of analysis to use. He argued that there is no alternative to

> some form of communication with the members of that society or group; and, to be valid and reliable, any such communication with the members presupposes an understanding of their language, their uses of that language, their own understandings of what the people doing the observations are up to, and so on almost endlessly. (1971: 9)

Douglas identified two alternatives to the *absolutist* (or objectivist) stance towards everyday life. The *natural* stance, the opposite extreme, is the largely taken-for-granted stance of individuals in their everyday life.[3] The other alternative, the *theoretic* (or phenomenological) stance, treats the everyday world as a phenomenon. 'To take the theoretic stance toward the everyday world is to stand back from, to reflect upon, to re-view the experience taken for granted in the natural stance' (Douglas 1971: 15). In addition to systematically studying the common-sense meanings and actions of everyday life on their own terms, the social scientist 'must then seek an ever more general, trans-situational (objective) understanding of everyday life' (1971: x).

---

[2] Douglas defined an absolutist perspective as one 'which assumes that human actions are independent of the specific situations in which they occur, in the sense that they are determined by some factors outside of the situation and outside of the individual's committing the actions' (1971: 9n).
[3] The natural stance, and its application as a research strategy, referred to as naturalistic sociology or naturalism, must be distinguished from the naturalism associated with positivism. The two are at opposite ends of the methodological spectrum.

A major feature of Douglas's position is that everyday life must be studied on its own terms.

> The first fundamental methodological commitment of those phenomenological sociologists committed to taking the theoretic stance toward everyday life is *to study the phenomena of everyday life on their own terms, or to make use only of methods of observation and analysis that retain the integrity of the phenomena.* This means most simply that the phenomena to be studied must be the phenomena as experienced in everyday life, not phenomena created by (or strained through) experimental situations. (Douglas 1971: 16)

Douglas was critical of the American branch of Interpretivism known as Behavioural Interactionism (represented by Denzin 1970); while it accepts the commitment to take everyday life as *the* social reality, it imposes its own concepts and forms of reasoning on it rather than using the concepts and forms of reasoning of the social actors (Douglas 1971: 17). In other words, these so-called Interpretivists tend to work with Positivistic (or absolutist) principles and, what is more, fail to see the conflict in adopting incompatible approaches. '[T]here remains a great difference between taking everyday life as the primary reality (but partially studying this reality with conventional absolutist methods and ideas) and systematically studying it in such ways as to consistently retain the integrity of the phenomena' (1971: 18).

Douglas was comfortable with the other American branch of Interpretivism known as Phenomenological Interactionism. However, he argued that a commitment to studying Phenomena on their own terms is not necessarily associated with the theoretic stance. Some Interpretivists have adopted a *naturalistic* approach in which any form of generalization is rejected. There is a lack of concern with issues of objectivity and subjectivity and an apparent belief that a presuppositionless understanding of social life is possible; there is no awareness of the problem of the theory-dependence of observations.

> By failing to make an initial commitment to the theoretic stance, all naturalistic sociologies, the most famous of which is the work of Erving Goffman, wind up largely restricting themselves to the description (or rendition, as Matza calls it) of experience and then treating that description as if it constituted the entirety of justifiable generalization (or theory). Even in their most serious forms, which Matza's certainly is, these naturalistic arguments have made the classical error of assuming it is possible to establish a presuppositionless understanding of everyday life, that is, an understanding that will somehow go beyond the common-sense understandings of the members in everyday life and yet be founded entirely on that experience and will, therefore, be entirely comprehensible (or recapturable) by any member retaining the natural stance of that common sense. (Douglas 1971: 20–1)

To some extent, Douglas regarded the manner in which Schütz's postulate of adequacy has been applied as encouraging naturalistic sociology. He preferred to use the postulate as a useful rule-of-thumb test in doing field research rather than a general principle which restricts any divergence from first-order descriptions of everyday life.

In taking the middle ground between the two extremes of absolutist (Positivist) and naturalist sociology, Douglas recognized that the problem of objectivity had to be addressed. If presuppositions do enter into the research process, and the positivistic strategies for establishing objectivity cannot be accepted, some other solution must be found. In brief, his solution was to define objective knowledge as useful knowledge and useful knowledge as shareable knowledge. The shareability of knowledge is achieved

> by progressively freeing the knowledge of concrete phenomena from the situation in which they are known ... Moreover, this freeing is done not by making the knowledge objectlike or thinglike but by so examining the situation in which we do the knowing that we are able to (partially) specify the ways in which another observer would go about constructing the same kind of situation. (Douglas 1971: 28)

He was not interested in establishing fundamental truths about everyday life but in seeking partial (objective) truths which will be replaced as 'deeper' analyses of everyday life are undertaken.

Therefore, Douglas not only separated his kind of sociology from the Positivistic versions predominant in the United States at the time, but he also distanced himself from the main versions of Interpretivism being practised there. His position, however, is derived from an understanding of the later figures in the Hermeneutic approach and turns out to have a close affinity with the British tradition represented by Winch, Rex and Giddens. Douglas summarized his position thus.

> The fundamental challenge of the sociological endeavour today must be to develop (objective) useful knowledge of the complex gamut of everyday life, from unspoken exchanges of love to scientists' explicitly detailed search for transsituational knowledge, from mindless passions of angry mobs caught up in 'the spirit of the moment' to systematic planning and construction of new societies – and a new world order in which pluralistic differences are balanced against universal orderings. To do this we must always begin with the members' understandings of their situations, but as we increase our understandings we must seek to transcend the members' understandings to create transsituational (objective) knowledge. Just as there is an essential tension between the situational and transsituational aspects of human existence, so is there an essential tension between the sociologist's new-found commitments to the integrity of the phenomena and to the theoretic stance. No doubt our objective knowledge will always remain partially grounded in the unexplicated situations of everyday use, but this is only to recognize that the scientific existence shares the ultimate absurdity of everyday life. (Douglas 1971: 44)

Rex's Neo-Weberianism

Like Schütz before him, Rex (1971, 1974) used Weber as the major foundation for his approach to sociology. He wished to develop Weber's view of sociology further, while at the same time avoiding the extremes of Positivism – which neglects actors' meanings – and what he called empirical phenomenology – which is concerned with them exclusively. Rex, like Giddens, also drew on Schütz and Garfinkel and he was sympathetic with Habermas's Critical Theory. In this latter respect, Rex regarded his approach as 'unashamedly a moral one' of liberating people from oppression, a position no doubt derived from his intense interest in racism. He was anti-positivist but not anti-science. For Rex, the subject matter of sociology is the 'structure of social relations, whether these be changing and conflictual or stable and harmonious, and whether they are based upon shared and agreed meanings or upon confusions and misunderstandings' (1974: 34). He regarded social structures as being these structures of social relations.

Rex also addressed the question of the relationship between actors' constructs and sociologists' theories. The language and meanings used by social actors in everyday life are the 'first and most elementary givens' for the sociologist; it is necessary to 'learn the language' before establishing ideal types. The question then becomes in what ways, and to what extent, are these ideal types different from the concepts and meanings used by the social actors.

While recognizing that actors' theories have some role in the process of formulating ideal types, he acknowledged that the former are distinct from the latter.

> For, whereas the actor's use of meanings is open-ended, situation-bound, and often inconsistent, the sociologist who uses these meanings in order to provide definitions and rules of transformation in his [sic] ideal typical theory when he uses it for explanatory purposes can, if he wishes, always subject the interpretations and meanings which he takes over from the actor to some kind of test, and he is likely to do so when he finds himself in dispute with his fellow sociologists. He may then argue with them about the internal consistency of the concepts being used and about whether or not the descriptions of the social and cultural world used by the actor are justifiable or not. It should be noted here that, although the ethnomethodologists and other phenomenologically-oriented sociologists believe that the 'integrity of the phenomenon' should be preserved and that meddling with or seeking to alter 'members' theories' is undesirable, they do none the less probe the members' meanings which they encounter ... One can, in fact, represent a very large part of the task of the sociologist as that of cleaning up and systematising the language of common sense and everyday life. (Rex 1974: 47, 49)

Therefore, Rex did not believe that actors' meanings and accounts should be accepted uncritically. Like Marx, he acknowledged that people may suffer from 'false consciousness', that they may have an inadequate understanding of the broader social context and their place within it. He argued that there has to be a role for social scientists to give different and competing accounts of social actors' activities. However, this creates a problem for social scientists in being able to demonstrate that their accounts have a greater claim to acceptance. In the end, Rex claimed that 'sociology can give a different and competing account of the meaning of action, not that it can give a true and objective account. None the less, this does not mean that the sociologist's account is yet another account, no better than that of any ideologist or of the actor himself [sic]' (1974: 48). He endeavoured to steer a course between justifications based on agreements between professionals, and those based on some belief system.

> An extreme view which is sometimes put in order to debunk sociological, as distinct from members', theories is that the question of what tests are to be used to decide between valid and invalid explanations rests upon agreement between the sociologists and that, therefore, the sociologist makes an 'act of faith' or is accused of subscribing to a religious or political theory of truth. There is some truth in this contention, but there are also ways of putting the matter which seem deliberately to distort what the sociologist does. If his [sic] procedures do depend upon agreement between his own sub-community of like-minded sociologists, and this is called a 'political theory of truth', it is still none the less important to bear in mind that we are not saying, for example, that what is true or not true is decided for political purposes by a political party. (Rex 1974: 48)

Ultimately, Rex believed in a non-trivial sociology, one which is 'able to describe the macro socio-political structures of the modern world, and the way in which more intimate and personal structures are articulated with them' (1974: 34). He was not interested in general theoretical systems but rather with systematically developed ideal types which make it possible to analyse aspects of social and historical situations. In the process, the ideal types remain linked to the language of everyday life.

> Unfortunately phenomenological sociologists and ethnomethodologists have too often sought to dissociate their work from all structural sociology, representing all that is not cast in terms of members' meanings or the actor's definition of the situation, as though it . . . takes no account of meaning . . . We believe that there is a kind of structural sociology of a Weberian kind which is based upon a dialogue of languages and which leads to a systematic sociological typology. It is in fact the closest of all sociologies to the work of the latter-day phenomenologists. But, unlike these, it still continues to interest itself in actual historical structures as they appear to the sociologist and not merely the structures which actors believe to exist, or believe that they make, in the process of thinking them to exist. (Rex 1974: 50)

Rex did not provide any details of how ideal types are to be derived from everyday language except to say that a process of abstraction was involved. He was nevertheless adamant that social theories are founded on everyday meanings. However, he was not averse to the sociologist both criticizing and generalizing from actors' accounts, and he wished, ultimately, to build sociological concepts and theories that include reference to 'real' social structures, or at least those that sociologists regard as real and of which social actors may be unaware. In this regard, he distanced himself from Schütz and Douglas and other phenomenologists and ethnomethodologists.

Giddens' Double Hermeneutic

Giddens' sociology is built on the fundamental principle that social life is a skilled performance which is made possible because competent members of society are practical social theorists who modify their theories about practical aspects of daily life on the basis of their experiences. The mutual knowledge which social actors use to negotiate their encounters with others and to make sense of social activity is regarded as the fundamental subject matter of social science. The social scientist cannot begin to describe any social activity without knowing what social actors know, either what they can report or what they tacitly assume, while engaging in social activity.

The processes involved in producing social scientific descriptions of this mutual knowledge are complex and diverse. According to Giddens, it depends on what has been described as 'the hermeneutic task of penetrating the frames of meaning' used by social actors, and requires the social scientist to immerse her/himself in the way of life of the group. This is particularly necessary when the culture of the group is very different from that of the researcher, as has traditionally been the case for anthropologists, but it is also necessary for social scientists who are conducting research within their own society. As developed societies are made up of many sub-cultures based, for example, on social class, ethnicity, age, gender and region, a researcher should not assume that the mutual knowledge used within his/her sub-culture is necessarily similar to that in other sub-cultures. Giddens has argued that while it is not necessary or usually possible for a social researcher to become a full member of such groups or communities, it *is* necessary that s/he learn enough about these ways of life to be able to participate in them at least to some degree.

The techniques available to the researcher to learn a way of life are the same techniques that are available to any person who wishes to become a member of a group or community. Understanding the meaning of what other people say and do is a skilled accomplishment of competent social actors, not the preserve of the professional social investigator (Giddens 1976b: 322). These techniques involve: observing and listening; asking questions about what is appropriate or inappropriate behaviour, and why it is appropriate or inappropriate; and reflexive monitoring of trial and error behaviour. The social scientist must draw on the same 'mutual knowledge' which social actors use to make sense of their activity. Without immersion there is no adequate understanding of what lies behind and structures overt behaviour. Social research has to deal with a social world that is already constituted as meaningful by its participants. In order to grasp this world it is necessary to get to know what social actors already know, and need to know in order to go about their daily activities.

The notion of the *double hermeneutic* is central to Giddens' view of the logic of the social sciences. Following Schütz and Habermas, he has argued that there is only a single hermeneutic in the natural sciences but there is a double hermeneutic in the social sciences.

> The social sciences operate within a double hermeneutic, involving two-way ties with the actions and institutions of those they study. Sociological observers depend upon lay concepts to generate accurate descriptions of social processes; and agents regularly appropriate theories and concepts of social science within their behaviour, thus potentially changing its character. (Giddens 1987: 30–1)

This process is identified as a double hermeneutic because it involves a dual process of translation or interpretation. First, the concepts and meanings used by social actors have to be translated into descriptions. Secondly, these descriptions can be translated into social theories. However, these translations are not just one-way: the relationship between lay concepts and technical concepts is a two-way process as social actors can reappropriate technical concepts into everyday language. 'There is a two-way relation involved between lay language and the language of social science, because any of the concepts introduced by sociological observers can in principle be appropriated by lay actors themselves, and applied as part of "ordinary language" discourse' (1979: 248).

Early in his work Giddens consolidated his views into a set of 'rules of sociological method'.

A1   *'Sociology is not concerned with a "pre-given" universe of objects, but one which is constituted or produced by the active doings of subjects.'* In transforming nature socially, human beings create history, and thence live *in* history, because the production and reproduction of society is not biologically programmed as it is in the lower animals.

A2   *'The production and reproduction of society thus has to be treated as a skilled performance on the part of its members,* not as merely a mechanical series of processes.'

C1   *'The sociological observer cannot make social life available as a "phenomenon" for observation independently of drawing upon his [sic] knowledge of it as a resource whereby he constitutes it as a "topic for investigation".* In *this* respect, his position is no different from that of any other member of society; "mutual knowledge" ... represents the interpretive schemes which both sociologists and laymen [sic] use, and must use, to "make sense" of social activity.'

C2 *'Immersion in a form of life is the necessary and only means whereby an observer is able to generate such characterizations ...* To "get to know" an alien form of life is to know how to find one's way about in it, to *be able* to participate in it as an ensemble of practices.' This mode of generating descriptions requires a transformation into the categories of social scientific discourse.

D1 *'Sociological concepts thus obey what I call a double hermeneutic:* (1) Any generalizing theoretical scheme in the natural or social sciences is in a certain sense a form of life in itself, the concepts of which have to be mastered as a mode of practical activity generating specific types of descriptions. That this is already a hermeneutic task is clearly demonstrated in the "newer philosophies of science" of Kuhn and others. (2) Sociology, however, deals with a universe which is already constituted within frames of meaning by social actors themselves, and reinterprets these within its own theoretical schemes, mediating ordinary and technical language. This double hermeneutic is of considerable complexity, since the connection is not merely a one-way one (as Schütz seems to suggest); there is a continual "slippage" of the concepts constructed in sociology, whereby these are appropriated by those whose conduct they were originally coined to analyse, and hence tend to become integral features *of* that conduct (thereby in fact potentially compromising their original usage within the technical vocabulary of social science).'

D2 *'In sum, the primary tasks of sociological analysis are the following: (1) The hermeneutic explication and mediation of divergent forms of life within descriptive metalanguages of social science; (2) Explication of the production and reproduction of society as the accomplished outcome of human agency'* (Giddens 1976a: 160–2).

Giddens, like Rex, was concerned that basing social theory on everyday language could lead to a 'paralysis of the critical will'.

It is right to claim that the condition of generating valid descriptions of a form of life entails being able in principle to participate in it (without necessarily having done so in practice). To know a form of life is to know a language, but in the context of the practices that are organised through the 'common sense' or tacit presuppositions against the background of which discourse is carried on. In this sense, hermeneutic tasks are integral to the social sciences. But it does not follow from such a conclusion that the beliefs and practices involved in forms of life cannot be subjected to critical assessment – including within this the critique of ideology. We must distinguish between *respect for the authenticity of belief* ... and the *critical evaluation of the justification of belief* ... [W]e must differentiate what I call 'mutual knowledge' from what might simply be called 'common sense' ... [M]utual knowledge is not corrigible to the sociological observer ... Common sense is corrigible in the light of claimed findings of social and natural science ... [W]e should not therefore succumb passively to a paralysis of the critical will ... [T]he critical evaluation of beliefs and practices is an inescapable feature of the discourse of the social sciences. (Giddens 1979: 251–3)

Mutual knowledge must be taken seriously if social activity is to be understood from the point of view of the participants; it is not corrigible to the social scientist. Common sense, on the other hand, is corrigible in terms of the findings of the natural and social sciences.

Glaser and Strauss's Grounded Theory

Finally, it is appropriate to review Grounded Theory, an Abductive strategy which is not necessarily Interpretive. Grounded Theory originated in the United States when Positivistic methods were in the ascendancy and Interpretive research was largely descriptive. Its founders, Glaser and Strauss, argued that sociological research methods in the 1960s were primarily concerned with improving the accuracy of measurement and with the rigorous testing of theory to the neglect of the prior step of discovering what concepts and hypotheses might be appropriate for the area under investigation. For them, the generation and testing of theories are of equal importance, and the two activities are intimately related. '[G]enerating theory goes hand in hand with verifying it; but many sociologists have been diverted from this truism in their zeal to test either existing theories or a theory that they have barely started to generate' (Glaser and Strauss 1968: 2).

Their solution was to generate theory from data by a process they described as inductive. This, they argued, will produce a theory that will fit and work, i.e. its concepts and categories will be appropriate, it will be meaningfully relevant, and it will be able both to explain and to predict the phenomena under study. Theory generation is seen to be intimately involved in the process of research rather than being something that precedes it. 'Generating a theory from data means that most hypotheses and concepts not only come from the data, but are systematically worked out in relation to the data during the course of the research' (Glaser and Strauss 1968: 6). This means that theoretical ideas that come from other sources – such as existing theories or one's own or other's insights – are not simply tested during the course of the research, as is the case with the Deductive strategy, but have to be worked out in relation to the data in a much less formal trial and error process. Theory generation is, therefore, an evolving process.

Glaser and Strauss advocated the use of the *constant comparative method*. As conceptual categories (or concepts) and their properties are generated from data gathered in one social context, their relevance can be explored in other contexts. In time it may be possible to establish the level of generality of these concepts.

[G]eneration by comparative analysis requires a multitude of carefully selected cases, but the pressure is *not* on the sociologist to 'know the whole
field' or to have all the facts 'from a careful random sample.' His [sic] job is
not to provide a perfect description of an area, but to develop a theory that
accounts for much of the relevant behavior. (Glaser and Strauss 1968: 30)

They used this process in their work with patients dying of cancer (Glaser
and Strauss 1965). For example, the concept of 'closed awareness context'
was developed to identify a feature of the research context in which
patients were not told that they were dying. The patient had to rely on
cues that might be hard to read until the last stages of their dying. Further
exploration of this phenomenon in other types of hospitals, and in other
countries, revealed that 'open awareness contexts' existed in a Japanese
hospital and in a prison medical ward. Hence cultural and structural differences began to emerge in what initially appeared to be a widespread
phenomenon.

In Grounded Theory, comparative analysis is used to generate two types
of theory – substantive and formal. Substantive theory is generated in
specific contexts and is related to a specific social process, such as dying.
Formal theory, on the other hand, is generated at a higher level of generality and involves concepts that can be applied to a number of substantive
areas.

By substantive theory, we mean that developed for a substantive, or empirical, area of sociological inquiry, such as patient care, race relations, professional education, delinquency, or research organizations. By formal theory,
we mean that developed for a formal, or conceptual area of sociological
inquiry, such as stigma, deviant behavior, formal organization, socialization,
status congruity, authority and power, reward systems, or social mobility.
(Glaser and Strauss 1968: 32)

While it is possible to borrow categories from existing theory, provided
it can be demonstrated that they fit the data, Glaser and Strauss preferred that new categories be developed. There is a tendency with borrowed
categories to select data to fit the category rather than using the data to
produce the category. They argued that there are many areas of everyday
life for which there are no appropriate categories and, even if borrowed
categories are used, their meanings are likely to undergo radical transformation.

The process of theory generation is one of trial and error in which
tentative hypotheses are entertained and informally tested in the context
of the continuing data gathering.

Whether the sociologist, as he [sic] jointly collects and analyzes qualitative
data, starts out in a confused state of noting almost everything he sees
because it all seems significant, or whether he starts out with a more defined
purpose, his work quickly leads to the generation of hypotheses. When he
begins to hypothesize with the explicit purpose of generating theory, the
researcher is no longer a passive receiver of impressions but is drawn natu-

rally into actively generating and verifying his hypotheses through comparison of groups. Characteristically, in this kind of joint data collection and analysis, multiple hypotheses are pursued simultaneously. Some are pursued over long periods of time because their generation and verification are linked with developing events. Meanwhile, new hypotheses are continually sought. (Glaser and Strauss 1968: 39)

The emphasis is on a process of observation and reflection, of continuing comparative analysis. As this proceeds, the emerging hypotheses may be integrated with other hypotheses into a formal theory. Glaser and Strauss suggested that the form of the theory is not important; it may be either a set of propositions, or a running argument. However, this integration should not be forced but, like the categories and hypotheses themselves, will go through a process of generation.

While Grounded Theory construction requires an integrated process of data collection, coding and analysis, Glaser and Strauss suggested that these aspects of research activity need to be separated into alternating stages. In the early stages, more time will be spent on collection than on coding and analysis but, as the research proceeds, the balance changes; towards the end, analysis predominates with only brief periods of collection to pick up loose ends. Analysis requires periods of detachment from the research site for coding and analytic memo-writing, for periods of reflection, especially in the early stages. Later, as categories become clearer, some analysis may occur simultaneously with data collection.

The authors used the concept of 'verification' of a theory ambiguously and uncritically; it is not clear whether they were referring to the Inductivist process of adding support, or the Deductivist process of testing. In practice, however, they considered the process of generation also to be a process of testing, and that no 'ultimate' critical testing is required. Grounded theories, they argued, are not easily refuted because they are intimately linked to data, but they are likely to be modified and reformulated as the research process continues. The publication of a report on the research is only a pause in the never-ending process of theory generation.

Grounded Theory was a reaction against the dominant Critical Rationalist methods of theory testing. As it makes little reference to the intellectual foundations of Interpretivism it must be regarded as a pragmatic strategy which has been developed in the context of research. Nevertheless, after all this time, Grounded Theory is still the most explicit exposition available of a genuine Abductive research strategy. However, its concepts are not explicitly derived from lay language but are labels which the researcher constructs for categories that are considered to organize the data. It is essentially a method of qualitative data-gathering and analysis, albeit one which departs radically from the linear logic and procedures characteristic of Positivism and Critical Rationalism.[4]

[4] For more recent expositions of the method see Turner (1981), Strauss (1987) and Strauss and Corbin (1990).

Combining Retroductive and Abductive Strategies

It is evident from the discussion in chapter 3 that aspects of the Abductive strategy have been incorporated into a number of contemporary approaches to social enquiry. Some form of Abduction provides the starting point for Critical Theory, Realism and Structuration Theory, and is the dominant strategy in Feminism. All these approaches accept that it is essential to have a description of the social world on its own terms, at least as the basis for the use of other strategies.

Habermas recognized the relevance of both Retroductive and Abductive strategies for an emancipatory social science, and Fay incorporated the Abductive strategy in his version of Critical Theory. However, it is in the work of Harré and Bhaskar that the combination of these two strategies is most fully realized. Harré's ethogenic approach is based on many features of an Interpretive ontology. The use of the Abductive strategy in this approach, to develop models of people, social episodes and the social order, is particularly clear. Harré and Secord have argued that lay explanations of behaviour provide the best model for psychological theory (1972: 29).

> At the heart of the explanation of social behaviour is the identification of the meanings that underlie it. Part of the approach to discovering them involves the obtaining of *accounts* – the actor's own statements about why he [sic] performed the acts in question, what social meanings he gave to the actions of himself and others. These must be collected and analysed, often leading to the discovery of the rules that underlie the behaviour ... An important tool in obtaining these meanings is ordinary language ... [which] should provide the basis for the concepts employed in a realistic psychology, and should serve as a model for other logical connections, and new concepts introduced by psychologists. (Harré and Secord 1972: 9–10)

In contrast to the dominant schools of psychology, which have been based on Positivism or Critical Rationalism, ethogeny insists that it is necessary to respect 'the intellectual capacities of ordinary human beings as managers and interpreters of the social world. Everyone is, in a certain sense, a fairly competent social scientist, *and we must not treat his (or her) theory about the social world and his place in it with contempt*' (Harré 1974: 244). However, while social actors' accounts are the starting point, and are taken seriously, they are not accepted uncritically. 'In order to be able to treat people as if they were human beings it must be possible to accept their commentaries upon their action as authentic, though reviseable, reports of phenomena, subject to empirical criticism' (Harré and Secord 1972: 101).

Review

As an alternative to Induction and Deduction, the long-standing strategy of Retroduction, associated with Realism in the natural sciences, has now been advocated as an appropriate strategy for the social sciences. Similarly, Abduction, an embryonic strategy in the Hermeneutic and Interpretive approaches to social enquiry, has been advocated as either the only suitable one for the social sciences, or as an essential adjunct to other strategies.

Retroductive reasoning, according to Peirce, differs fundamentally from inductive and deductive logic. It is the process of devising a theory which will account for some surprising observed phenomenon, such that if the theory were true the phenomenon would no longer produce 'why' questions. It entails working back from observations to an explanation; once the explanatory idea has emerged it will be overwhelming and irresistible. He viewed the process of generating a theory, such as Kepler's idea of elliptical planetary orbits, as being gradual and iterative rather than being a quantum leap. The process for testing it, which he argued involves both Deduction (drawing a logical conclusion from the theory) and Induction (using data to test the theory in the manner of Hempel's broad view of induction), is largely mechanical and lacks the creativity required in Retroduction.

The Retroductive research strategy is used by Realists as the process for generating hypothetical models of the structures and mechanisms which are assumed to produce observed phenomena. By the use of disciplined scientific imagination, a plausible model of what is producing an observed regularity is invented. In constructing these models of mechanisms that have usually never been observed, ideas may be borrowed from known structures and mechanisms in other fields. The reality of the hypothesized structures and mechanisms are initially assumed but have to be empirically demonstrated. Once this has been achieved, and their status is transformed from the 'real' to the 'actual', they become the phenomena to be explained.

Harré has applied the use of models in his Realist approach to the natural sciences to the social sciences in what he has labelled as the ethogenic approach. It involves building homeomorphic models of social episodes and paramorphic models of the largely unknown natures of people – psychological mechanisms. These person models are of four kinds: the ethogenic model of the actions of aware people engaged in rule-following or goal attainment; the cybernetic model in which the ethogenic model is expressed in formal and abstract terms; the system-theoretic model which provides abstract mechanisms for the cybernetic model; and the physiological model which hypothesizes real structures of the nervous system corresponding to the system-theoretic model. This chain of person models is supplemented by models of the social order based on the images of it that social actors use to manage their social action when rules and habits no longer work.

Abduction is the strategy that characterizes those branches of Interpretivism that are concerned with deriving expert accounts of social life from the everyday accounts that social actors can provide. In its most fundamental form this strategy is primarily concerned to produce understanding by means of second-order descriptions of these first-order accounts. However, in its more liberal and less inhibited form, it is concerned with explanation, and possibly prediction, rather than just description.

In view of the fact that much of social life is routine and habitual, and takes place in an unreflective, taken-for-granted attitude, the accounts of social actors do not usually reveal the largely tacit meanings that underpin their interactions. It is therefore necessary for the social scientist to piece together the fragments of meanings that can be gleaned from these accounts. It is a hermeneutic process of trying to grasp the unknown whole from the known parts.

While the versions of the Abductive strategy discussed here have many features in common, they also differ in important respects thus making it impossible to produce a synthesis. They differ on the issue of retaining the integrity of the phenomenon, on the extent to which it is appropriate to generalize from and thus decontextualize lay accounts, on the extent to which explanation is the aim, and on whether it is appropriate to correct or interpret lay accounts in the light of sociological theory. These issues will be discussed in chapter 7. Much still remains to be done to develop appropriate techniques for generating second-order concepts from first-order concepts, for moving from lay language to technical language (Blaikie et al., in preparation).

Further Reading

Key References

Douglas, J.D. 1971. *Understanding Everyday Life.*
Giddens, A. 1976. *New Rules of Sociological Method.*
—— 1984. *The Constitution of Society,* ch. 6.
Glaser, B.G. and Strauss, A.L. 1968. *The Discovery of Grounded Theory.*
Harré, R. 1974. 'Blueprint for a New Science'.
—— 1976. 'The Constructive Role of Models'.
—— 1977. 'The Ethogenic Approach: Theory and Practice'.
—— and Secord, P.F. 1972. *The Explanation of Social Behaviour.*
Rex, J. 1974. *Sociology and the Demystification of the Modern World.*
Schütz, A. 1963a. 'Concept and Theory Formation in the Social Sciences'.
—— 1963b. 'Common-sense and Scientific Interpretation of Human Action'.
Weber, M. 1962. *Basic Concepts in Sociology.*
—— 1964. *The Theory of Social and Economic Organization.*
Winch, P. 1958. *The Idea of Social Science and its Relation to Philosophy.*

General References

Bauman, Z. 1978. *Hermeneutics and Social Science.*
Bernstein, R.J. 1976. *Restructuring Social and Political Theory.*
—— 1983. *Beyond Objectivism and Relativism.*
Bhaskar, R. 1975. *A Realist Theory of Science.*
—— 1979. *The Possibility of Naturalism.*
Douglas, J.D. 1977. 'Existential Sociology'.
Gadamer, H-G. 1989. *Truth and Method.*
Giddens, A. 1976. 'Hermeneutics, Ethnomethodology and the Problem of Interpretive Analysis'.
Harré, R. 1970. *The Principles of Scientific Thinking.*
—— 1972. *The Philosophy of Science.*
Outhwaite, W. 1975. *Understanding Social Life.*
—— 1983a. 'Towards a Realist Perspective'.
—— 1983b. *Concept Formation in Social Science.*
Schütz, A. 1970. 'Interpretive Sociology'.
—— 1976. *The Phenomenology of the Social World.*

Part III
Some Methodological Issues

7

Choosing between
Approaches and Strategies

Introduction

The existence of an array of divergent approaches and strategies for social enquiry poses the problem of choice for the social researcher. How can the best approach and strategy be selected? It should be clear from the previous discussion that there is no neutral ground on which to stand to evaluate their relative merits. It is possible to entertain arguments about the logic of the various methods of theory construction and testing but, ultimately, a conclusion about the strengths or weaknesses of any approach or strategy will entail the adoption of a particular set of ontological and epistemological assumptions, usually those of one of the approaches or strategies. It is possible to adopt a pragmatic position and to try to match a strategy to the nature of a particular research project and the kind of research questions that have been selected for consideration. A choice might also be made in terms of how the approaches relate to the worldview of the researcher; there may be a conscious or unconscious preference for the maintenance of some compatibility between ontological assumptions and ideological or religious beliefs and values, particularly on issues such as a preference for an absolutist versus a relativist worldview. This should not be surprising in view of the work of Kuhn (1970a) and the sociology of knowledge and science (see, for example, Mulkay 1979). The preference for a particular set of epistemological assumptions may also be the result of personality factors; the choice between an 'outsider' or an 'insider' research strategy is likely to be determined by a perceived preference for predetermined, linear procedures as against a perceived ability to manage flexible, ambiguous processes.[1] The professional socialization of the

[1] This hypothesis has been developed from the observation of colleagues and students over many years.

researcher, in terms of both discipline and academic institution, will have influenced exposure to and experience with particular approaches and strategies. Further, the social context in which the researcher works is likely to influence the choice; the preferences of the funders and consumers of the research, and the research culture of the academic or research organization in which it takes place, need to be taken into account. There is a price to be paid for adopting an unpopular or 'deviant' approach. In short, past experiences and present social circumstances will together have a bearing on the choice. Hopefully, the review and critique of the approaches and strategies in the previous chapters will contribute to a more informed choice and, perhaps, a desire to break with old habits and conventions.

It should now be evident that the basic questions outlined in chapter 1 do not have single or simple answers. In order to answer them it is necessary to consider a range of fundamental methodological issues which distinguish the approaches and strategies. The issues to be considered here are: the ontological and epistemological assumptions adopted; the purpose of social enquiry; the processes of theory construction and testing; the relationship between lay concepts and social science discourse; the relationship of the researcher to the researched; and, the meaning and relevance of the notions of objectivity and truth. The approaches and strategies are compared on these issues. However, as only the core elements can be reviewed here, the more subtle differences must be ignored.

Methodological Issues

Ontological and Epistemological Assumptions

Approaches to social enquiry can be divided into two groups in terms of their ontological assumptions: they are either realist or constructivist. Positivism, Critical Rationalism and Realism all assume that social reality exists independently of the observer and the activities of social science, that this reality is ordered, and that these uniformities can be observed and explained. However, they differ in their view of the elements that constitute social reality, particularly the explanatory elements, and on whether this reality also exists independently of social actors. The ontological positions of Positivism and Critical Rationalism entail a deterministic view of social life in which social action and interaction are the product of the operation of 'external' forces (such as social norms) on social actors. The structuralist version of Realism (Bhaskar) tends to share this 'external' view, although it would look for the forces in different places, while the social psychological version (Harré) would look more to 'internal' cognitive resources.

The other major approaches, Interpretivism, Critical Theory, Structuration Theory and Feminism, are all fully or partly constructivist in their ontological assumptions, and Realism also includes some elements of it. A constructivist ontology entails the assumption that social reality is produced and reproduced by social actors; it is a preinterpreted, intersubjective world of cultural objects, meanings and social institutions. A consequence of this position is that in any social situation there may be multiple realities.

While Critical Theory, Structuration Theory, Feminism and, to some extent Realism, are all built on this constructivist foundation of Interpretivism, they recognize that the production and reproduction of social reality occurs either in wider social conditions of which social actors may not be fully or even partly aware or, in the case of Structuration Theory, within the limitations produced by the social structures which are products of these processes (the duality of structure).

The approaches which adopt Realist assumptions differ in their view of whether social reality can be directly observed and, if so, to what extent. Positivism accepts as reality only the discrete events that can be directly observed by the senses, Critical Rationalism accepts that knowledge of reality can be achieved, and then only tentatively, by explicitly using theoretical concepts to determine what can and needs to be observed, and structural Realism recognizes domains of reality only one of which, the empirical, is or can be directly observed. Interpretivism, Structuration Theory, social psychological Realism and Feminism all accept that knowledge of the social world must be achieved by immersion in some part of it in order to learn the 'local' language, meanings and rules. What is then done with this 'inside' knowledge is a matter of considerable disagreement. The position of Critical Theory is somewhat mixed because of its willingness to use a combination of *historical–hermeneutic* and *empirical–analytic* traditions for different aspects of an investigation with emancipatory aims.

There is, then, a fundamental choice to be made by the social researcher, a choice between very different ontological (realist v. constructivist) and epistemological (outside v. inside) positions. These differences will be elaborated further in the discussion of the other issues.

Purpose of Social Enquiry

Social enquiry has a range of purposes: exploration, description, understanding, explanation, change and evaluation. At the most basic level, it is concerned with exploring some social phenomenon that is not well understood, possibly to inform further stages of an investigation. This can be followed by a description of its characteristics, an understanding or explanation of its regularities, prediction of possible outcomes under particular circumstances, and an attempt to change it in some way and perhaps to monitor such change. While there is a tendency to underestimate the importance and difficulty of exploration and description, and to see explanation as the pinnacle of scientific achievement, without an adequate grasp of the regularities that exist, there is nothing to be understood or explained, except, perhaps, a figment of the researcher's imagination.

The various approaches differ in what they consider to be achievable in social enquiry. Some branches of Interpretivism (e.g. Garfinkel and Winch) wish to do nothing more than report social actors' accounts of their experiences, how they interpret their world, the motives they attribute to their actions, or the rules which direct their actions; the purpose is limited to description of specific social situations which, it is claimed, will produce all the understanding that is possible and necessary. Positivism is also primarily interested in description, with recording observed regularities. It argues that generalizations inductively derived from these observations allow for explanation and prediction; observed regularities can be explained as being a special case of what is known in general (Kaplan 1964). In this way descriptions become explanations.

Other branches of Interpretivism (e.g. Weber, Schütz, Douglas) wish both to generalize about and to explain social life. Structuration Theory rejects the distinction between understanding (or interpretation) and explanation and, while it is interested in the latter, accepts that all social generalizations and explanations are limited by time and space. In terms of its emancipatory concerns, Critical Theory is prepared to seek description, interpretation and explanation. Critical Rationalism offers the extreme position in that it aims to transcend such limitations to achieve tested universal propositions that will make both explanation and prediction possible. However, Realism rejects the possibility of prediction because the social world cannot be experimentally closed in the way that is possible in some natural sciences; decisive test situations cannot be devised (Bhaskar 1979: 58). It is content to describe regularities and then seek explanation by demonstrating the existence of hypothesized underlying structures and mechanisms.

The extent to which the approaches can be used to answer a particular research question will partly depend on the form of the question. Some approaches are well suited to deal with 'what' (descriptive) questions, while others are more suited to answering 'why' (explanatory) questions. With the exception, perhaps, of Critical Theory and Feminism, the extent to which understanding and explanation are used to bring about change, to answer 'how' questions, is more a matter of the social and political concerns of the researcher than a core element of the approach to social enquiry. Critical Theory regards its emancipatory aim as central to its concerns, while Feminist social science is committed to rectifying the androcentric nature of the natural and social sciences, and contemporary societies.

Theory Construction and Testing

The four research strategies provide fundamentally different processes for constructing and testing theories, and have different positions on the status of these theories. The choice of approach, and its accompanying strategy or strategies, will determine where the research begins, how it will proceed, what kinds of research techniques will be appropriate, in what sequences they will be used, and the nature of the outcome.

Induction in Positivism and Deduction in Critical Rationalism offer polar opposite starting points and procedures. The former builds generalizations, or constant conjunctions, out of observations of specific events; it starts with observations and ends up with general propositions which it claims provide explanations; it does this by believing in the possibility of pure, theoretically neutral observation. The latter accepts the theory-dependence of observation and begins explicitly with theoretical propositions of some sort, ideally a fully worked out theory from which hypotheses can be drawn, and proceeds to use observations selectively to test the hypotheses. Inductivism produces generalizations of relationships while Deductivism produces a set of propositions which form an argument.

Realism has rejected both of these strategies as being unsatisfactory, the former because it is essentially descriptive and does not really explain anything – it does not uncover the causes of the generalized conjunctions, and the latter because it is a myth that the ideal form of knowledge is deductive. Harré has argued that the logic of mathematical systems does not reflect the order in the world, not even the time order of causes and consequences. It is in fact rare to find deductive sequences in science; 'mostly scientists come up with descriptions of structures, attributions of powers and laws of change' (Harré 1970: 10), and these cannot be logically deduced from a set of premises. Realism starts with observed regularities and proposes models of structures and mechanisms to explain them. A combination of reason and imagination is required to 'invent' the model, and then research has to be undertaken to try to establish its existence.

In so far as Interpretivists – or those approaches which include or are founded on Interpretivism – are concerned with explanation, the process of theory construction is one of Abduction. The hermeneutic task of penetrating the frames of meaning of social actors is the first and essential stage of the process, and the generation of ideal types is the major aim. Typical social actors with typical meanings and motives, engaged in typical courses of action in typical situations, are derived from everyday concepts, meanings and accounts. Explanation is achieved by constructing these ideal types, these abstracted models, and using them to provide the ingredients for testable theoretical propositions.

Lay Language and Social Science Discourse

A central question for the practitioner, and particularly for one who adopts an Interpretive approach, is what position to adopt on the relationship between lay language (concepts, meanings and accounts) and social science discourse (concepts and theories). Positivism and Critical Rationalism both explicitly reject any role for lay language in either description or explanation. On the other hand, both Realism, in its interpretive foundations, and Interpretivism place great emphasis on the importance of lay language. However, within the broad spectrum of positions included within Interpretivism, there are disagreements about its status and how it is to be used.

The Positivist position is well illustrated in Durkheim's injunction that the sociologist should formulate new concepts at the outset and not rely on lay notions. In his quest to establish social facts as the subject matter of sociology, and to achieve what he regarded as objective methods, Durkheim argued that it was necessary to leave aside any reference to the way social actors conceptualize their world. For him, everyday concepts include fallacious ideas and merely express the 'confused impressions of the mob'.

The type of social science which is consistent with Positivism and Critical Rationalism, the orthodox consensus, has adopted a traditional view of language as a medium for describing the world. In this view, the basic features of language have a one-to-one relationship with objects in the real world; language is regarded as providing pictures of corresponding aspects of reality. There is a preference for the precision which is believed to be possible in a discipline-based language rather than the vague and imprecise language of everyday life. It is assumed that this meta-language can improve upon and correct the inadequacies of lay language.

Another feature of the orthodox consensus is its reliance on a revelatory view of science in which science is seen to demystify common-sense beliefs about the natural world by offering more profound explanations than are available in everyday knowledge. Science checks out common-sense knowledge in order to show that some of it is wrong, or that it can be improved on. However, social science based on this principle has frequently been criticized by lay people as expressing what they know in an obscure language.

An alternative view states that description is only one of the things that language can do; it is also a medium of social life and is therefore a central element in all the activities in which social actors engage. As a result, it is necessary for social scientists to build their accounts of social life on lay language. 'Ordinary or lay language cannot be just dismissed as corrigible in the light of sociological neologisms, since lay language enters into the very constitution of social activity itself' (Giddens 1979: 246). Further, Giddens has argued that

> social life cannot even be accurately described by a sociological observer, let alone causally elucidated, if that observer does not master the array of concepts employed (discursively or non-discursively) by those involved. All social science, to put it bluntly, is parasitic upon lay concepts. (Giddens 1987: 18–19)

It is evident from the discussion of the Abductive strategy that this relationship has been approached from many directions within Interpretivism.

For some writers, ordinary language, concepts and meanings, are all there is; even the language of science is just another ordinary language. However, those who accept a role for lay language in the construction of social theory differ in a number of important ways: on the issue of retaining the integrity of the phenomenon; on the extent to which they are prepared to generalize from and thus decontextualize sociological accounts; on the extent to which explanation is the aim; and on whether it is appropriate to correct or interpret lay accounts in the light of sociological theory.

Retaining the Integrity of the Phenomenon

Schütz, Winch, Douglas, Rex and Giddens are in basic agreement about the importance of and the 'logic' for generating technical language from lay language; that it is necessary for social scientists first to grasp lay concepts, to penetrate hermeneutically the particular form of life; that social theories need to be built on everyday concepts. However, they appear to take rather different positions on the critical issue of whether these theories can also incorporate concepts which are not derived from lay concepts, i.e. the extent to which 'foreign' concepts and theoretical ideas can be imported into the social scientist's account before it ceases to be authentic and useful. Schütz and Douglas wished to anchor sociological discourse to lay discourse by insisting that social actors should be able to recognize themselves and others in sociological accounts, thus retaining the integrity of the phenomenon. However, this was not seen to inhibit their desire to produce decontextualized social theories. Winch also wished to keep the two languages tied together but was prepared to allow the use of technical concepts that are not derived directly from lay concepts. His main restriction was that such concepts must at least be based on a previous understanding of lay concepts. The interest of both Rex and Giddens in social contexts and structures, which are beyond the direct experience or even awareness of social actors, requires the use of at least some elements of technical language which are independent of lay language.

Schütz's postulate of adequacy appears to have been interpreted in different ways. Douglas preferred to use it as a rule-of-thumb and Pawson (1989) has regarded it as requiring a one-to-one translation of lay concepts into sociological concepts. Giddens appears to have misunderstood it entirely but ended up adopting Schütz's position on the relationship between lay and technical language. He has accepted that 'there is necessarily a reciprocal relation between the concepts employed by members of society and those used by sociological observers' (Giddens 1976a: 153), but he suggested that Schütz had this relationship the wrong way around. Giddens has interpreted Schütz's postulate as meaning that 'the technical concepts of social science have to be in some way capable of being reduced to lay notions of everyday action' (1976a: 158), a position similar to that adopted by Pawson. Instead, and in fact consistent with Schütz, Giddens has argued that 'the observing social scientist has to be able first to grasp those lay concepts, i.e. penetrate hermeneutically the form of life whose features he [sic] wishes to analyse or explain' (Giddens 1976a: 158–9).[2]

> The 'logical tie' implicated in the double hermeneutic does not depend upon whether the actor or actors whose conduct is being described are able to grasp the notions which the social scientist uses. It depends upon the social scientific observer accurately understanding the concepts whereby the actors' conduct is oriented. (Giddens 1982: 13)

Decontextualizing, Generalizing and Explaining

Within Interpretivism there is also a variety of views on whether it is legitimate to try to go beyond description of social actors' accounts to some kind of explanation. At one extreme, ethnomethodology insists that both lay accounts and sociological accounts must be considered in the context in which they are used. It has no interest in or need for general propositions, except in the sense of the ontological claims made about the reality of interest to ethnomethodology. It takes the everyday world as a phenomenon in its own right and its focus of enquiry (Johnson 1977). Ethnomethodologists study everyday practical reasoning, the accounts that members produce to describe the factual status of their experiences and activities. They are not concerned with developing causal explanations of observed patterns of social activity. Rather, ethnomethodology '*is* concerned with how members of a society go about the task of *seeing, describing*, and *explaining* order in the world in which they live' (Zimmerman and Wieder 1971: 289). Meanings, rules and norms are not resources to be used by the social scientist to construct explanations, they are topics to be studied. It is the manner in which social actors describe the order in their situation, in terms of such rules and norms, how the ideas and language of rationality are used to describe the orderly character of their social activities, that is of interest to the ethnomethodologist.

Other writers are willing to accept some degree of decontextualizing. Winch implied an interest in such a process and Weber, Schütz, Douglas, Rex and Giddens all explicitly aimed to achieve it. Schütz expressed this as a process of moving from the 'subjective' contexts of everyday life to the 'objective' contexts of social science. Douglas argued that while it is essential to ground our understanding of everyday life on the situations in which it occurs, it is important to recognize that there is considerable variability in the degree to which everyday knowledge is contextually determined. He argued that just as there is a tension between situational and trans-situational aspects of human existence, there is also a similar

---

[2] For a critical discussion of Giddens' position, see Bauman (1989: 47–8).

tension between the need to retain the integrity of the phenomenon and to produce useful knowledge about everyday life. As it is not possible to completely decontextualize this knowledge, Douglas recognized that it constitutes only partial truths.

If it is accepted that lay language can be decontextualized and generalized at least to some degree, particularly by the development of ideal types, then it is a small step to the development of explanations, even if these are limited in time and space. Weber, Schütz and Rex all agree that ideal types can provide the foundation for testable propositions.

Corrigibility of Lay Accounts

Garfinkel regarded any attempt to correct or pass judgement on social actors' accounts as being completely inappropriate. Rex, on the other hand, argued that the social scientist should be able to give a different and competing account of social life from that offered by social actors. Giddens drew a distinction between 'mutual knowledge' and 'common sense' and argued that only the latter is open to correction. The largely tacit mutual knowledge upon which social actors draw to make sense of what each other says and does, and on which the social scientist draws to generate descriptions of their conduct, must be regarded as authentic and not open to correction by the social scientist. However, it is nevertheless possible to provide a rational evaluation of this knowledge. Common sense, on the other hand, is corrigible in terms of the findings of the natural and social sciences. Thus, the 'critical evaluation of beliefs and practices is an inescapable feature of the discourse of the social sciences' (Giddens 1979: 253). In any case, the relationship between this everyday knowledge, and the accounts of it produced by social scientists, is a shifting one. Just as social scientists adopt everyday concepts and use them in a specialized sense, 'so lay actors tend to take over the concepts and theories of the social sciences and embody them as constitutive elements in the rationalization of their own conduct' (Giddens 1976a: 159) – the double hermeneutic.

Bhaskar has described as the *linguistic fallacy* the claim by many Interpretivists that social actors' concepts are not corrigible. This fallacy is a failure to recognize that there is more to reality than is expressed in the language of social actors. As social actors' constructions of reality comprise only one element in a Realist social science, rather than being its entire concern, it is the case

that the conditions of being are not the conditions of the linguistic expression of being, that lay accounts are corrigible and susceptible to critique, and that social science (and, at a remove, philosophy) always and necessarily consists in a semantic, moral and political intervention in the life of the society under study. (Bhaskar 1979: 199)

In a manner reminiscent of critical theory, Bhaskar claimed that

> [s]uch a critique is both emancipatory and self-reflexive – *emancipatory*, in as much as the necessity for false ideas can be explained; *self-reflexive*, in as much as social science is a part of the totality it seeks to explain. Such a critique ... constitutes an explanatory production, not simply a semantic exchange. (Bhaskar 1979: 202)

Explicitly or implicitly the researcher takes a stand on this complex issue. As was suggested at the beginning of this chapter, the choice is likely to be influenced by pragmatic, personal and contextual factors. Researchers need to be aware of the nature of the issue and the consequences of a particular choice.

The Researcher and the Researched

The approaches to social enquiry and the accompanying research strategies entail a view of the relationship between social scientists and social actors, ranging from the position of detached observer to a fully engaged participant. In the name of achieving their conception of objectivity, Positivism and Critical Rationalism have adopted the extreme detached position. Research is conducted from the 'outside', from the point of view of the researcher's conceptual and theoretical frameworks, and the research methods used are linear and standardized. The social actors' concepts and meanings are either ignored or intentionally rejected and any hint of 'subjective' involvement on the part of the researcher is to be deplored.

From its initial concern with the interpretation of ancient texts, Hermeneutics has provided the foundation for the other extreme. One version has taken *verstehen* to mean that the investigator places him/herself in the shoes of the author or social actor, while another version has viewed the relationship as involving the investigator in the mediation of languages. These alternatives are reflected within Interpretivism: Weber used the first version in his historical studies; Winch focused on the relationship between languages and, like Schütz and Rex, argued that the researcher must first learn the language of the social actors; Giddens stressed the need for the researcher to immerse her/himself in the actors' world and he incorporated the mediation of languages.

Critical Theory sees the researcher and the researched engaged in dialogic communication. The researcher is a reflective partner – a co-participant whose task is to facilitate the emancipation of the victims of social, political and economic circumstances, to help people to transform their situations and hence resolve their needs and deprivations.

Feminism has adopted the most extreme position on this issue and has presented a manifesto which provides a useful summary of the 'involved' alternative. It argues that social scientists should not be detached and impersonal but should use their thoughts, feelings and intuitions as part of the research process. Social research should mediate the experiences of the researcher and the researched; it should facilitate understanding and change in their lives and situations. This manifesto also relates to the emancipatory aspects of Critical Theory and Bhaskar's Realism, and places stress on participatory action research (see, for example, Whyte 1991).

(1) The postulate of *value free research*, of neutrality and indifference towards the research objects, has to be replaced by *conscious partiality*, which is achieved through partial identification with the research objects. (Mies 1983: 122)

Conscious partiality recognizes the larger social context and the researcher's place in this. It is different from mere subjectivity or empathy as it involves a critical distance between the researcher and the researched.

(2) The vertical relationship between researcher and 'research objects', the *view from above*, must be replaced by the *view from below* ... Research, which so far has been largely an instrument of dominance and legitimation of power elites, must be brought to serve the interests of dominated, exploited and oppressed groups, particularly women. (Mies 1983: 123)

(3) The contemplative, uninvolved 'spectator knowledge' must be replaced by *active participation in actions, movements and struggles* for women's emancipation. Research must become an integral part of such struggles. (1983: 124)

(4) Participation in social actions and struggles, and the integration of research into these processes, further implies that the *change of the status quo* becomes the starting point for a scientific quest. The motto for this approach could be: 'If you want to know a thing, you must change it.' (1983: 125)

(5) *The research process must become a process of 'conscientization'*,[3] both for the so-called 'research subjects' (social scientists) and for the 'research objects' (women as target groups) ... People who before were objects of research become subjects of their own research and action. This implies that scientists who participate in this study of the conditions of oppression must give their research tools to the people. (1983: 126)

Again, this fundamental issue cannot be glossed over lightly. As it has ethical and political as well as methodological aspects, it needs to be considered independently of other issues and may therefore influence the choice of approach and strategy.

Objectivity and Truth

This last issue is probably the most contentious of all those discussed in this chapter and is one on which there is a great deal of confusion in science and in everyday life. The belief that the so-called scientific method is the ultimate way to acquire reliable knowledge and, therefore, of establishing truths about the world, continues to be accepted as dogma in many

---

[3] This concept is derived from Freire (1970), and means 'learning to perceive social, political and economic contradictions and to take action against oppressive elements of reality'.

circles. For many scientists and lay people, any approach to social enquiry that does not achieve both objectivity and truth is to be rejected. However, there is a dominant trend in the philosophy of science which argues that 'science is not a path to truth at all, let alone the only one. It sometimes looks as if some philosophers are saying that there is no such thing as truth' (Trigg 1985: 19). This latter position regards all knowledge as contextual and therefore relative, and is contrasted with absolutist claims about the existence of reality and our capacity to determine what is true. However, many writers point to the logical circularity of asserting that knowledge and truth are relative as it leaves the proponents with nowhere to stand to make such a claim; it can be nothing more than an assertion based on an act of faith. However, this criticism of relativism does not mean that absolutism is therefore supported.

The approaches to social enquiry adopt different positions on this continuum. The extreme absolutist position is taken by Positivism in its claim that objective knowledge can be achieved through the use of pure observation, uncontaminated by theoretical notions, and accompanied by the separation of facts and values. It is argued that the truth of generalizations from such observations is the result of the one-to-one correspondence between observation statements and 'reality'. Critical Rationalism also adopts this *correspondence* theory of truth and argues that objectivity is achieved by the use of logical (deductive) reasoning to criticize false or bad theories. It aims to produce truths about the world, it accepts the view that observations are theory-dependent, and it believes in the superiority of the logic of falsification. This leads to the view that scientists can never know when a theory is true, only when it is false (although even this latter claim has been challenged).

Some versions of Hermeneutics and Interpretivism provide the alternative relativistic extreme. One branch of Hermeneutics has argued that there is no objectively valid interpretation of a text or social situation; it is not possible for a researcher to stand outside history or become detached from culture. All that is possible is culturally and historically situated accounts which lead to an unlimited number of interpretations. However, when meanings in any social situation are shared by the participants, they may be regarded as being objective in the sense of being *their* reality, and *their* truth can be communicated.

By separating the transitive and intransitive objects of science, the tools for explaining reality from reality itself, Realism has tried to avoid the problems of objectivity. If the mechanism that is hypothesized in a model can be shown to exist and act in the manner postulated, then it must be true. Theories are regarded as being either true or false, a claim that is regarded as being unproblematic.

Critical Theory has rejected the 'objectivist illusion' that the world is made up of facts independent of the observer. The three forms of knowledge (empirical–analytical, historical–hermeneutic and self-reflection) are each associated with particular interests and deal with different aspects of social existence. These interests determine the way reality is viewed and, therefore, what is regarded as knowledge. Truth is not a matter of evidence from observations but is achieved in an 'ideal speech situation' through open and equitable critical discussion. This is a *consensus* view of truth founded on reason; competent people, freed from constraints and distorting influences, could be expected to achieve consensus. This capacity for rational criticism is used in the interests of human emancipation. However, some latter-day Critical Theorists (e.g. Fay) have adopted a *pragmatic* view of truth; if a theory leads to action which overcomes the felt needs and privations caused by structural conflicts and contradiction, it must be true.

Giddens addressed the issue of truth in the context of notions such as 'multiple realities' (Schütz), 'alternate realities' (Casteneda) and 'competing paradigms' (Kuhn). He distinguished between *relativism on the level of meaning*, the view that forms of life have mutually exclusive constructions of reality such that translation between these frames of meaning is impossible, and *judgemental relativism* which views these different realities as being logically equivalent and inaccessible to rational evaluation. He argued that 'authenticity on the level of meaning has to be distinguished from the validity of propositions about the world expressed as beliefs within a particular meaning-frame' (Giddens 1976a: 144). While he was concerned to go beyond lay accounts in producing explanations, he accepted time and space limitations on all social theories. The consequence of this view is that ultimate truths are impossible in social science.

The standpoint branch of Feminism shares much in common with the relativistic branch of Hermeneutics and it is in this approach that a great deal of the contemporary debate about objectivity is taking place. Some Feminists see a concern with achieving objectivity and overcoming subjectivity in science as being part of the dualistic way in which men view the world. Instead, it has been argued that dynamic objectivity can be achieved through the use of subjective processes by which other people can be understood. This knowledge is gained from shared feelings and experiences; the use of subjectivity increases objectivity and decreases the false claims of objectivism.

Some of the dilemmas and possible solutions to this issue can be illustrated by reviewing how they have been dealt with by some Feminists. The most radical version has been developed by the biologist, Haraway (1986), in her analysis of primatology. She has taken Kuhn and Feyerabend seriously and has regarded all scientific knowledge claims as social constructions, and the concepts, theories, methods and results as historically and culturally specific. For Haraway, facts are laced with values: '[L]ife and social sciences in general, and primatology in particular, are story-laden; these sciences are composed through complex, historically specific story-telling practices. Facts are theory-laden; theories are value-laden; values are story-laden. Therefore, facts are meaningful within stories' (Haraway 1986: 79). She has suggested that, in their efforts to describe and explain the world, scientists are also searching for the limits of possible worlds. A good story is one that fits with available visions of these possible worlds. 'Description is determined by vision; facts and theories are perceived within stories; the worlds of human beings are made of meanings. Meanings are tremendously material forces – much like food and sex. And, like food and sex, meanings are social constructions that determine the quality of people's lives' (Haraway 1986: 80). On the basis of different histories, experiences and worldviews, feminist scientists have reconstructed existing stories. The result is that the structure of a field of study like primatology can be radically changed; it is not a case of replacing false stories but of creating new ones. 'Feminist science is not biased science; nor is it disinterested in accurate description and powerful theory. My thesis is that feminist science is about changing possibilities, not about having a special route to the truth about what it means to be human – or animal' (Haraway 1986: 81).

These aspects of feminist method have produced some contradictions; feminists want a new kind of science while at the same time recognizing the historically situated character of knowledge. While this could be seen to lead to a form of relativism, Haraway has rejected such implications in her work; one account of monkeys and apes is not as good as another; some stories are better than others. 'To count as better stories, they have to better account for what it means to be *human* and *animal*. They have to offer a fuller, more coherent vision, one that allows the monkeys and apes to be seen more accurately' (Haraway 1986: 80–1). The problem is what will count as a more accurate, fuller, more coherent story is part of the craft of constructing good stories. And all stories are related to matters of power, race, sex and class, and the struggles people have in telling each other how we might live together.

Dugdale (1990) has argued against drawing a relativist conclusion from Haraway's social constructivist position. Relativism,

> understood as equivalence of all personal assertions or as anything goes, is not necessarily the outcome of recognizing that all knowledge-claims are moves in power strategies, rather than moves towards truth. Certainly social constructionism leaves no value-free or neutral position from which to make knowledge-claims. But in recognizing the stakes involved in the conversion of knowledge-claims to facts, social constructivism leaves no innocent positions. It undermines the universalist perspective usually attributed to science and opens science up as a field of political struggle. All knowledge-claims are partial, situated and locatable in political projects; solidarities are structured on and through the construction of shared visions; the world as we know it is always the production of a particular community with a particular vision of the future. It seems to me that feminists have an interest in asserting precisely such a politics of truth. (Dugdale 1990: 61)

In the context of social research, relativism would mean that using women's experiences as a basis for social research produces results which are equally as plausible as those produced by using men's experiences. However, Harding has rejected this claim and has argued that 'women's and men's characteristic social experiences provide different but not equal grounds for reliable knowledge' (1987b: 10). In fact, she went further to claim that women's experiences should be used in preference to men's. Nevertheless, she has accepted that men can make, and have made, important contributions to feminist research and scholarship. Men can bring a feminist perspective on some aspects of masculine thought and behaviour to which women do not have access. The only requirement for research conducted by men to be designated 'feminist' is that it must satisfy the same standards that women must satisfy to earn the label, particularly the struggle against the exploitation of women (1987b: 12). The outcome is a *political* view of truth.

Conclusion

At the risk of oversimplification, it is possible to summarize these issues as involving choices between a number of alternative positions (see table 2). Some of these alternatives are mutually exclusive, others involve a continuum, while others provide choices that may be appropriate under certain conditions. For example, belief in single or in multiple realities is mutually exclusive, at least in a particular social context, a choice between being a detached or an involved researcher can be a matter of degree, and it is possible to regard some aspects of lay accounts (mutual knowledge) as authentic and not corrigible and others (common sense) as open to correction in the light of technical knowledge.

The use of dualisms to characterize the world and our knowledge of it has been criticized by both Structuration Theory and Feminism. The intention of this summary is not to perpetuate this tendency but rather to highlight the complex range of choices which any researcher needs to consider. It should be clear that the various approaches to social enquiry imply positions on all these issues, whether or not this is made explicit, and that they are related to the position taken on the more fundamental issue of the relationship between the methods of the natural and social sciences.

In adopting an approach to social enquiry, the researcher is buying into a set of choices with far-reaching implications. They therefore need to be given careful attention. No one approach or strategy, and its accompanying choices on these issues, provides a perfect solution for the researcher; there is no one ideal way to gain knowledge of the social world. All approaches and strategies involve assumptions, judgements and compromises; all are claimed to have deficiencies. However, depending on where one stands, it is possible to argue their relative merits. It is hoped that this review and critique of the approaches and strategies will assist both the novice and experienced researcher in this process.

Table 2 Choices between methodological issues

Issue	Alternative positions	
Nature of reality	Realist Single	Constructivist Multiple
Starting point	Theory Technical language Outside	Observation Lay language Inside

Role of language	1:1 correspondence
	  with reality
		Constitution of
		  social activity

Lay accounts	Irrelevant Corrigible Trans-situational	Fundamental Authentic Situational

Social science accounts	Generalizable across
	  social contexts
		Specific in time
		  and space

Researcher	Subject-to-object Detached Outside expert	Subject-to-subject Involved Reflective partner
Objectivity	Absolutist Static	Relativist Dynamic
Theory of truth	Correspondence Political	Consensus Pragmatic
Aim of research	Explain Evaluate	Understand Change

References

Abbagano, N. 1967. 'Positivism', in P. Edwards (ed.), *The Encyclopedia of Philosophy*, Vol. 6. New York: Macmillan.

Achinstein, P. 1968. *Concepts of Science*. Baltimore: Johns Hopkins Press.

—— 1971. *Law and Explanation: An Essay in the Philosophy of Science*. Oxford: Oxford University Press.

Adorno, T.W. 1976. 'Introduction', in T.W. Adorno et al., *The Positivist Dispute in German Sociology*, pp. 1–67. London: Heinemann.

Adorno, T.W., H. Albert, R. Dahrendorf, J. Habermas, H. Pilot and K.R. Popper. 1976. *The Positivist Dispute in German Sociology*. Translated by G. Adey and D. Frisby. London: Heinemann.

Albert, H. 1969. *Traktat über kritische Vernunft*, 2nd edn. Tübingen: Mohr.

—— 1976a. 'The Myth of Total Reason: Dialectical Claims in the Light of Undialectical Criticism', in T.W. Adorno et al., *The Positivist Dispute in German Sociology*, pp. 163–97. London: Heinemann.

—— 1976b. 'Behind Positivism's Back? A Critical Illumination of Dialectical Digression', in T.W. Adorno et al., *The Positivist Dispute in German Sociology*, pp. 226–57. London: Heinemann.

Atkinson, J.M. 1978. *Discovering Suicide*. London: Macmillan.

Bacon, F. 1889. *Novum Organon*. Translated by G.W. Kitchin. Oxford: Clarendon Press.

Bauman, Z. 1978. *Hermeneutics and Social Science*. London: Hutchinson.

—— 1989. 'Hermeneutics and Modern Social Theory', in D. Held and J.B. Thompson (eds), *Social Theory of Modern Societies: Anthony Giddens and his Critics*, pp. 34–55. Cambridge: Cambridge University Press.

—— 1990. 'Philosophical Affinities of Postmodern Sociology', *Sociological Review* 38: 411–44.

Benton, T. 1977. *Philosophical Foundations of the Three Sociologies*. London: Routledge & Kegan Paul.

—— 1981. 'Realism and Social Science: Some Comments on Roy Bhaskar's "The Possibility of Naturalism"', *Radical Philosophy* 27: 13–21.

Berger, P.L. 1963. *Invitation to Sociology*. New York: Doubleday.

—— 1967. *The Sacred Canopy: Elements of a Sociological Theory of Religion*. Garden City, NY: Doubleday.

—— and T. Luckmann. 1966. *The Social Construction of Reality*. Garden City, NY: Doubleday.

Bernard, J. 1973. 'My Four Revolutions: An Autobiographical History of the ASA', *American Journal of Sociology* 78: 773–91.

Bernstein, R.J. 1976. *Restructuring Social and Political Theory*. Oxford: Blackwell.

—— 1983. *Beyond Objectivism and Relativism: Science, Hermeneutics and Praxis*. Oxford: Blackwell.

—— 1989. 'Social Theory as Critique', in D. Held and J.B. Thompson (eds), *Social Theory of Modern Societies: Anthony Giddens and his Critics*, pp. 19–33. Cambridge: Cambridge University Press.

Betanzos, R.J. 1988. 'Introduction', in Wilhelm Dilthey, *Introduction to the Human Sciences*, pp. 9–63. Detroit, Mich.: Wayne State University Press.

Betti, E. 1962. *Die Hermeneutik als Allgemeine Methodik der Geisteswissenschaften*. Tübingen: Mohr.

Bhaskar, R. 1975. *A Realist Theory of Science*. Leeds: Leeds Books.

—— 1978. *A Realist Theory of Science*, 2nd edn. Hassocks: Harvester Press.

—— 1979. *The Possibility of Naturalism: A Philosophical Critique of the Contemporary Human Sciences*. Brighton: Harvester.

—— 1982. 'Realism in the Natural Sciences', in L.J. Cohen et al. (eds), *Logic, Methodology and Philosophy of Science*, pp. 337–54. Amsterdam: North-Holland.

—— 1983. *Dialectical Materialism and Human Emancipation*. London: New Left Books.

—— 1986. *Scientific Realism and Human Emancipation*. London: Verso.

Black, M. 1962. *Models and Metaphors: Studies in Language and Philosophy*. Ithaca, NY: Cornell University Press.

Blaikie, N.W.H. 1991. 'A Critique of the Use of Triangulation in Social Research', *Quality and Quantity* 25: 115–36.

—— et al. In preparation. *The Dialogic Method*.

Bleier, R. (ed.). 1986. *Feminist Approaches to Science*. New York: Pergamon.

Bottomore, T. 1984. *The Frankfurt School*. London: Tavistock.

Braithwaite, R.B. 1953. *Scientific Explanation*. Cambridge: Cambridge University Press.

Brody, B.A. and N. Capaldi (eds). 1968. *Science: Men, Methods, Goals*. New York: W.A. Benjamin.

Bryant, C.G.A. 1985. *Positivism in Social Theory and Research*. London: Macmillan.

—— 1991. 'The Dialogical Model of Applied Sociology', in C.G.A. Bryant and D. Jary (eds), *Giddens' Theory of Structuration: A Critical Appreciation*, pp. 176–200. London: Routledge.

—— and D. Jary. 1991. *Giddens' Theory of Structuration: A Critical Appreciation*. London: Routledge.

Bubner, R. 1982. 'Habermas's Concept of Critical Theory', in J.B. Thompson and D. Held (eds), *Habermas: Critical Debates*, pp. 42–56. London: Macmillan.

—— 1988. *Essays in Hermeneutics and Critical Theory*. New York: Columbia University Press.

Butts, R.E. (ed.). 1968. *William Whewell's Theory of Scientific Method*. Pittsburgh, Penn.: University of Pittsburgh Press.

—— 1973. 'Whewell's Logic of Induction', in R.N. Giere and R.S. Westfall (eds), *Foundations of Scientific Method: The Nineteenth Century*, pp. 53–85. Bloomington, Ind: Indiana University Press.

Chalmers, A.F. 1982. *What is this Thing Called Science?* St Lucia, QLD: University of Queensland Press.

—— 1988. 'Is Bhaskar's Realism Realistic?', *Radical Philosophy* 49: 18–23.

Churchland, P.M. 1985. 'The Ontological Status of Observables: In Praise of the Superempirical Virtues', in P.M. Churchland and C.A. Hooker (eds), *Images of Science*, pp. 35–47. Chicago, Ill.: University of Chicago Press.

Churchland, P.M. and C. Hooker (eds). 1985. *Images of Science*. Chicago, Ill.: Chicago University Press.

Clark, J., C. Modgil and F. Modgil (eds). 1990. *Anthony Giddens: Consensus and Controversy*. Brighton: Falmer Press.

Clegg, S. 1979. *The Theory of Power and Organization*. London: Routledge & Kegan Paul.

Cohen, I.J. 1987. 'Structuration Theory and Social *Praxis*', in A. Giddens and J. Turner (eds), *Social Theory Today*, pp. 273–308. Cambridge: Polity Press.

—— 1989. *Structuration Theory: Anthony Giddens and the Constitution of Social Life*. London: Macmillan.

Cohen, P.S. 1968. *Modern Social Theory*. London: Heinemann.

Comte, A. 1970 (1830). *Introduction to Positive Philosophy*. Indianapolis, Ind.: Bobbs-Merrill.

Connerton, P. (ed.). 1976. *Critical Sociology*. Harmondsworth: Penguin.

Craib, I. 1992. *Anthony Giddens*. London: Routledge.

Cuff, E.C. and G.C.E. Payne. 1979. *Perspectives in Sociology*. London: Allen & Unwin.

Dallmayr, F.R. 1982. 'The Theory of Structuration: A Critique', in A. Giddens, *Profiles and Critiques in Social Theory*, pp. 18–27. London: Macmillan.

Denzin, N.K. 1970. *The Research Act in Sociology*. London: Butterworths.

Douglas, J.D. 1967. *The Social Meanings of Suicide*. Princeton, NJ: Princeton University Press.

—— 1971. *Understanding Everyday Life*. London: Routledge & Kegan Paul.

—— 1977. 'Existential Sociology', in J.D. Douglas and J.M. Johnson (eds), *Existential Sociology*, pp. 3–73. Cambridge: Cambridge University Press.

Doyal, L. and R. Harris. 1986. *Empiricism, Explanation and Rationality: An Introduction to the Philosophy of the Social Sciences*. London: Routledge & Kegan Paul.

Dugdale, A. 1990. 'Beyond Relativism: Moving On – Feminist Struggles with Scientific/medical Knowledge', *Australian Feminist Studies* 12: 51–63.

Durkheim, E. 1952. *Suicide*. Translated by J.A. Spaulding and G. Simpson. London: Routledge & Kegan Paul.

—— 1964. *The Rules of Sociological Method*. Glencoe, Ill.: Free Press.

Fay, B. 1975. *Social Theory and Political Practice*. London: Allen & Unwin.

—— 1987. *Critical Social Science: Liberation and its Limits*. Ithaca, NY: Cornell University Press.

Fee, E. 1981. 'Is Feminism a Threat to Scientific Objectivity?', *International Journal of Women's Studies* 4: 378–92.

—— 1986. 'Critiques of Modern Science: The Relationship of Feminism to Other Radical Epistemologies', in R. Bleier (ed.), *Feminist Approaches to Science*, pp. 42–56. New York: Pergamon.

Feyerabend, P.K. 1978. *Against Method: Outline of an Anarchistic Theory of Knowledge*. London: Verso.

Feynman, R. 1967. *The Character of Physical Law*. Cambridge, Ma.: MIT Press.

Filmer, P., M. Phillipson, D. Silverman and D. Walsh. 1972. *New Directions in Sociological Theory*. London: Collier-Macmillan.

Flax, J. 1983. 'Political Philosophy and the Patriarchal Unconscious: A Psychoanalytic Perspective', in S. Harding and M.B. Hintikka (eds), *Discovering Reality*, pp. 245–81. Dordrecht: Reidel.

van Fraassen, B.C. 1980. *The Scientific Image*. Oxford: Clarendon Press.

Freire, P. 1970. *Pedagogy of the Oppressed*. New York: Seabury Press.

Friedrichs, R.W. 1970. *A Sociology of Sociology*. New York: Free Press.

Gadamer, H-G. 1960. *Wåhrheit und Methode*. Tübingen: Mohr.

—— 1975. *Truth and Method*. London: Sheed and Ward.

—— 1989. *Truth and Method*, rev. 2nd edn. New York: Crossroad.

Garfinkel, H. 1967. *Studies in Ethnomethodology*. Englewood Cliffs, NJ: Prentice-Hall.

Giddens, A. 1974. *Positivism and Sociology*. London: Heinemann.

—— 1976a. *New Rules of Sociological Method*. London: Hutchinson.

—— 1976b. 'Hermeneutics, Ethnomethodology, and the Problem of Interpretive Analysis', in L.A. Coser and O. Larsen (eds), *The Uses of Controversy in Sociology*, pp. 315–28. New York: Basic Books. Also published in A. Giddens, *Studies in Social and Political Theory*, pp. 165–78. London: Hutchinson, 1977.

—— 1977a. 'Positivism and its Critics', in A. Giddens, *Studies in Social and Political Theory*, pp. 29–89. London: Hutchinson.

—— 1977b. 'Habermas's Critique of Hermeneutics', in A. Giddens, *Studies in Social and Political Theory*, pp. 135–64. London: Hutchinson.

—— 1979. *Central Problems in Social Theory: Action, Structure and Contradiction in Social Analysis*. London: Macmillan.

—— 1981. *A Contemporary Critique of Historical Materialism*. London: Macmillan.

—— 1982. *Profiles and Critiques in Social Theory*. London: Macmillan.

—— 1984. *The Constitution of Society: Outline of the Theory of Structuration*. Cambridge: Polity Press.

—— 1987. *Social Theory and Modern Sociology*. Cambridge: Polity Press.

—— 1989. 'A Reply to my Critics', in D. Held and J.B. Thompson (eds), *Social Theory of Modern Societies: Anthony Giddens and his Critics*, pp. 249–301. Cambridge: Cambridge University Press.

—— 1991. 'Structuration Theory: Past, Present and Future', in C.G.A. Bryant and D. Jary (eds), *Giddens' Theory of Structuration: A Critical Appraisal*, pp. 201–21. London: Routledge.

Giedymin, J. 1975. 'Antipositivism in Contemporary Philosophy of Social Science and Humanities', *British Journal for the Philosophy of Science* 26: 275–301.

Glaser, B.G. and A.L. Strauss. 1965. *Awareness of Dying*. Chicago, Ill.: Aldine.

—— 1968. *The Discovery of Grounded Theory*. London: Weidenfeld & Nicolson.

Glennon, L.M. 1979. *Women and Dualism*. New York: Longman.

—— 1983. 'Synthesism: a Case of Feminist Methodology', in G. Morgan (ed.), *Beyond Method*, pp. 260–271. Beverly Hills, Ca: Sage.

Gouldner, A.W. 1971. *The Coming Crisis in Western Sociology*. London: Heinemann.

Gregory, D. 1989. 'Presences and Absences: Time-space Relations and Structuration Theory', in D. Held and J.B. Thompson (eds), *Social Theory of Modern Societies:*

Anthony Giddens and his Critics, pp. 185–214. Cambridge: Cambridge University Press.

Gregson, N. 1989. 'On the Irrelevance of Structuration Theory to Empirical Research', in D. Held and J.B. Thompson (eds), *Social Theory of Modern Societies: Anthony Giddens and his Critics*, pp. 235–48. Cambridge: Cambridge University Press.

Grünbaum, A. and W.C. Salmon (eds). 1988. *The Limitations of Deductivism*. Berkeley, Ca: University of California Press.

Guba, E.G. (ed.). 1990a. *The Paradigm Dialog*. Newbury Park, Ca: Sage.

—— 1990b. 'The Alternative Paradigm Dialog', in E.G. Guba (ed.), *The Paradigm Dialog*, pp. 17–27. Newbury Park, Ca: Sage.

Habermas, J. 1970. 'Knowledge and Interest', in D. Emmet and A. MacIntyre (eds), *Sociological Theory and Philosophical Analysis*, pp. 36–54. London: Macmillan.

—— 1971. *Towards a Rational Society*. London: Heinemann.

—— 1972. *Knowledge and Human Interests*. London: Heinemann.

—— 1976. 'A Positivistically Bisected Rationalism: A Reply to a Pamphlet', in T.W. Adorno et al., *The Positivist Dispute in German Sociology*, pp. 198–225. London: Heinemann.

——1987. *The Theory of Communicative Action, Vol. 2: Lifeworld and System: The Critique of Functionalist Reason*. Cambridge: Polity Press.

Hacking, I. 1983. *Representing and Intervening: Introductory Topics in the Philosophy of Natural Science*. Cambridge: Cambridge University Press.

Halfpenny, P. 1982. *Positivism and Sociology: Explaining Social Life*. London: Allen & Unwin.

Hanson, N.R. 1958. *Patterns of Discovery*. Cambridge: Cambridge University Press.

—— 1965. 'Notes Towards a Logic of Discovery', in R.J. Bernstein (ed.), *Perspectives on Peirce*, pp. 42–65. New Haven, Conn.: Yale University Press.

Haraway, D. 1986. 'Primatology is Politics by Other Means', in R. Bleier (ed.), *Feminist Approaches to Science*, pp. 77–118. New York: Pergamon.

Harding, S. 1986. *The Science Question in Feminism*. Milton Keynes: Open University Press.

—— 1987a. *Feminism and Methodology*. Bloomington, Ind.: Indiana University Press.

—— 1987b. 'Introduction: Is There a Feminist Method?', in S. Harding (ed.), *Feminism and Methodology*, pp. 1–14. Milton Keynes: Open University Press.

—— 1987c. 'Conclusion: Epistemological Questions', in S. Harding (ed.), *Feminism and Methodology*, pp. 181–90. Milton Keynes: Open University Press.

—— 1987d. 'The Instability of the Analytical Categories of Feminist Theory', in S. Harding and J.F. O'Barr (eds), *Sex and Scientific Inquiry*, pp. 283–302. Chicago, Ill.: University of Chicago Press.

Harding, S. and M.B. Hintikka (eds). 1983a. *Discovering Reality: Feminist Perspectives on Epistemology, Metaphysics, Methodology and Philosophy*. Dordrecht: Reidel.

—— 1983b. 'Introduction', in S. Harding and M.B. Hintikka (eds), *Discovering Reality*, pp. ix–xix. Dordrecht: Reidel.

Harman, G. 1965. 'The Inference to the Best Explanation', *Philosophical Review* 74: 88–95.

——1968. 'Numerative Induction as Inference to the Best Explanation', *Journal of Philosophy* 65: 529–33.

Harré, R. 1960. *An Introduction to the Logic of the Sciences*. London: Macmillan.
—— 1961. *Theories and Things*. London: Sheed & Ward.
—— 1970. *The Principles of Scientific Thinking*. London: Macmillan.
—— 1972. *The Philosophy of Science: An Introductory Survey*. London: Oxford University Press.
—— 1974. 'Blueprint for a New Science', in N. Armistead (ed.), *Restructuring Social Psychology*, pp. 240–49. Harmondsworth: Penguin.
—— 1976. 'The Constructive Role of Models', in L. Collins (ed.), *The Use of Models in the Social Sciences*, pp. 16–43. London: Tavistock.
—— 1977a. 'The Ethogenic Approach: Theory and Practice', in L. Berkowitz (ed.), *Advances in Experimental Social Psychology*, vol. 10, pp. 284–314. New York: Academic Press.
—— 1977b. 'The Ethogenic Approach: Theory and Practice', *Advances in Experimental Social Psychology* 10: 283–314.
—— 1979. *Social Being: A Theory for Social Psychology*. Oxford: Blackwell.
—— 1986. *Varieties of Realism: A Rationale for the Natural Sciences*. Oxford: Blackwell.
—— and P.F. Secord. 1972. *The Explanation of Social Behaviour*. Oxford: Blackwell.
Harstock, N.C.M. 1983. 'The Feminist Standpoint: Developing the Ground for a Specifically Feminist Historical Materialism', in S. Harding and M.B. Hintikka (eds), *Discovering Reality*, pp. 283–310. Dordrecht: Reidel.
Hawking, S.W. 1988. *A Brief History of Time: From the Big Bang to Black Holes*. London: Batman Press.
Held, D. 1980. *Introduction to Critical Theory*. London: Hutchinson.
—— and J.B. Thompson (eds). 1989. *Habermas: Critical Debates*. Cambridge: Cambridge University Press.
Hempel, C.E. 1966. *Philosophy of Natural Science*. Englewood Cliffs, NJ: Prentice-Hall.
Hesse, M.B. 1953. 'Models in Physics', *British Journal for the Philosophy of Science* 4: 198–214.
—— 1974. *The Structure of Scientific Inference*. London: Macmillan.
—— 1976. 'Models Versus Paradigms in the Natural Sciences', in L. Collins (ed.), *The Use of Models in the Social Sciences*, pp. 1–15. London: Tavistock.
Hindess, B. 1977. *Philosophy and Methodology in the Social Sciences*. Hassocks: Harvester.
Hollis, M. 1977. *Models of Man: Philosophical Thoughts on Social Action*. Cambridge: Cambridge University Press.
Homans, G.C. 1964. 'Contemporary Theory in Sociology', in R.E.L. Faris (ed.), *Handbook of Modern Sociology*, pp. 951–77. Chicago, Ill.: Rand McNally.
Hughes, J. 1980. *The Philosophy of Social Research*. London: Longman.
—— 1991. *The Philosophy of Social Research*, 2nd edn. London: Longman.
Hume, D. 1888. *A Treatise of Human Nature*. London: Oxford University Press.
Inkeles, A. 1964. *What is Sociology?* Englewood Cliffs, NJ: Prentice-Hall.
Jevons, W.S. 1958/1874. *The Principles of Science*. New York: Dover.
Johnson, J.M. 1977. 'Ethnomethodology and Existential Sociology', in J.D. Douglas and J.M. Johnson (eds), *Existential Sociology*, pp. 153–73. Cambridge: Cambridge University Press.
Johnson, T., C. Dandeker and C. Ashworth. 1984. *The Structure of Social Theory: Dilemmas and Strategies*. London: Macmillan.
Kant, I. 1929. *Critique of Pure Reason*. London: Macmillan.

Kaplan, A. 1964. *The Conduct of Inquiry: Methodology for Behavioral Science*. San Francisco, Ca: Chandler.

Keat, R. 1971. 'Positivism, Naturalism and Anti-naturalism in the Social Sciences', *Journal for the Theory of Social Behaviour* 1: 3–17.

Keat, R. and J. Urry. 1975. *Social Theory as Science*. London: Routledge & Kegan Paul.

—— 1982. *Social Theory as Science*, 2nd edn. London: Routledge & Kegan Paul.

Keller, E.F. 1978. 'Gender and Science', *Psychoanalysis and Contemporary Thought* 1: 409–33.

—— 1985. *Reflections on Gender and Science*. New Haven, Conn.: Yale University Press.

—— 1987. 'Feminism and Science', in S. Harding and J.F. O'Barr (eds), *Sex and Scientific Inquiry*, pp. 233–46. Chicago, Ill.: Chicago University Press.

Kilminster, R. 1991. 'Structuration Theory as World-view', in C.G.A. Bryant and D. Jary (eds), *Giddens' Theory of Structuration: A Critical Appreciation*, pp. 74–115. London: Routledge.

Kolakowski, L. 1972 (1966). *Positivist Philosophy: From Hume to the Vienna Circle*. Harmondsworth: Penguin.

Kuhn, T.S. 1970a. *The Structure of Scientific Revolutions*, 2nd edn. Chicago, Ill.: Chicago University Press.

—— 1970b. 'Logic of Discovery or Psychology of Research,' in I. Lakatos and A. Musgrave (eds), *Criticism and the Growth of Knowledge*, pp. 1–23. Cambridge: Cambridge University Press.

—— 1970c. 'Reflections on my Critics', in I. Lakatos and A. Musgrave (eds), *Criticism and the Growth of Knowledge*, pp. 231–78. Cambridge: Cambridge University Press.

Lakatos, I. 1970. 'Falsification and the Methodology of Scientific Research Programmes', in I. Lakatos and A. Musgrave (eds), *Criticism and the Growth of Knowledge*, pp. 91–230. Cambridge: Cambridge University Press.

—— and A. Musgrave (eds). 1970. *Criticism and the Growth of Knowledge*. Cambridge: Cambridge University Press.

Laudan, L. 1977. *Progress and its Problems: Towards a Theory of Scientific Growth*. London: Routledge & Kegan Paul.

Layder, D. 1981. *Structure, Interaction and Social Theory*. London: Routledge & Kegan Paul.

—— 1985. 'Power, Structure and Agency', *Journal for the Theory of Social Behaviour* 15: 131–49.

Lengermann, P.M. and J. Niebrugge-Brantley. 1988. 'Contemporary Feminist Theory', in G. Ritzer, *Sociological Theory*, 2nd edn, pp. 400–43. New York: Alfred A. Knopf.

Lichtenstein, Ben Y.M. 1988. 'Feminist Epistemology: A Thematic Review'. *Thesis Eleven* 21: 140–50.

Lincoln, Y.S. and E.G. Guba. 1985. *Naturalistic Inquiry*. Beverly Hills, Ca: Sage.

Linge, D.E. 1976. 'Editor's Introduction', in H-G. Gadamer, *Philosophical Hermeneutics*, pp. xi–lviii. Berkeley, Ca: University of California Press.

Longino, H. 1981. 'Scientific Objectivity and Feminist Theorizing', *Liberal Education* 67.

Luckmann, T. 1967. *The Invisible Religion*. New York: Macmillan.

Makkreel, R.A. 1975. *Dilthey: Philosopher of the Human Studies*. Princeton, NJ: Princeton University Press.

Masterman, M. 1970. 'The Nature of a Paradigm', in I. Lakatos and A. Musgrave (eds), *Criticism and the Growth of Knowledge*, pp. 59–90. Cambridge: Cambridge University Press.

McCarthy, T. 1973. 'A Theory of Communicative Competence', *Philosophy of the Social Sciences* 3: 135–56.

—— 1984. *The Critical Theory of Jürgen Habermas*, 2nd edn. Cambridge: Polity Press.

Medewar, P.B. 1969a. *Induction and Intuition in Scientific Thought*. London: Methuen.

—— 1969b. *The Art of the Soluble: Creativity and Originality in Science*. Harmondsworth: Penguin.

Merton, R.K. 1957. *Social Theory and Social Structure*. Glencoe, Ill.: Free Press.

Mies, M. 1983. 'Towards a Methodology for Feminist Research', in G. Bowles and R.D. Klein (eds), *Theories of Women's Studies*, pp. 117–139. London: Routledge & Kegan Paul.

Mill, J.S. 1947 (1879). *A System of Logic*. London: Longman Green & Co.

Millman, M. and R.M. Kanter (eds). 1975. *Another Voice: Feminist Perspectives on Social Life and Social Science*. New York: Anchor Books.

Mulkay, M. 1979. *Science and the Sociology of Knowledge*. London: Allen & Unwin.

Musgrave, A. 1985. 'Realism Versus Constructive Empiricism', in P. Churchland and C.A. Hooker (eds), *Images of Science: Essays on Realism and Empiricism*, pp. 197–221. Chicago, Ill.: University of Chicago Press.

Nagel, E. 1961. *The Structure of Science: Problems in the Logic of Scientific Explanation*. London: Routledge & Kegan Paul.

Oakley, A. 1974. *The Sociology of Housework*. Oxford: Martin Robertson.

O'Hear, A. 1989. *An Introduction to the Philosophy of Science*. Oxford: Clarendon Press.

Outhwaite, W. 1975. *Understanding Social Life: The Method Called Verstehen*. London: Allen & Unwin.

—— 1983a. 'Towards a Realist Perspective', in G. Morgan (ed.), *Beyond Method*, pp. 321–30. Beverly Hills, Ca: Sage.

—— 1983b. *Concept Formation in Social Science*. London: Routledge & Kegan Paul.

—— 1987a. *New Philosophies of Social Science: Realism, Hermeneutics and Critical Theory*. London: Macmillan.

—— 1987b. 'Laws and Explanations in Sociology', in R.J. Anderson, J.A. Hughes and W.W. Sharrock (eds), *Classic Disputes in Sociology*, pp. 157–83. London: Allen & Unwin.

Palmer, R.E. 1969. *Hermeneutics: Interpretation Theory in Schleiermacher, Dilthey, Heidegger, and Gadamer*. Evanston, Ill.: Northwestern University Press.

Pawson, R. 1989. *A Measure for Measures: A Manifesto for Empirical Sociology*. London: Routledge.

Peirce, C.S. 1908. 'A Neglected Argument for the Reality of God', *Hibbert Journal* 7: 90–112.

—— 1931a. *Collected Papers*, Vol. I. Edited by Charles Hartshorne and Paul Weiss. Cambridge, Ma: Harvard University Press.

—— 1931b. *Collected Papers*, Vol. II. Edited by Charles Hartshorne and Paul Weiss. Cambridge, Ma: Harvard University Press.

—— 1934a. *Collected Papers*, Vol. V. Edited by Charles Hartshorne and Paul Weiss. Cambridge, Ma: Harvard University Press.

—— 1934b. *Collected Papers*, Vol. VI. Edited by Charles Hartshorne and Paul Weiss. Cambridge, Ma: Harvard University Press.

Phillips, B.S. 1966. *Social Research: Strategy and Tactics*. New York: Macmillan.

Phillips, D.C. 1987. *Philosophy, Science and Social Inquiry*. Oxford: Pergamon.

Polanyi, M. 1962. *Person Knowledge: Towards a Post-Critical Philosophy*. London: Routledge & Kegan Paul.

Popper, K.R. 1959a. *The Logic of Scientific Discovery*. London: Hutchinson.

—— 1959b. 'Prediction and Prophesy in the Social Sciences', in P. Gardiner (ed.), *Theories of History*, pp. 276–285. New York: Free Press.

—— 1961. *The Poverty of Historicism*. London: Routledge & Kegan Paul.

—— 1970. 'Normal Science and its Dangers', in I. Lakatos and A. Musgrave (eds), *Criticism and the Growth of Knowledge*, pp. 51–8. Cambridge: Cambridge University Press.

—— 1972. *Conjectures and Refutations*. London: Routledge & Kegan Paul.

—— 1976. 'The Logic of the Social Sciences', in T.W. Adorno et al., *The Positivist Dispute in German Sociology*, pp. 87–104. London: Heinemann.

—— 1979. *Objective Knowledge: An Evolutionary Approach*, rev. edn. Oxford: Clarendon Press.

Quinton, A. 1980. *Francis Bacon*. Oxford: Oxford University Press.

Reichenbach, H. 1948. *Experience and Prediction*. Chicago, Ill.: University of Chicago Press.

Rex, J. 1971. 'Typology and Objectivity: A Comment on Weber's Four Sociological Methods,' in A. Sahay (ed.), *Max Weber and Modern Sociology*, pp. 17–36. London: Routledge & Kegan Paul.

—— 1974. *Sociology and the Demystification of the Modern World*. London: Routledge & Kegan Paul.

Richards, S. 1983. *Philosophy and Sociology of Science: An Introduction*. Oxford: Blackwell.

Rickman, H.P. (ed.). 1976. *Wilhelm Dilthey – Selected Writings*. Cambridge: Cambridge University Press.

—— 1979. *Wilhelm Dilthey: Pioneer of the Human Sciences*. Berkeley, Ca: University of California Press.

—— 1988. *Dilthey Today: A Critical Appraisal of the Contemporary Relevance of his Work*. New York: Greenwood.

Ricoeur, P. 1981a. 'What is a Text? Explanation and Understanding', in J.B. Thompson (ed.), *Paul Ricoeur, Hermeneutics and the Human Sciences*, pp. 145–64. Cambridge: Cambridge University Press.

—— 1981b. 'Appropriation', in J.B. Thompson (ed.), *Paul Ricoeur, Hermeneutics and the Human Sciences*, pp. 182–93. Cambridge: Cambridge University Press.

Riggs, P.L. 1992. *Whys and Ways of Science: Introducing Philosophical and Sociological Theories of Science*. Melbourne: Melbourne University Press.

Ritzer, G. 1975. *Sociology: A Multiple Paradigm Science*. Boston, Ma: Allyn & Bacon.

Rose, H. 1983. 'Hand, Brain and Heart: Towards a Feminist Epistemology for the Natural Sciences', *Signs* 9: 73–90.

—— 1986. 'Beyond Masculinist Realities: A Feminist Epistemology for the Sciences', in R. Bleier (ed.), *Feminist Approaches to Science*, pp. 57–76. New York: Pergamon.

Rubinstein, R.A., C.D. Laughlin and J. McMannis. 1984. *Science as Cognitive Process: Towards an Empirical Philosophy of Science*. Philadelphia, Penn.: University of Pennsylvania Press.

Runciman, W.G. 1969. *Social Science and Political Theory*, 2nd edn. Cambridge: Cambridge University Press.

—— (ed.). 1977. *Max Weber: Selections in Translation*. Translated by E. Matthews. Cambridge: Cambridge University Press.

Ryan, A. 1970. *The Philosophy of the Social Sciences*. London: Macmillan.

Sahay, A. 1971. 'The Importance of Weber's Methodology in Sociological Explanation', in A. Sahay (ed.), *Max Weber and Modern Sociology*, pp. 67–81. London: Routledge & Kegan Paul.

Salleh, A. 1984. 'Contributions to the Critique of Political Epistemology', *Thesis Eleven* 8: 23–43.

Salmon, W.C. 1988. 'Rational Prediction', in A. Grünbaum and W.C. Salmon (eds), *The Limitations of Deductivism*, pp. 47–60. Berkeley, Ca: University of California Press.

Sayer, A. 1984. *Method in Social Science: A Realist Approach*. London: Hutchinson.

Schütz, A. 1963a. 'Concept and Theory Formation in the Social Sciences', in M.A. Natanson (ed.), *Philosophy of the Social Sciences*, pp. 231–49. New York: Random House.

—— 1963b. 'Common-sense and Scientific Interpretation of Human Action', in M.A. Natanson (ed.), *Philosophy of the Social Sciences*, pp. 302–46. New York: Random House.

—— 1970. 'Interpretive Sociology', in H.R. Wagner (ed.), *Alfred Schütz on Phenomenology and Social Relations*, pp. 265–93. Chicago, Ill.: University of Chicago Press.

—— 1976. *The Phenomenology of the Social World*. London: Heinemann.

—— and T. Luckmann. 1973. *The Structures of the Life-World*. Translated by R.M. Zaner and H.T. Engelhardt. Chicago, Ill.: Northwestern University Press.

Schwandt, T.R. 1990. 'Paths to Inquiry in the Social Disciplines: Scientific, Constructive, and Critical Theory Methodologies', in E.G. Guba (ed.), *The Paradigm Dialog*, pp. 258–76. Newbury Park, Ca: Sage.

Sherif, C.W. 1987. 'Bias in Psychology', in S. Harding (ed.), *Feminism and Methodology*, pp. 37–55. Milton Keynes: Open University Press.

Sica, A. 1986. 'Locating the 17th Book of Giddens', *Contemporary Sociology* 15: 344–6.

Smart, C. 1976. *Women, Crime and Criminology*. London: Routledge & Kegan Paul.

Smart, J.J.C. 1963. *Philosophy and Scientific Realism*. London: Routledge & Kegan Paul.

Smith, D.E. 1974. 'Women's Perspective as a Radical Critique of Sociology', *Sociological Inquiry* 44: 7–13.

—— 1979. 'A Sociology for Women', in J.A. Sherman and E.T. Beck (eds), *The Prism of Sex: Essays in the Sociology of Knowledge*, pp. 135–87. Madison, Wis.: University of Wisconsin Press.

Stanley, L. and S. Wise. 1983. *Breaking Out: Feminist Consciousness and Feminist Research*. London: Routledge & Kegan Paul.

Stockman, N. 1983. *Antipositivist Theories of the Sciences*. Dordrecht: Reidel.

Strauss, A. 1987. *Qualitative Analysis for Social Scientists*. New York: Cambridge University Press.

—— and J. Corbin. 1990. *Basics of Qualitative Research: Grounded Theory Procedures and Techniques*. Newbury Park, Ca: Sage.

Suppe, F. 1977. 'The Search for Philosophic Understanding of Scientific Theories', in F. Suppe (ed.), *The Structure of Scientific Theories*, pp. 3–241. Urbana, Ill.: University of Illinois Press.

Thomas, D. 1979. *Naturalism and Social Science: A Post-empiricist Philosophy of the Social Sciences.* Cambridge: Cambridge University Press.

Thomas, W.I. 1928. *The Child in America.* New York: Alfred K. Knopf.

Thompson, J.B. 1981a. *Critical Hermeneutics: A Study in the Thought of Paul Ricoeur and Jürgen Habermas.* Cambridge: Cambridge University Press.

—— 1981b. *Paul Ricoeur: Hermeneutics and the Human Sciences.* Cambridge: Cambridge University Press.

—— 1984. *Studies in the Theory of Ideology.* Cambridge: Polity Press.

—— 1989. 'The Theory of Structuration', in D. Held and J.B. Thompson (eds), *Social Theory of Modern Societies: Anthony Giddens and his Critics*, pp. 56–76. Cambridge: Cambridge University Press.

—— and D. Held (eds). 1982. *Habermas: Critical Debates.* London: Macmillan.

Thrift, N. 1985. 'Bear and Mouse or Bear and Tree? Anthony Giddens's Reconstruction of Social Theory', *Sociology* 19: 609–23.

Trigg, R. 1985. *Understanding Social Science: A Philosophical Introduction to the Social Sciences.* Oxford: Blackwell.

Tudor, A. 1982. *Beyond Empiricism: Philosophy of Science in Sociology.* London: Routledge & Kegan Paul.

Turner, B.A. 1981. 'Some Practical Aspects of Qualitative Data Analysis: One Way of Organizing the Cognitive Process Associated with the Generation of Grounded Theory', *Quality and Quantity* 15: 225–47.

Turner, S.P. 1980. *Sociological Explanation as Translation.* New York: Cambridge University Press.

Tursman, R. 1987. *Peirce's Theory of Scientific Discovery.* Bloomington, Ind.: Indiana University Press.

Wallace, W.L. 1971. *The Logic of Science in Sociology.* Chicago, Ill.: Aldine-Atherton.

—— 1983. *Principles of Scientific Sociology.* Chicago, Ill.: Aldine.

Watkins, J.W.N. 1968. 'Non-inductive Corroboration', in I. Lakatos (ed.), *The Problem of Inductive Logic*, pp. 61–6. Amsterdam: North-Holland.

—— 1984. *Science and Scepticism.* Princeton, NJ: Princeton University Press.

Weber, M. 1949. *The Methodology of the Social Sciences.* Translated and edited by E.A. Shils and H.A. Finch. Glencoe, Ill.: Free Press.

—— 1958. *The Protestant Ethic and the Spirit of Capitalism.* New York: Scribners.

—— 1962. *Basic Concepts in Sociology.* New York: The Citadel Press.

—— 1964. *The Theory of Social and Economic Organization.* Translated by A.M. Henderson and T. Parsons. New York: Free Press.

Weiss, C.H. 1979. 'The Many Meanings of Research Utilization', in M. Bulmer (ed.), *Social Science and Social Policy*, pp. 31–40. London: Allen & Unwin.

—— 1983. 'Ideology, Interests and Information: The Basis of Policy Positions', in D. Callahan and B. Jennings (eds), *Ethics, the Social Sciences, and Policy Analysis*, pp. 213–45. New York: Plenum Press.

Weiss, C.H. and M.J. Bucuvalas. 1980. *Social Science Research and Decision-making.* New York: Columbia University Press.

Whewell, W. 1847. *The Philosophy of the Inductive Sciences*, 2 vols. London: Parker.

Whyte, W.F. (ed.). 1991. *Participatory Action Research.* Newbury Park, Ca: Sage.

Willer, D. 1967. *Scientific Method: Theory and Method.* Englewood Cliffs, NJ: Prentice-Hall.

Winch, P. 1958. *The Idea of Social Science and its Relation to Philosophy.* London: Routledge & Kegan Paul.

Winch, P. 1964. 'Understanding a Primitive Society', *American Philosophical Quarterly* 1: 307–24.

Wolfe, A.B. 1924. 'Functional Economics', in R.G. Tingwell (ed.), *The Trend of Economics*. New York: Alfred A. Knopf.

Wolff, K.H. (ed.). 1984. *Alfred Schütz: Appraisals and Developments*. Dordrecht: Martinus Nijhoff.

von Wright, G.H. 1971. *Explanation and Understanding*. London: Routledge & Kegan Paul.

Zimmerman, D.H. and D.L. Wieder. 1971. 'Ethnomethodology and the Problem of Order: Comment on Denzin', in J.D. Douglas (ed.), *Understanding Everyday Life*, pp. 285–98. London: Routledge & Kegan Paul.

Index